I Never Walked Alone

I NEVER WALKED ALONE

The Autobiography of an American Singer

Shirley Verrett

with

Christopher Brooks

WILEY

John Wiley & Sons, Inc.

Published by John Wiley & Sons, Inc., Hoboken, New Jersey
Published simultaneously in Canada

Photo credits: pp. 132 (top), 133 (both), 134 (top right), 144 (bottom), 146 (both), 147 (top and bottom), and 148 (bottom) courtesy of Shirley Verrett; p. 132 (bottom) courtesy of John H. McCoy, Jr.; pp. 134 (bottom) and 147 (middle) courtesy of Henry Grossman; p. 134 (top left) photograph by Impact Photo Inc., courtesy of Shirley Verrett; pp. 135 (top), 137 (top), 138 (both), and 140 (top) courtesy of the Metropolitan Opera Archives; p. 135 (bottom) photograph by Isaac Berez, courtesy of Shirley Verrett; p. 136 (top) courtesy of United Press International Photo; p. 136 (bottom) photograph by Stephanie Rancou, courtesy of Shirley Verrett; p. 137 (bottom) photograph by Louis Melancon, courtesy of the Metropolitan Opera Archives; p. 139 photograph by Foto Piccagliani, courtesy of Shirley Verrett; p. 140 (bottom) from the Donald Southern Collection, courtesy of the Royal Opera House Archives; pp. 141, 142 (top), and 143 (both) photographs by Milton I. Feinberg; p. 142 (bottom) courtesy of Louis LoMonaco; p. 144 (top) photograph by J. Hefferman, courtesy of the Metropolitan Opera Archives; p. 145 photograph by Winnie Klotz, courtesy of the Metropolitan Opera Archives; p. 148 (top) photograph by Lattelle Solomon.

For general information about our other products and services, please contact our Customer Care Department within the United States at (800) 762-2974, outside the United States at (317) 572-3993 or fax (317) 572-4002.

Wiley also publishes its books in a variety of electronic formats. Some content that appears in print may not be available in electronic books. For more information about Wiley products, visit our web site at www.wiley.com.

Library of Congress Cataloging-in-Publication Data:

Verrett, Shirley.
I never walked alone : the autobiography of an American singer /
Shirley Verrett with Christopher Brooks.
p. cm.
Includes index.
Discography: p.
ISBN 0-471-20991-0 (cloth : alk. paper)
1. Verrett, Shirley. 2. Mezzo-sopranos—United States—Biography. I. Brooks, C. W. II. Title.
ML420.V3515A3 2003
782.1'092—dc21   2003002601

Printed in the United States of America

10 9 8 7 6 5 4 3 2 1

To the memory of my parents

Leon Solomon Verrett, Sr.
(1908–1988)
and
Elvira Augustine Harris Verrett
(1906–2001)

Contents

PART THREE

PART FOUR

Foreword

by Luciano Pavarotti

I FIRST met Shirley Verrett at the Marina alla Scala in 1967. It was a small hotel across the street from the La Scala theater where young singers often stayed. We were there to sing a UNESCO benefit performance of Verdi's *Messa de Requiem,* with Maestro Herbert von Karajan conducting. She was such a striking woman, and I will never forget the first time that I heard her glorious voice in rehearsal. We became friends from that time on.

Over the next twenty-five years, Shirley and I sang in operas, made joint orchestral appearances, and, of course, recorded together. I have so many special memories of her and her supreme artistry, but a few occasions do stand out. One was a 1975 San Francisco Opera performance of *Il Trovatore,* starring Joan Sutherland and me. The scheduled Azucena became ill, and Shirley flew in at the eleventh hour to replace her. Her portrayal of the tormented gypsy was so strong that she received a standing ovation at the end of the opera! As beautifully as she sang throughout the performance, I especially remember how well we blended in the duet "Ai nostri monti," in the last act. Her voice was so tender, it was as if she were singing a lullaby.

By the late 1980s, we had sung together in several other operas, including *Un Ballo in Maschera* at La Scala and *La Favorita* and *Tosca* at the Met. In 1988, I made my debut as a stage director with La Fenice (Venice Opera). I chose Donizetti's *La Favorita* because I knew the opera well and I was able to persuade Shirley to sing Leonora in the production. I will always appreciate her generosity because some divas of her caliber would not have sung with such a young cast. Around the same time she rescued a recording of *Rigoletto* that I was in, by agreeing to sing Maddalena as a personal favor to me. This is a role that she had never even considered doing onstage. She has been that kind of colleague.

Throughout my career I have performed with many great artists, but I continue to hold a special place in my heart for Shirley Verrett. Reading her autobiography has given me, and the world, the opportunity to gain an even greater insight into this special colleague, artist, charming lady, and, most especially, dear friend. She is surely one of the great artists of our time.

Foreword

by Plácido Domingo

ETWEEN 1968, when we first did a concert performance of
Carmen in Saratoga, New York, and 1990, when we last sang
Samson et Dalila at the Met together, Shirley Verrett and I have
sung nearly one hundred performances. When I think back on those
performances, I see before me an artist of rare vocal beauty, of physical and histrionic endowment, and a consummate musician.

My first impression of Shirley, even before I heard her sing a note,
was of her preparation. When she arrived at a rehearsal or in the
recording studio, there was no question that she was ready to work.
Nowhere was her professionalism more apparent to me than when we
recorded *Don Carlo* with Carlo Maria Giulini, which to this day remains one of my favorite recordings.

Although the *Carmen* in Saratoga was our first performance together, our first fully staged opera came in the 1972 revival of Meyerbeer's *L'Africaine*. This production marked the return of the opera
after a ninety-year absence in this country. Shirley looked stunning as
Princess Selika and sang beautifully. Sixteen years later we appeared in
the same production, and again she delivered a wonderful performance.

Shirley was totally believable in her portrayals not only to the audience but also to her colleagues. This is especially important to the tenor, who so often must show love or jealousy for his operatic partner. How much easier it is to feel love or jealousy when singing opposite a woman with such beauty of voice and physical allure. And the fact that she is not just a voice and a beauty but a true musician and a charming human being makes her a treasure in the world of opera.

Preface

*The important thing is this: To be ready to sacrifice
what you are for what you could become.*

—CHARLES DUBOIS

PEOPLE ALWAYS think I'm joking when I say this, but it's true:
I was bored selling real estate. Unhappily married and already
twenty-four years old, I sat in my Southern California office,
thinking, "This career is ridiculous. I'm really a singer, and I'm ready
to sing."

And that's how I made up my mind to study. I found a teacher,
switched from that teacher to another one, and, not long afterward,
arrived in New York to appear on a hugely popular, nationally televised talent show. I won, and for the next few years, as a student at
Juilliard, it was almost as if I could do no wrong. The people I listened to were the right people to listen to. I knew what would be
good for me and at what moment. I knew what I was ready for and
what I wasn't.

The whole truth is another matter, more complicated than this
version of the story. I've skipped over my strict religious upbringing,
my father's dream, my passion for singing and acting, the days of
sheer struggle and incredible luck. But in all honesty, for a long time

in the beginning and for years afterward, it seemed as if everything just came to me, changing my life into what it was meant to be.

Perhaps you've heard my voice in recital or in recordings over the years. Or you may have an image of me on the opera stage in *Oedipus Rex* in Washington; *Aida* and *La Favorita* in Dallas; *Maria Stuarda* at the Maggio Musicale; *Don Carlo* at Covent Garden; *Les Troyens, Siege of Corinth, The Dialogue of the Carmelites,* or *Il Trovatore* at the Metropolitan; *L'Africaine* in San Francisco; *Samson et Dalila* and *Macbeth* at La Scala; *Tosca* in Verona; *Norma* in Boston; or, after I left the opera stage, *Carousel* on Broadway.

Those were a few of the numerous productions where I delivered the performances I knew I could. Naturally, like a good many other singers, I had my share of disasters, too, like the infamous 1987 *Macbeth* in Rome. Fortunately, I had far more performances in the first category than in the second.

What mattered most was that from childhood on, through each more astonishing, unpredictable year, I never let anything, including disappointment or the fear of rejection, slow down my intellectual curiosity or my personal development. With God's help, I always figured out what I needed, what I was all about as an artist and a woman.

"WHEN WILL I be ready to do this?" students ask.

I say, "Let's not worry about it; let's just do the work. The other things will take care of themselves. Appreciate the work you do and whatever results you get, because it all passes so quickly."

"Hurry slowly," as one of my most important mentors used to tell me.

That's how I see my life. To be an artist, you cannot rush into something you are not ready for or think of your career solely as a means to financial security. You have to remember that you never stop learning. You never stop needing close, authentic relationships. You must constantly pull on whatever knowledge, essence, energy, or belief that motivates and guides you. And for the sake of your career, you must see, without a doubt, where you stand in the world. If you're not honest with yourself, many terrible mistakes can be made.

Believe me, I've learned how imperative it is to be devastatingly honest with yourself as a person and a performer. Otherwise, I would have quite a different story to tell.

I never imagined I would write an autobiography, although over the years several people asked me to tell my story. Then one day I received a call from Christopher Brooks, an African American professor and biographer. As it turned out, he had heard me sing when he was an undergraduate student and followed my career from then on. He motivated me to think about how few books there were by African American singers. The only ones I've seen are by or about Marian Anderson, Paul Robeson, Simon Estes, and Leontyne Price. In the end, I realized that it was necessary and important to give my own account as well.

Writing this book with Christopher has made me think a little more about certain things that were possibly always inside me and hadn't come out before. It's also given me a chance to set the record straight about what was happening behind the scenes, as well as onstage and in the recording studio, during my highs and lows over a long international career. At the back of the book you'll find the storyline of every opera in which I've appeared.

Now I will take you on my journey.

The road has been long and full of personal challenges, triumphs, joys, regrets, and resurgences. And here I am, telling you my story. Just entering my seventies, I feel strongly that the beginning has only begun.

PART ONE

1

My Mother's Voice

THE FIRST sound I remember is the sound of my mother singing. Hers was a rich, full lyric soprano voice that seemed to soar when she sang certain notes, but could be soothingly mellow in the lower register. I suppose at some point I started to imitate her because the quality of my adult voice bears a similarity to hers. Mother called some of the songs she sang all day "long meters." Others were church hymns. I am sure my affinity for singing spirituals is related to these expressions of her spirit. It was the basis of a profound bond between us.

When I was about five, Mother realized I could hold a tune. I imagine she paused, pleased and thinking that there was something special about what I was doing. So she taught me my first song, "Jesus Loves Me." I sang it in our Seventh-Day Adventist church one Sabbath. I felt I sang it well. Dad really paid attention to what I was doing. I saw in his eyes that he was focusing on me with a seriousness beyond the usual. He leaned forward and put his hand to his chin, nodding his head and smiling slightly. Dad loved music. He conducted our church choir. He also had a smooth baritone voice, though not as rich as Mother's soprano.

"Do you know you have a very lovely voice, little girl?" he said after the service. Suddenly, I felt a foot taller. I think it was at that exact moment that I became a singer.

MOTHER LOVED music, but spirituality and family were her deepest passions. She passed these feelings on to me, though not quite in the way she anticipated.

Mother's Catholic ancestors arrived in New Orleans in the late eighteenth century from Haiti, in the first wave of refugees from the 1791 Haitian Revolution. One of them, my great-great-grandfather Paul E. Morel, nicknamed "Deauville," fought in the American Civil War, initially for the Confederacy in 1862 as part of a volunteer group of blacks. Later that year, General Benjamin Butler persuaded the group to switch sides and fight for the Union. They were known as the Native Guards. According to family history, every Sunday Grandpa Morel dressed in his Union uniform and shouldered his gun. He received a government pension until he died in 1915.

Grandpa Morel's daughter Eugénie Morel, known as "Mamal," married a man whose surname was Joseph. Mamal's first child, Grandma Rita, was born and baptized in 1883. Mamal had another child, born in 1893, who died in infancy, and a daughter, Emily, born in 1895 after the death of her husband. Great-aunt Emily, whom we called "Malie," was very light skinned, while my grandmother Rita Joseph was dark brown. Like the rest of her family, Grandma Rita spoke French or patois, with English as her second language. Mamal made sure she had a strict New Orleans Catholic upbringing.

But Grandma Rita broke with Mamal's religious tradition when she decided to marry Walter Harris from Covington, Louisiana. He was a very light-skinned man, most probably a mulatto, what New Orleaneans then called *passant blanc*. In other words, he was able to pass for white. More important to Mamal and Grandma Rita, however, was the fact that he was a Methodist, and the Catholic Church did not officially recognize a marriage outside the faith.

Grandma Rita and Grandpa Harris eventually had seven children, Noella, Elvira (Mother, born August 1, 1906), Gladys, Vivian, Hilda, Walter Jr., and Hazel. They spoke English instead of French as a first language, the first generation of Mother's family to do so.

Although the Catholic Church did not officially recognize her marriage, Grandma Rita raised all her children as Catholics just as she had been raised by Mamal. But in the early 1920s, after being rigorously recruited during what was called a "tent effort" of the Seventh-Day Adventist faith, Grandma Rita left the Catholic church. In time, I learned the story of her conversion to the religion that shaped my life.

When the Adventists came to New Orleans, Grandma Rita was moved by their marathon preaching sessions under huge tents. There she learned about the second coming of Christ. The preachers declared that Christ would appear in clouds coming from heaven, that God's law was still set out in the Ten Commandments, and that the true Sabbath was Saturday. Adventists held that although they were in the world, they were not of the world. This, of course, presented many restrictions. Adventists rejected divorce and lawsuits in general. They disapproved of opera, theater, and movies. Jazz, blues, or any hybrid of these traditions was taboo, as were card playing, gambling, and dancing.

To be an Adventist, Grandma Rita knew she would have to dress modestly. She could no longer wear clothes that accentuated her hips or breasts. Nor could she wear lipstick, jewelry, or elaborate hairstyles, because they called attention to her beauty. Dietary observances prohibited "unclean" foods like pork and shellfish. If one could not be a strict vegetarian, meats like beef, lamb, chicken, and fish (but not shellfish) were allowed. Of course, alcoholic beverages were forbidden, as was tobacco. After sunset on Friday evenings, she could no longer attend certain kinds of musical performances. Instead, she would have to prepare for the Sabbath.

Yet this was the faith she embraced. Several of those practices have changed now, but under the tent Grandma Rita converted from one strict religion to a stricter one and brought her children with her, though not all at once.

MY MOTHER, in her late teens then and nearing marrying age, was allowed to make her own decisions about religion. Apparently, she liked what she heard from the Adventists because she joined the church after marriage, along with her sister Noella. Mother's sense of spirituality ran deep. Not only had she been raised as a Catholic, but, because of her Haitian background, she also knew something about the voodoo practices in New Orleans and strongly disapproved of anyone who practiced those negative arts.

MOTHER MET Dad at a house party in 1925.

In later years, Dad liked to say that he already knew her name was Elvira, because he had had a dream about her. He had also seen her a few times before but hadn't spoken to her, perhaps because he was only seventeen, two years younger than she was. At the party, he apparently seized his opportunity to meet her formally.

Young as he was, Leon Solomon Verrett was already a person of substance and action. He came from a line of builders and carpenters with a long history in Louisiana. According to Dad, the name Verrett originally belonged to a large family of carpenters and builders who had emigrated from France in the early nineteenth century and lived and worked on a plantation in Louisiana, close to where Dad was born years later.

Dad's father was named Joseph Verrett. He was born in the mid-1870s outside New Orleans. Around the turn of the century, Joseph married a woman named Mary Lee, who was definitely an African. "Lee" was obviously a plantation name. Joseph and Mary Lee Verrett settled in New Orleans and had eight children. Their oldest son, Harrison, was born in 1906. Dad was born in 1908. Then came Walter, Gus, Alphonse, Joseph Jr., Rosemary, and Selena. I knew them all very well.

Granddad Joseph Verrett was a master builder and carpenter. He could hang wallpaper, build beautiful furniture—you name it and he could do it. If a project had anything to do with construction or carpentry, my grandfather did it. He also loved words. He used to read the dictionary and correct people if they mispronounced anything. The man was a walking dictionary.

Granddad was also apparently a soft touch and sometimes did not get paid on time for the jobs he completed. When that happened, Dad went to demand the money.

Grandmother Mary Lee Verrett, who had learned to look up to this son, was well aware of this scenario and began saying to her husband, "If you can't get the money, let Leon do it. He'll get it done." This created some hard feelings between father and son, but not enough to disturb the business. Dad helped train his younger brothers as carpenters, painters, paperhangers, or all-around maintenance men. By the time Dad met Mother, he was already on his way to becoming a well-respected carpenter and painter, with increasing contact with the white world.

Since Dad and Mother were then both still in their late teens, they courted for more than three years. After they married, on January 30, 1929, they joined the Seventh-Day Adventists. Their firstborn, my brother David, arrived on November 13, 1929. I was born on May 31, 1931, at the Toureau Infirmary in New Orleans. Mother and Grandma Rita said I looked like a little Turk, with straight hair sticking out of my ears. Leon Jr. was born when I was two. Elvira came along in 1935; two years after that came Milton. Within eight years there were five of us.

Following in the path of Grandma Rita, Aunt Noella, and most black women of the New Orleans of her day, Mother had worked as a domestic in her youth. Proudly now, she managed her own home and family. Before we left home for any occasion, David, Leon, and I lined up for her inspection. My hair had to be neatly braided or combed and my teeth brushed. There could be no ashy knees, hands, or elbows. Mother was equally particular about her own appearance, setting out her dress and shoes the evening before, to make sure everything matched. All of her life, she was conscious of what she wore and how she looked. Mother and Dad were both big on dressing appropriately. Dad often said, "Clothes do not make the man, but they can open the door."

As far as I know, Mother's only regret was never finishing high school. She often said that if circumstances had been different, she would like to have received her high school diploma and gone to college. At Dad's insistence, she remained a homemaker, but she wanted us to have all the opportunities she had missed. Her dictum was "Learn all that you can, because you never know when you'll need it." As our first teacher, she taught us to spell, recite poetic verse, and do simple addition and subtraction before we started school.

We also learned that outside our family, the world was not to be trusted. For our protection, Mother decided that we were never to eat in anyone else's home. Fearing New Orleans's old occult tradition, she never let anyone other than a close relative cook in her house, because they might put something in her cooking pots. When we children visited other people, we would generally go after dinner. And if we hadn't eaten, we were to politely say, "No, thank you very much, but we won't have any." We were not even allowed to drink water away from home. In case someone pressed us, Mother taught us to say we had to eat at home.

BY 1935, Mother and Dad had moved to 2135 New Orleans Street, between Miro and Galvez. My best friend in the neighborhood was Iris Charles. We did almost everything together, playing jacks, hopscotch, and with our dolls. Iris was also one of the few children Mother allowed to come into our home because she was so well behaved and polite.

It was an integrated neighborhood, not unusual for New Orleans in the 1930s, filled with working-class blacks and whites, many of them blue-collar laborers. Outside our neighborhood, however, the racial lines were more clearly drawn. Even if we rode on the same bus as a white neighbor who had just borrowed some sugar from us, the white neighbor still sat toward the front of the bus while we stayed toward the back.

I got to see another side of the skin color issue through the eyes of a best friend and playmate from church. Jacqueline Mathieu and I were the same age and remained good friends up until her death just a few years ago. Her family had also left the Catholic Church to become Adventists. We didn't live in the same neighborhood, so we saw each other mostly on weekends or at church activities.

Both of Jackie's parents were very light-skinned. Her father was passant blanc. Several members of Mr. Mathieu's family passed as white. It was hard even for us to tell. Jackie, on the other hand, was darker than either of her parents or her brothers and sisters, who were also very light. Jackie's hair texture was closer to mine. Her other brothers and sisters had what was called "good hair," which was softer in texture and closer to white people's. This reality chafed Jackie throughout childhood and into adult life. When she visited her father's people, they treated her like a second-class citizen—unlike her brothers and sisters, who enjoyed a much warmer welcome from Mr. Mathieu's family. It got to the point where Jackie refused to see them. To compensate for his family's disgraceful behavior, Mr. Mathieu spoiled Jackie. He not only gave her material possessions, he allowed her to speak to him in an unheard-of manner. Even in front of me she called him names like "stupid" or told him, "Shut up!"

If I had ever tried that with Dad, he would have strapped me on my legs before I got out the "sh" of "shut up."

I WAS always a bit of a renegade. I barely escaped from one particular misadventure with my favorite uncle, Dad's brother Harrison. Ironically, music was involved. Uncle Harrison had left the building trade and become a full-time jazz musician. He had once played the banjo and piano with Papa Celestin's band in New Orleans. Sometimes when he came to our house to baby-sit, he played boogie-woogie tunes on the piano. Uncle Harrison encouraged me to dance and I complied. I would shake, shake, shake, shake, shake my little hips to the music. Sometimes I even put my hands on my hips and shook like a grown person.

I knew it was against my religion. Mother and Dad did not approve of such music, much less dancing, even though Dad had once been a good dancer and had won a few community contests in his youth. So neither Uncle Harrison nor I ever said anything to Mother and Dad about our boogie-woogie dance sessions.

One day when I was alone, practicing my hands-on-the-hips shake, Mother came up behind me. She didn't punish me. She just stared at me, which was more than enough to make me stop. I wondered if she knew I had learned the dance from Uncle Harrison. She never said a word about it to me, but I wouldn't be at all surprised if she mentioned it to Dad. They were always very close.

One of my earliest memories is of Dad singing love songs to Mother. The most memorable was a delightful, simple little tune, "Just a Cottage Small by the Waterfall." Mother always smiled in silence while he sang to her. I heard that song so much, I memorized some of the words. Dad also played the saxophone. When I listened to him practice, something about those notes made me feel I could float away on the sound.

Music captivated me. After I sang "Jesus Loves Me" in church, Dad became my voice teacher. We started with simple church songs. As I became better at memorizing them, he taught me others that were more difficult because they required communicating more feeling. In one song, "I Stood on the River o' Jerdan," there was a passage, "just to see the ships com'a sailing over." I had a hard time singing those words as expressively as Dad wanted. We worked on that passage for a long time before he felt I was ready to sing it publicly.

Soon, I was singing at other Adventist churches in the New Orleans area, as well as at our own, at socials, or at regional church meetings with large audiences. Leon Jr. also had a very beautiful voice. Although we were young, we occasionally had family sing-ins, where all the children joined our parents to sing songs like "Dry Bones"; "Certainly,

Lord"; and "Swing Low, Sweet Chariot." We sometimes sang for little parties at my parents' home.

Dad taught me rituals to observe on days I performed. He said I should minimize my talking and not eat anything that could produce phlegm. He also told me to drink a lot of pineapple juice, because it contains a good digestive agent. I still find that's a helpful thing for me. The performance-day rituals set me apart from my brothers and sister. I liked the attention I received when I was getting ready for an engagement.

Sometimes after my voice lessons, Dad rehearsed the church choir. Curiously, this was my introduction to opera, even though the church did not approve of opera performances or the stories from operas. Years later at Juilliard I discovered that many of our church songs came from operas. Melodies from opera arias or choruses were given sacred words and adapted as four-part choir hymns sung in the Adventist church. When I first heard the melody of the Pilgrims' chorus from Wagner's *Tannhäuser*, despite knowing nothing about the opera, I envisioned large numbers of people praying.

Dad also belonged to a choral group affiliated with Dillard University that was directed by a certain Dr. Hall. Dad learned a great deal about the mechanisms of the human voice from Dr. Hall. Dad carefully explained how to position my mouth, how to enunciate the words, and how to hold my diaphragm. I had no idea what a diaphragm was in those years, but I followed his example. When I sang solos in church, he sat in the audience. My eyes were glued to him, and I followed any gesture he indicated, including standing upright with my chest out, with fingers interlaced at the midsection. This was the singer's stance. You can date singers of a certain generation by that stance. I broke many of Dad's rules as I learned more about voice production myself.

Once, I was supposed to sing in church but had a cold. Dad told me I shouldn't sing, but I wanted to do it anyway. I sang and the performance went badly, as far as I was concerned. After I finished, I walked out of the church and climbed into the backseat of our car, to be alone with my disgrace. The next thing I recall was Dad opening the car door. He got in, sat beside me, and, after keeping silent for what seemed like an eternity, finally spoke.

"Shirley, you knew you had a cold and wouldn't sing well, but you did it anyway. We won't go over that again. But you did some good things in the performance." He told me what he had liked and was very specific. He even demonstrated it for me right there, on the spot. He was always my greatest fan.

Dad was absolutely adamant about my having a career as a recitalist. He would not permit anyone to touch my voice. He told me I had a mature voice for my age and predicted for me a career like those of the great African American concert singers Dorothy Maynor and Marian Anderson. He was a big fan of Dorothy Maynor's expressive soprano voice, particularly her interpretation of spirituals. He played Maynor's and Anderson's recordings for me. Even though I was a child of seven, the sounds of their voices fascinated me.

When I was a little older, Miss Maynor and Miss Anderson came to New Orleans to give recitals. I was in their audiences with Dad and Mother. Many other wonderful black singers delighted me in recital, but I have forgotten their names. I also enjoyed choral groups like the Wings Over Jordan and the Fisk Jubilee Singers, both of which specialized in singing spirituals.

I ENTERED the Adventist school when I was five. I didn't want to be at home alone, so my parents let me go to school with David. My third-grade teacher was Miss Bradford, a tall, light-skinned young lady of about twenty. It was her first year in the classroom. One afternoon, Miss Bradford assigned the entire class an eight-stanza poem to be memorized and recited the next day. She said any child who didn't learn that poem would be in trouble. I timidly protested that it was too much for us to learn overnight, since we also had math and other homework to do.

She said, "You can do it. Especially *you,* Miss Shirley Verrett, who are always reciting poems in church." The tone of her remark didn't seem friendly, so it put more pressure on me. That night, Mother coached me. She always loved to drill me.

"Shirley, can you say this? Now give it a little more emphasis on some of the words," she used to say. She would give me a clue.

"I got it, I got it!" I'd reply.

As a result of all her coaching, I became a very good speller in my youth, in addition to learning the art of memorization. Eventually, when I entered college, I was told I had the highest scores in English of any freshman. To this day, I get very involved when I'm reading a book. I could never be a speed-reader, because I get bogged down in the beauty of words. As I read, I listen to the words in my head, painting pictures as I go along.

The following day, no one in the class knew all eight stanzas. When Miss Bradford came to my desk and asked me to recite, I looked at the floor and replied shyly, "Miss Bradford, I learned six of the eight verses, but I couldn't do it all." I looked up and saw in her face that she wasn't going for this explanation, and I didn't plan to take my punishment lying down. The standard punishment for misbehavior was a rap on the hands with a ruler. Miss Bradford gave me one rap. When it appeared that she intended a second one, I pulled back my fist, punched her in the stomach, and immediately began crying. The other children looked around at each other in disbelief.

Mother came to school immediately. She told Miss Bradford that the assignment was too much for a child to master overnight, because she herself had coached me through the material. But when we got home, she administered my punishment anyway, strapping me on my legs and hands, and made me apologize to Miss Bradford.

ONE DAY Aunt Noella, Uncle Walter, and Aunt Hilda arrived at our house and seemed unusually quiet. I couldn't hear what they said to Mother, but her hands flew up to her head as if she were shocked. She fell on Aunt Noella's shoulder and began crying softly. Aunt Noella hugged her and patted her back. I got real quiet and watched. Mother got her coat and left without saying a word.

"It was pressure," I heard one of the grown people say, but I had no idea what it meant. Then David whispered to me that Grandma Rita had died.

She was one of the most important people in my life. I remember Aunt Noella's wedding in August 1935, because Grandma Rita made my flower girl's white dress and took me shopping for white shoes and socks. It mattered to me that she let me pick out the shoes and that we went out to eat afterward. When the day of the wedding finally arrived, I carried out my flower girl assignment without a hitch, and Grandma Rita was proud of me.

The sense of security I felt holding her hand still warms me. She was such a beautiful woman, tall and regal, with dark chiseled features and marvelous hair pulled back so you could see her striking face. Mother told me even then that I resembled her.

I don't remember the funeral well, but I know I was there. It was the custom in New Orleans for children to go to wakes and funerals. Sometimes children were encouraged to touch the dead person, but I never did. There wasn't a lot of talk about Grandma Rita's death, but I understood that I wouldn't see her again. A picture of her appeared on our fireplace mantel, tied with a black ribbon. For a while, Mother wore black dresses, as did my aunts. I often saw Mother looking at Grandma Rita's picture. Even though she said nothing, I felt her sadness. One day, I went to her and hugged her. Tears rolled down our cheeks.

THE FOLLOWING year, Grandma Rita's mother, Mamal, died. She was living with us at the time. She always called me Baby and told me what a pretty and well-behaved little girl I was. She slept in a brass bed with shiny knobs that I believed in my mind had once belonged to a royal person. When I waited on Mamal and brought her tea, I imagined that she was a queen and I was her servant.

Mamal died in the brass bed I loved so much. I wanted to keep it in our household, but Mother gave it to one of her sisters. In a brief time, I saw two generations of our family pass away.

2

My Father's Dream

DAD'S MOTHER, Mary Lee Verrett, lived on. She was a true matriarch. There was no question about who wore the pants in her household. She could curse like a sailor. Whenever she did, Dad told us to put our hands over our ears.

Although I loved that old woman dearly, she and Mother did not get along at all. Dad was Grandma Verrett's pride and joy. She did not feel that Mother was pretty enough for her son. She had wanted him to marry someone not only prettier, but also lighter. I believe those were just excuses, because her other sons married women of varying complexions, and this apparently didn't matter to her. She really just wanted Dad to stay with her, because she had some sense of where he was going and what he would become. Grandma, I am convinced, was jealous of Mother.

Mother did not like Grandma Verrett, either. Mother didn't like her children being around Grandma when she was cursing "up a blue streak." I never heard Mother say anything hostile, but when we went to Grandma's house for a visit, Mother seldom got out of the car. We children were just dropped off or picked up.

Grandma Verrett had once owned a restaurant, although at that point she was primarily a homemaker. She made fabulous cakes, turkeys, stuffing, pies, breads, gumbo, red beans and rice, and other foods. I loved being in the kitchen with her because she let me help her cook. Among other things, I learned to roll dough for bread and pastry, cut meat for gumbo, separate the good rice from the bad, shuck corn, and boil potatoes. Being at her house was very different from being at home. When we ate at her house, my brother David and I could eat meat and not be punished. Although we were lacto-ovo vegetarians, Grandma Verrett, the matriarch, told us to eat the meat, that it was good for us. We, of course, did as she said. On these occasions she overruled both of my parents, and neither of them ever said anything.

"Yes, I told them to eat the meat and you will not touch them," she told Dad once while she stood in front of us. Dad merely looked at the floor in response, as if to say, "Yes, ma'am."

Grandma broke other rules that Adventists were supposed to observe. When she sent me to a movie with my aunts Rosemary and Selena, it was the first time in my life that I had ever been to one. I was close to ten years old and had a good time watching the Lone Ranger, Tonto, and Silver, the horse. I knew I shouldn't have gone, but Grandma Verrett had authorized it and that was that.

Back at Grandma's house, I felt uneasy. "What's going to happen when my daddy comes?" I asked. "He's going to give me a whipping."

"No, he won't. I'll talk to him when he gets here," she said calmly. When Daddy arrived to pick me up, she told him that *she* had sent me to the movies. *She* paid for it, it wasn't a bad movie, and he wasn't to punish me for going. He didn't. He explained to me later that it wasn't my fault, but his mother's.

In retrospect, it's obvious Dad and Grandma Verrett were born actors. Dad used to tell dark Southern ghost stories, with singing so scary that all of us children would try to get through one doorway at once when it was bedtime.

"Honey, why are you doing that to the kids?" Mother used to ask. And he'd reply, "Like father, like son." His father used to do that to him, and he didn't think anything of it. For years afterward, I would look under the bed and in closets, thinking I'd see a dead person or a spirit.

Dad also told me that Mamal was once a "street" actress. At the time I was born, she was sixty and not performing anymore. But I recognized in her movements the theatrics of an actor. Apparently, all these natural actors inspired me. They awakened something inside me.

Grandma Verrett was a spiritualist and had her own church. In that setting, she was known and beloved as "Mother Verrett." The church was a large room in her home, filled with burning candles and incense, which created a kind of eerie, but very effective, setting for the service. Aunt Selena played a prelude at the piano as the members and visitors arrived. Sometimes she played standard hymns like "Nearer My God to Thee" and "What Are They Doing in Heaven Today?" and at other times, the kind of songs one still hears today in Baptist or Sanctified churches. When Aunt Selena shifted to entrance music, it announced Mother Verrett's arrival.

Grandma Verrett appeared, dressed in a long white robe, with her arms stretched out like Christ's on the cross. Her head swayed from side to side; her eyes were half-closed, as if in a partial trance. As she walked down the aisle, an ample woman, she shifted her hips from one side to the other, in time with her swaying head, with a slight bounce to her knees. It looked, when I think back on it, somewhat mechanical, but it enthralled the church members. Some had their eyes fixed on her every movement; others sat in chairs with their eyes closed, rocking back and forth, humming or mumbling quietly to themselves as if they were in a trance. Sometimes Grandma let out a soft groan or a moan that gradually swelled.

Her voice rose with almost rhythmic precision. Everyone waited with great anticipation for her to begin her healings and blessings. Even people who were not regular members came for this part, because they, too, believed in her healing powers.

I lapped it all up like a kitten drinking milk. It was pure theater. There were times when I got caught up in the moment.

"Amen!" "Thank you, Jesus!" or "Hallelujah!" I yelled with the other members of the church.

Grandma Verrett could hold her own with any man who stepped into a pulpit. Grandpa Verrett preached and he was good, but I preferred Grandma, because she had all the hand gestures. She rubbed her hands together very fast, almost like a clap. Then she blew on them three times, did a quick clap-clap-clap, and laid her hands on someone who might just fall back with arms outstretched, as if hit by an electric charge.

I paid close attention to these dramatic hand motions and routinely practiced them at home in front of a mirror. I learned them so well I teased Elmo Serrao, one of my friends next door, into thinking I was putting a curse on him. He told his mother and she said if I didn't stop, she would tell my parents. David, Leon, and I thought Mother Verrett's healing was mostly make-believe.

It amused me that Grandma Verrett terrified my sister, Elvira. Elvira had been sickly in her childhood and had to be given tonics and herbal remedies to combat constant illnesses. She was afraid of the candles and all the incense in Grandma's church. That didn't sit well with Grandma, who didn't like squeamish and "scary" little children. Sometimes, throwing her hands up in a threatening manner, she deliberately frightened Elvira. Elvira immediately cried, as if on cue. It was kind of funny to me as a small child. Although Elvira never said anything negative, I could tell she didn't like being at Grandma's. My brothers David and Leon Jr. were like me. We all loved being around her. She was particularly fond of Leon Jr., whom she thought resembled her precious son.

GRANDMA VERRETT died when I was about ten, so it had to be at the beginning of the 1940s. Mother remembers it as what was then called a "hard death," when the person doesn't want to leave this life and fights death's onset. Grandma Verrett evidently suffered a lot. Mother said—with some sarcasm I suppose—that she could heal everyone else, but she couldn't heal herself.

Being at the funeral with David and Leon Jr. was a traumatic experience because for the first time I saw our daddy crying. He stood next to Grandma's graveside. He had to take his glasses off because the tears were streaming down his face so hard. Even though I was young, I really felt bad about him losing his mother. It was the saddest moment of my young life.

IN THESE early years, I started absorbing the harsh lessons of race from my father. He taught me my race's "place," and I learned better than to ask any questions. As a little girl, I was taken to the "Colored Only" bathrooms in stores, and I accepted that as the custom. But it wasn't this easy for Dad, and I knew it. Sometimes black men were insulted, even assaulted, for merely looking at a white person the wrong way.

Dad could not abide the omnipresent racial prejudice. He and Mother took every opportunity to fill us with pride in our race. He always said bitterly that for black men to be successful, "You had to be ten times better than a white man, *and* humble." He wanted to change these rules for his children. At the same time, while he wanted us to know what was happening in those years—the lynchings and other unspeakable acts that haunted black life in the South—he did not want us to develop what he called a "chip on our shoulder."

I vividly remember the bigotry of the South. Everywhere we went, we could be made to feel like criminals. I was very angry about this and had violent feelings myself. I wished a bomb would just blow all the benighted, cruel people away. I was angry each time we were treated like second-class citizens, as if we didn't belong anywhere. I was angry when we weren't allowed to go into certain stores or to try on clothes because the fitting room was for whites only. I was angry when we had to go around to back doors to buy food or had to eat in the car because we couldn't be served in a restaurant. I was angry when we had to drink from separate water fountains. But I kept the fury bottled up inside.

As I got older, I realized that many white people were involved in the struggle for civil rights and that a bomb was not the answer. But now, when I encounter the racism of another person who assumes I'm not as smart or talented as him, it takes me right back to my childhood rage.

AFTER THE attack on Pearl Harbor in 1941, Dad traveled around the country, building barracks and bungalows—at first in the South, but later going west to Seattle and Tacoma. Dad liked what he saw and fell in love with Washington State. For the first time, he began to visualize a new home, not in the South, but in a community far more tolerant of black people. We would have moved right away had Grandma Verrett not been ill. After her death, Dad decided it was time to leave New Orleans. His word was law. If he and Mother had a disagreement over leaving, none of us knew.

I was more than ready to go. In fact, when the day came, I didn't even want to stay around and say good-bye to anyone. We piled into a small house trailer, a mobile home Dad had bought for us to live and travel in until he could build us a home wherever we finally put down roots.

Traveling during the war was difficult, especially for seven people on a long trip who were riding in a trailer built for four or five. It seemed as if a tire blew out every two miles. Few places served "Coloreds." We followed an "underground" road system to the black sections of towns to get food or go to the bathroom.

Our first big stop was in Los Angeles, California. Dad wanted to see his brother, Uncle Harrison, who was stationed at Port Hueneme, five miles outside of Oxnard, a flat suburban landscape with few trees. We parked our trailer in a very nice black family's backyard. I hated the arrangement and so did Mother, but Dad saw possibilities in Oxnard for the start of his construction company. Uncle Harrison confirmed that it was a good place to start a business, so Dad decided to stay. The decision horrified Mother and me, but he determined this was the place and moved our trailer to another black couple's yard.

Within a year, with the help of David, who was barely a teenager, Dad built a new home for us from scratch, on land he had purchased. When he finally sold our trailer home, Mother celebrated.

This began a beautiful time in my social life as an Adventist. In Oxnard, we joined an all-white congregation, including the Peak and the Porter families, which had children the same ages as ours. We visited back and forth at each others' houses. We had wonderful potluck picnics, played softball, and staged sack races. Dad became the choir director, and Mother and I often sang solos or duets. Elder Scully, our pastor, was a very good leader, kindly and attractive. His mother-in-law, Mrs. McKim, became one of my teachers in high school. This kind of community was what Dad had wanted for us—to not feel like second-class citizens.

Meanwhile, Dad's construction company was booming. He acquired more property, on which he built apartments to rent. We became middle-class, with the wherewithal to afford a housekeeper and cook. Of course, Mother wouldn't have it. As far as she was concerned, she was the only person who cooked in her kitchen, with the exception of her sisters. She held on to that fear of someone tampering with her pots. Mother also washed and pressed the clothes. When my sister, Elvira, was old enough, she did a lot of the ironing. I had to wash dishes and hated it. Thank God, Dad put in a dishwasher.

FOR ME, what mattered most didn't change. Mother and Dad still ruled the household, and, like it or not, their decisions were the law. One memory sums up my growing frustration.

When I was about fifteen, I had to ride a bus ten miles to an Adventist school. I had gone to a nearby public school for a brief period after we arrived in Oxnard, but I felt that the white children were getting more from the teachers than I was being offered. Mother and Dad agreed and enrolled me in our church's school in Ventura. Consequently, I had to get up and leave early and was frequently late.

One day, a train crossed my path and held me up as I rushed to catch the bus. I missed it. By chance, one of my neighborhood friends offered to drive me to school in his car. He was a nice young man from a good family, so I got in. I was in that car for only a few minutes when I heard a loud horn blowing behind us. Dad roared up beside us and yelled, "Get *out* of that car and get in here!"

In those days you didn't question your father, especially not mine. I was never so humiliated and embarrassed. I tried to explain to him that he knew the boy's family, but he didn't care. He was thinking about his fifteen-year-old daughter in a teenage boy's car and let his imagination run wild with what that might lead to. I told him I had accepted that ride because I was always late.

"We will figure that out!" he said. "But in the meantime I don't want to see you in any boy's car again."

By the time I got home from school that day, he had decided two things. First, he would build a home closer to Ventura, so I would no longer have a reason to be late. And second, he would let me drive. That afternoon he had gotten permission from the Department of Motor Vehicles for me to get a driver's permit six months early. When he found a little car I called a "flivver," which was *very* used, I was allowed to drive myself back and forth to school, as long as I promised not to pick up anyone.

There was another change—my new baby brother, Ronald. When Dad suggested that we had a large enough family, Mother responded, "It's up to you, brother." Ronald *was* the last. There were now six Verrett children.

We moved to the new house when I was sixteen and in my junior year of high school. Dad built a playroom, as well as a small movie theater above the detached three-car garage so we could see movies at home. I suppose he and Mother relaxed a little, watching the films with us.

At first, Dad chose all of the movies we saw. One of my favorites was *The Imitation of Life,* with the African American actress Louise Beavers. Mother and I cried at the suffering of Beavers's character.

She was unfairly treated by her daughter and by a society that saw her as a second-class citizen because of her color. I'm sure Dad chose this movie with some deliberation because he used it to have a discussion with us about the importance of not forgetting from whence we had come. As time passed, Dad relented and let us suggest the films.

We remained a close-knit family. We all went together on occasional weekend trips to Los Angeles, sixty miles away, to attend black Adventist social gatherings. We were not the only family from New Orleans who had migrated to California. My friend Iris Charles and her family, Jackie Mathieu's family, and several of Dad's brothers followed us to the West Coast. Dad helped his brothers settle when they came, and they continued the Verrett family building tradition in Southern California. To encourage us children in learning business principles, Dad even built a little soda shop for us to run. Our business didn't last long, because we were more interested in socializing than in selling sodas.

ALL ALONG, Dad never gave up on his dream of *me* becoming famous. I always seemed to have known that he had painted me into his dreams. Once when I was quite young, a nurse came through the church school and looked down at my nails. She said, "Shirley, if you're going to be a singer and perform for large audiences, you'll have to stop biting your nails." That did it. Nothing anyone had said before had affected my nervous habit, but this did.

Nevertheless, when Dad wanted to pay for me to take voice lessons as a teenager, I was convinced it would be a waste of his money, because I didn't feel ready to study. So, he let me spread my wings a little, under the supervision of his cousin Artemease. I attended the Adventists' Los Angeles Academy during the week and came home on the weekends.

I loved getting away from home and just being myself. One of the jokes among the students was that I talked so much, I could give a wrong answer and make it seem right just by talking around it. I was voted the junior class president.

I sang with the Los Angeles Academy school choir, but only after the director and Dad agreed that I would be the principal singer in any performances that required a soloist. Dad continued to acquire recordings and take me and Mother to concerts whenever Marian Anderson or other notable African American singers came to Los Angeles. Leon still sang but lacked my interest; I seized every opportunity. Still, I was not fired up by the idea of committing myself to a singing career.

When I graduated at seventeen, and went to Ventura Junior College to study bookkeeping and economics, it was because Dad wanted me to have another skill besides singing. In time I became a pretty good bookkeeper and kept the company books, which were then sent to his accountant. Whenever Dad claimed he didn't have money for something I asked him for, I would just give him a "know it all" look, because I knew differently. I must say, my bookkeeping knowledge came in handy on several occasions throughout my life.

Whenever Dad and I talked about my future as a singer, he asked me when I thought I might be ready to study. I couldn't answer or explain it to him at the time, but somehow I felt I would know. Meanwhile, I continued to sing at local and regional events.

In 1948, at a fundraiser for a big organization, I had a brush with fate that tested my instincts. That day, I happened to be singing on the same program with a very fine African American singer named Georgia Lasster. She was several years older than me and had already embarked on a professional career. Georgia had a wonderful instrument, a very rich soprano voice, a broad face and nose, and a complexion and eyes that suggested she might have some Asian ancestry. She was very complimentary of my singing and told me about her teacher, Madame DeSanctis. Subsequently, I took a few lessons from this nice lady, who taught me the *Vaccai* vocal exercises and a few early Italian songs.

Georgia also told me about an upcoming vocal competition she had been a finalist in a year or so earlier, sponsored by Atwater Kent, the electrical company. Dad reminded me that we had heard Georgia singing in the Atwater Kent finals on the radio.

"Shirley, *you* could win that contest!" Dad said later with quiet enthusiasm. He thought I could do anything. So I entered the competition.

Some weeks later, Dad drove me to the first round, held in a beautiful home in Santa Barbara, about thirty miles from Oxnard. I was the only African American contestant. While I was waiting around with the other young singers, they talked about having studied in Europe with this person and that person, and I began to get nervous.

How could I hold my own against these contestants, I wondered? Dad saw that I needed reassurance and immediately stepped in.

"Shirley, don't *ever* listen to what people tell you they've done. You just go out and do what you have to do. I can tell you that most of those girls can't sing." Just then, a girl who had bragged about her travels and her vocal studies began to sing. It was horrible. I thought to myself, "Where did she study?"

When it was my turn, I sang the Italian song "O Cessate di Piegarmi" (O stop this anguish). Dad told me later the well-known operatic and musical theater baritone John Charles Thomas had been standing in the hall at that moment. The Italian song seemed to have caught his attention. Next, I sang my own solo arrangement of the duet "Come, Come, I Love You Only" from *The Chocolate Soldier,* with music by Oscar Strauss.

Dad said Thomas was about to walk off, but he turned, came back, and listened attentively. Thomas had an established name in operetta repertory and became quite celebrated in the dual roles of Karl Lang and Vasili Vasilovich Varonofsky in *The Chocolate Soldier.* Dad and I had seen him perform it onstage and had listened to several of his recordings, with no idea that he was connected to the competition, much less that he was its principal judge and artistic sponsor.

That evening, the judges announced that *Shirley Verrett* had won the first round. I was nearly floored. I know Dad could have done back flips at this news, but he was very reserved and nodded his appreciation when others came around to congratulate me. When we got home, Dad gathered the family around and told them that I had won. Everyone was excited. Mother hugged me. When she loosened her embrace, I could see tears welling in her eyes. The other kids kept jumping up and down. I stood there and smiled.

"I said you could win," Dad kept repeating with a grin.

As a result of my winning that first round, John Charles Thomas recommended me to study with the celebrated soprano Lotte Lehmann at the Music Academy of the West. Madame Lehmann had been one of the opera world's superstars. She had an enormous repertoire and an extensive recorded legacy. I had heard several of her recordings among Dad's huge record collection.

I realized that Mr. Thomas might have arranged the Lehmann offer on his own, but I had already decided I would not accept it. I felt that Madame Lehmann was definitely out of my league as a teacher at this time in my life.

I met Mr. Thomas at the Music Academy of the West in Santa Barbara, in a large room full of musical scores, all very neatly arranged and catalogued. He kept his sheet music in several large file cabinets, which were also beautifully arranged. I am sure he could have put his hand on any piece of music he wanted. Pictures of him in various opera roles hung on his wall. I recognized him with his fellow Baltimorean Rosa Ponselle from a Metropolitan Opera production of Verdi's *La Traviata*.

After singing, with Thomas's accompanist at the piano, I declined the offer to study with Madame Lehmann. I could see John Charles Thomas's surprise. Assuming I must not know of Madame Lehmann's celebrity as a world-class opera singer or of the doors that could open for me if I studied with an artist of her stature, he asked me if I knew who she was. When I told him I knew but wasn't ready for that level of commitment, he told me he respected my honesty. After an awkward pause in the conversation, he wished me well in the later rounds of the Atwater Kent competition, and I left.

After the Atwater Kent competition, I never saw John Charles Thomas again. He eventually became director of the Music Academy of the West. I only hope he felt vindicated years later when I began to emerge as a singer in the region. I advanced to the second round of the Atwater Kent competition, but, competing against people who had been studying for a long time, I was eliminated.

"This was just luck," I told Dad. "I have a good voice, but I am not ready for this yet." Most of what I knew about singing at that time, Dad had taught me. I had taken only three other lessons. As it turned out, I didn't study voice again for another five years.

Instead, in 1949, I enrolled at Oakwood College, a Seventh-Day Adventist school in Huntsville, Alabama. I begged for months before Mother and Dad agreed to let me go.

"We took you out of the South so you wouldn't experience that kind of treatment again, and you are going right back!" Dad said incredulously. But I was headstrong and determined to go and follow some of my friends.

I sensed early on that Dad was right, again. The college had a very restrictive dress code. We couldn't wear revealing clothes. Once, I decided to wear a sleeveless blouse to see how far I could get. Before I even made it to my first class, the matriarch of the campus, Mother Cunningham, saw me.

"Aren't we a little cold, dear?"

I feigned surprise at her remark, but I also went back to my room and got a sweater.

I adjusted more easily to the dietary rules that excluded meat, unlike the students who had not grown up as Adventists. Some of them slipped off campus to eat meat, or they got it cooked elsewhere and brought it back to their rooms.

I found that I missed singing. Dad had made it clear that he didn't want me to sing in a choir anymore because mine was not a choir voice but a soloist's voice. He believed that a choir director would force me to blend in with the other singers and mute the soloist quality of my voice. Whether he was correct or not, I followed his advice. When my psychology professor discovered I could sing, word spread and I was urged to join the Aeolians. Even then, this campus choral group had regional celebrity and had toured in other parts of the country. I politely declined the invitation, though.

After one semester I left, despite making the dean's list. I had come to college expecting to enjoy more freedom. Instead, I was more cloistered than before. And to be completely honest, I wanted to leave for another reason. I had been dating a man back home. We wrote to each other during the semester I was in Huntsville, and he occasionally called. When I told my colleagues I was dating an "older" man, they were green with envy. After I got back to California, he proposed marriage.

3

Mrs. James Carter

MET James Carter during a weekend trip that my family took to Los Angeles. He was fourteen years older than I was and a member of Wadsworth Seventh-Day Adventist Church in Los Angeles. James Carter was handsome, in uniform when I first met him, and eligible. He was a tall, light-skinned, muscular man with a small mustache and had very large hands.

Many young ladies were interested in him in that congregation, not to mention outside the church—including Georgia Lasster. He had persuaded her to become an Adventist by first inviting her to prayer meetings and Bible studies. Not only did she join, but her mother and brother did, too. Georgia became disillusioned with the progress of her singing career and, in compensation, became almost evangelistic in the Adventist faith. She went preaching at airports and shopping malls. Georgia died tragically in a car accident en route to one such engagement.

It was hard to believe that James Carter took notice of me, because I was so much younger than many other young ladies in the church. I had had the usual boyfriends, and then there was the man, James

Carter. I have asked God to forgive me, because even though I may have been infatuated for a brief time, I realized later that I never really loved him.

Mother and Dad had misgivings, but they let James Carter court me. He was loud and overbearing. Mother wondered aloud why a thirty-year-old man would be interested in a young girl—almost a child—when there were so many eligible older women. As much as I loved Mother, she could be a nag, so I let her wondering go in one ear and out the other.

After James Carter left the army, he became a Los Angeles County deputy sheriff and sold real estate on the side. When I reflect back, I find his job choice puzzling, because Adventists did not believe in carrying firearms.

Mother and Dad agreed to the marriage, but only after James Carter promised to let me continue my education and to sing after we were wed. Meanwhile, my school-girlish enthusiasm for the match slowly turned to ashes. By the time I came to my senses, it was too late.

The wedding took place on July 22, 1951, with twelve bridesmaids and groomsmen, several flower girls, and other attendants. I was told that a few girls who had pined for James Carter for years literally cried at the ceremony or did not attend. We had the reception at a huge mansion in Los Angeles. I received three truckloads of gifts. It was all such a waste. If you look at the photographs of the wedding, you can see my unhappy face. If not for the preaching I would have surely gotten from Dad, I would have canceled it. I was afraid of his anger and a lecture on wasting money.

The morning after the wedding confirmed what I'd suspected. It was a mistake. We were not compatible. I really didn't love him. That was the tragedy of the situation. The trick was on me. I found myself bound to a person who was more restrictive than my parents.

As a little girl growing up in the Adventist church, I constantly heard "Jesus is coming," today or tomorrow, to end the world as we knew it. You can't imagine the fear such a notion generated in me as a child. I wanted to be a grown-up and make my own decisions before the world ended. In my rush to become an adult, I thought James Carter could liberate me and give me some semblance of a free life while I was young enough to enjoy it.

Accepting my parents' devout religious beliefs had left me feeling caged and claustrophobic. I went through a tricky period as a teenager. Religion scared me to death. You couldn't do this. You couldn't do that. It was fire and brimstone every five seconds, it seemed. I was also a very obedient child. Yes, being the young singer in the family was great in some ways, but I preferred to believe I was valued more for being the biggest help to my mother.

In obedience to the commands of the church, I always tried to hide my sexuality as a young woman. Being an openly sexual woman was *verboten*. Dancing was *verboten*. Showing off your body was *verboten*. I tried to keep my body under wraps. According to our religion, the private, intimate display of sexuality was fine, but you never wanted to show it too much in public. You didn't want to bring it out into the open.

It would be many more years, long after I had become an adult, before I stopped carrying around these feelings. Working with the great acting teacher Stella Adler helped me to see things differently. She helped me to learn more about my body, about the moves I needed to make, and how to be freer and more sexual when I was onstage. As a young woman with a strict upbringing, I still hadn't gotten over the restraints I'd put on my body. I suspect that all these restrictions had led me to marry at a very early age.

Given our family backgrounds, with both of us "middle-class" and not having the financial strains of many young couples, we should have been okay. James Carter's family was good to us. His parents, who had been divorced, both loved me very much. Even his sisters and I got along very well. My father-in-law, who had been a teacher, came to California from the South and acquired a good deal of property in Lancaster County, including a large ranch. He gave us the down payment on two apartment buildings in a nice Los Angeles neighborhood. We lived in one apartment and rented out the other seven units. When Dad asked me what I wanted for a wedding gift from him and Mother, I mentioned furniture, and he took me shopping.

I stayed in close touch with Mother and Dad and became a pseudo-parent to my baby brother, Ronnie. He was such a cute, quick little boy, with a beautifully innocent smile like Mother's. He was about four then. People often thought he was my child. I didn't correct them because I felt such a sense of pride while looking out for him. I taught Ronnie the alphabet and how to count, and I read to him.

I wanted to grow up quickly, to be an adult. I wanted to be in a position where I could make decisions for myself, before Jesus came out of the clouds of Heaven. That was my fear and my driving force. I liked being a grown-up. I still like the idea of adult responsibility.

I'll be the first to admit, though, that back in those days I had a smart mouth. I guess I still have it, to a degree. My brother David told me before I got married, "Shirl, you are going to have to curb your tongue. Husbands aren't going to take what brothers take." I didn't heed that advice. I had a husband who was jealous of my young friends, and in less than a month he wanted to dictate who they would be. For someone who cherished freedom as much as I did, this was bound to cause friction.

One evening I was talking to Elvira on the phone. A real sisterly bond had developed between us. I could remember a time, years earlier, when she'd ask me to braid her hair and I routinely said, "No," partly because I resented her curling up around Daddy, while I was always working around the house, by Mother's side—the obedient one. Feeling such resentment toward my sister seemed like a sin. Now she was no longer a whining kid sister but had grown into a lovely young woman. What's more, she was about to leave home for Oakwood College. Because I was a good seamstress, she had asked for my help in making a suit. She had a million questions about life in Huntsville.

While we were on the phone, James Carter complained that I was talking too long. When I hung up, he demanded a say in whom I spoke to and associated with.

"Are you crazy? You can't tell *me* who to see. I'm going to see and talk to whomever I wa—"

Whoop! He slapped me right in the mouth, midsentence. He hit me so fast, I didn't even see it coming. I think I was more stunned and angry than hurt by the blow. But I was no shrinking violet. I immediately called my father. Dad was an Adventist, but he kept a gun at his office for protection and was ready to drive the sixty miles from Oxnard to deal with this situation.

James Carter screamed, "You tell him if he comes, he'd better be ready to deal with the consequences!" Mother calmed Dad down, and after I thought about it, I got back on the phone and told him to stay home. The next day, James Carter and Dad talked things over calmly.

I wanted a divorce even then, but our religion didn't allow it. I sometimes cried to myself at night, feeling that I had made a terrible mistake. Then I went to stay with my Aunt Hazel, Mother's youngest sister in Los Angeles. I got a job and didn't tell James Carter. Being a policeman, though, he found me. Church people persuaded me to return.

BY LATE 1953 or early 1954, James Carter and I looked like a successful couple, but I was unhappy and directionless. We had moved to Pacoima, California, a small town in the San Fernando Valley. We bought quite a few houses and owned prime property on a corner lot. We installed another office there and then built several shops to lease. For close to three years, I was no more than an average student at Los Angeles State College. Then I gave up, enrolled in a real estate course, and got my salesperson's license. In the San Fernando Valley, in Los Angeles, and also in Las Vegas, Nevada, I sold what were known as development houses, mostly in areas designated for African Americans or other minorities. At a point, however, I became tired of making a sales pitch, of always figuring out how to persuade a prospective buyer.

One day I said to myself, I should be singing instead of selling
houses. It was that simple. I was finally ready to do what Dad had
urged for years.

I looked in the yellow pages and from the listings chose a Madame
Consoli. The name was Italian, so I assumed she knew how to teach
voice. She had been a young singer in Italy. Her referrals came from
several major movie studios. Occasionally, stretch limousines arrived
at her studio. The starlets wanted to be incognito, and Madame Consoli maintained their privacy.

She charged very little. I drove up once a week to her Hollywood
home, while I was still selling real estate in the San Fernando Valley
area. She liked me so much I became her "thing," and she took me to
local music events. When the Young Musicians Foundation sponsored a televised competition in Los Angeles, Madame Consoli took
me. The foundation identified and assisted young pianists, singers,
instrumentalists, and conductors. Sylvia Kunin, the president, was a
wonderful pianist whose terrible stage fright had prevented her from
having a major career. Instead, she dedicated her life to helping young
musicians fulfill their ambitions.

Meeting Sylvia Kunin was one of the most fortunate things that
could have happened at that time. Sylvia and the foundation connection eventually transported me from invisibility to national visibility,
and I have Madame Consoli to thank for it.

Yet I was in Madame Consoli's studio for no more than five months
when her studio accompanist, Dean Mauk, pulled me aside.

"Your voice is too good to be wasting time with this lady," he said.

I didn't think I had wasted my time but asked, "Do you have someone else in mind?"

"Yes, but she will only take people who are serious about having careers. No matter how fine the voice, she won't take you if you are not
serious." That teacher was Anna Fitziu. I switched to her studio and
never saw Madame Consoli again. I often thought of her, though,

and felt sad that I had to leave her studio. She was a very encouraging teacher, but I needed more than she could give me. I was on a mission.

Anna Fitziu questioned me at length about what I wanted to do with my voice and my life. After hearing me, she was convinced I was a soprano. Madame Consoli hadn't pronounced me anything and said only that I had a wide range. Anna Fitziu and I began working in what she called the European manner. Five days a week I drove up from Pacoima to her house in Hollywood Hills. I am told the house once belonged to Rudolph Valentino. Since I came from such a distance, I stayed all day and had lessons in the morning and the afternoon. In-between, we ate lunch. When she taught other students, I repaired lace tablecloths in another part of the house. Sometimes she and I worked on them together.

We talked incessantly about music, and she played recordings of many great singers. We talked about her singing career and how one had to study in order to have success. She exposed me to a lot of vocal literature. When she assigned me the "Alleluia" from Mozart's *Exsultate Jubilate,* I learned that God had given me the facility for coloratura singing. I also learned Santuzza's big aria from *Cavalleria Rusticana* and even sang "Ritorno Vincitor!" from *Aida.*

DURING THIS period, another major influence came into my life—the great chorus master, composer, and arranger Dr. Hall Johnson. I must credit James Carter with that meeting. He knew I had sung spirituals since I was young, and he, too, had a love of music. He thought that Hall Johnson, a well-known interpreter and internationally renowned choir director, could strengthen my performances. Johnson lived in Los Angeles then but still maintained an apartment in New York City, where he had risen to fame during the Harlem Renaissance.

By the mid-1950s, Hall Johnson was already in his late sixties but very imposing and dignified. He was a tall, lanky man, with light brown-reddish skin and sandy-brown hair. He held his shoulders up in a tense position, antithetical to the correct singing posture. The stance was somewhat intimidating, given his height, but he was an extremely gracious and polished man.

I sang several spirituals for Hall Johnson the day we met. After listening awhile, he said, "You have the right musical instincts to sing spirituals. Not all Negro singers do." He suggested a few changes. He thought I needed only a couple of lessons to polish my interpretations.

Then, quite unexpectedly, he recommended that I learn German lieder, saying, "That's where your life will be, in song recital." Hall Johnson became my first German teacher. He was fluent in French and German. When speaking English, he had a slight stutter that vanished when he spoke foreign languages. He started me on some Brahms songs, and to this day Brahms is one of my favorite lieder composers. His songs have such pathos and emotion.

When I eventually went to Juilliard, my German teacher there was flabbergasted at my facility and asked where I had learned the language. I told her from Hall Johnson, whom I am sure she had never heard of, much less suspected was a black man who had graduated from the University of Pennsylvania and had also studied at Juilliard.

"I don't care who taught you. He did a good job," she said.

FOR A young singer, making a commitment to have a singing career is one thing. But being propelled into an arena beyond local competitions and performances is quite another, psychologically. It was the chance to sing on the *Arthur Godfrey's Talent Scouts* show that taught me that invaluable lesson. By this time I had won musical competitions sponsored by the Young Musicians Foundation in Los Angeles and had performed at Adventist regional conventions.

New York, however, was the big time for singers. So it was a huge lucky break when talent scouts from the Godfrey show contacted Sylvia Kunin, and she recommended two young performers: me and a pianist. *Arthur Godfrey's Talent Scouts* had a viewership of more than one million people a week. Each program reached a much wider audience than the weekly Texaco Metropolitan Opera radio broadcast did. After I sang two songs for the Godfrey talent scouts, they said the audition was over and asked me to sing something else just for their pleasure. I knew then that I would be selected for the show.

What would I sing? This was a huge question, considering the impact I believed it could have on my career. At first, Madame Fitziu and I decided on "Dich teure Halle" (Hail Great Hall) from Wagner's *Tannhäuser*, but she worried that it was not well known outside of opera circles. She wanted me to sing something the television audience—that is, non–opera listeners—would appreciate. Around that time, a black singer named Herbert Jeffrey (also known as Herb Jeffries) had popularized "When I Write My Song," set to the melody of Delilah's aria, "Mon coeur s'ouvre a ta voix" (My heart opens at thy voice), from *Samson et Dalila*. Anna Fitziu decided that I should sing the first verse and the ending, a perfect blend for the three minutes allowed, as well as for the audience's taste. With that performance, Shirley Carter, the mezzo-soprano, was born.

KNOWING I was going to the East Coast, I made another important decision: to explore the possibility of competing in the Marian Anderson voice competition, which was being in held in Philadelphia soon after the Godfrey show. I applied and was accepted. Then, to my delight, I found out that Marian Anderson would give a recital in California just before I left for New York. I asked the concert promoters if I could sing for her. They told me she was not available, but that I could sing for her personal manager, Mr. Jaffe.

At the appointed time, we met at a piano company. Shoppers browsed, as I began to sing Franz Schubert's "Du Bist di Ruh" (You Are the Rest), among other works. Franz Rupp, Marian Anderson's accompanist, played for me. Rupp played like an angel. It was the first time I had performed with someone of his caliber. His hands moved across the keys with such ease, his body attuned to the music. The shoppers stopped to listen and applauded when we finished our performance. Both Rupp and Mr. Jaffe were very encouraging about my voice.

* * *

MEANWHILE, EVERYONE in Pacoima found out that I was going to be on the Godfrey show. A lady who rented space in my building for her beauty parlor arranged for me to stay with her sister Mary Lou in New York.

As it turned out, Mary Lou was also a beautician and a part owner in a beauty salon in Harlem called Casdulan. Soon after arriving, I asked her to do my hair for the show, and she suggested that I meet Charles Beaver, an attorney across the street from her shop. Charlie was the husband of Camilla Williams, the well-known black concert and opera singer, who at the time was on a tour sponsored by the U.S. State Department. When Charlie learned I would be on the Godfrey show, he said he would ask Camilla's teacher, Madame Freschl, to watch.

The day of the show, I felt a little out of my element. Mary Lou had cut off all of my hair. I wore a blue dress with elbow-length sleeves, because I had gained weight and I thought that the style would be flattering. It wasn't. Once Godfrey found out I was "Mrs." Shirley Carter and my husband was with me, he invited James Carter to be on the telecast. James Carter's quick and witty responses to Arthur Godfrey's questions made the studio audience laugh. He was a real comedian.

Several contestants appeared with me, including an excellent jazz singer and an instrumentalist. At the end of the show, the three of us were declared winners and invited to stay a week longer for additional radio appearances. To curry favor and improve my chances of winning a longer engagement, James Carter encouraged me to flirt with one of the Godfrey producers. I acted as if I didn't hear him. The little regard I had for him weakened all the more. Although I didn't know it then, he could do nothing for me ever again.

Still savoring the Godfrey show victory, I set out to meet Marion Freschl. I owned one of Camilla Williams's recordings and knew that Madame Freschl was once known as Marion Szekely and had enjoyed a singing career in Hungary and Vienna. After marrying an Austrian psychiatrist, she eventually began teaching in the United States, first in Philadelphia and then at Juilliard.

In her late fifties then, Madame Freschl was elegant and tall, with nearly all-white hair, pulled back in a bun.

"I think you can be the most beautiful mezzo-soprano!" she said.

I started to list the soprano arias I had studied with Anna Fitziu. But Madame Freschl said that her ears told her I was a mezzo. I think she was conditioned more by having heard me sing the *Samson* aria when she watched the Godfrey show. I deferred to her judgment, but not before I put up a struggle. The next thing I knew, she suggested that I come to Juilliard as a student. She told me that if I stayed, became a student at Juilliard, and got a good musical foundation, I was certain to have a fine career.

Madame Freschl was not the first person that week to point out that remaining in the city might be the best thing for me. Sometime earlier, I had met Robert McFerrin, the celebrated baritone. Hall Johnson had written me a letter of introduction to him, thinking he might be helpful. This was the year McFerrin had broken the color barrier for African American men at the Metropolitan Opera, following Marian Anderson in a leading role.

Robert was a kind and beautiful man, just as Hall Johnson had said. Robert told me later that he had also auditioned for the Godfrey show but had not passed the qualifying round. I found that incredible. It seemed obvious that he hadn't qualified because he was a black man. In the history of the concert and opera world, no group has suffered more discrimination. McFerrin had won the national Met audition and was on his way to making his historic debut with the most prestigious opera house in the country, but he couldn't pass a preliminary round on the Godfrey show. This was a great singing voice that *could not* be overlooked.

McFerrin took me to his voice teacher, Ignaz Zitomirsky, also a kind and wonderful man and one of Dorothy Maynor's teachers.

"You study with me and I'll teach you for free!" Maestro Zitomirsky said after I sang for him. "You won't have to pay a cent. I guarantee you, in a year's time, you'll be at the Met!" He talked about some of his successful students, including Maynor and the legendary baritone Lawrence Tibbett.

Originally, I hadn't thought about staying in New York beyond the Marian Anderson competition. Now I had an entirely new perspective on the future. Freschl's vision promised a musical education, including performance practice, languages, and piano. I would finish up with a strong musical foundation. In contrast, James Carter, who was with me when I met both teachers, urged me to take the Zitomirsky offer because of the free lessons and the promise of the Metropolitan Opera.

It was not a hard choice to make. I was quite focused on what I needed for a successful career in the long run. And I thought opera was barely a serious consideration, given my race and religion. I thanked Maestro Zitomirsky but decided to go to the Juilliard School of Music.

Hall Johnson had made a prophecy when he learned I would be on the Godfrey show: "When you arrive in New York, you won't be back. They will keep you."

His words came true.

4

City of Dreams

HAVE to give the old devil his due. Some husbands might have said no to their wives staying in New York, but James Carter didn't.

Mary Lou said I could live with her and her mother in their Fifth Avenue apartment. The building had recently opened up to blacks. Lola Hayes, the African American singer and celebrated voice teacher, had an apartment there, as did Marian Anderson years later. I accepted Mary Lou's offer and paid a portion of the rent, bought and cooked my own food, mopped and waxed the floors, and generally kept the place clean. Cleaning the place was not part of the original deal, but I had been raised to pitch in and help wherever I lived, no matter what I paid in rent.

The arrangement didn't last long. After a few weeks, I overheard Mary Lou comment to her mother, with whom I shared a room, that she thought I was sitting on the living room sofa too much. Suddenly, it seemed as if I were a burden. I didn't know about stress then, but I immediately began to have vomiting spells for the first time in my life. I remembered that I was not a starving student and had means from my husband with which to support myself. I owned not only my own home but a few other properties as well. So I decided to look for another place.

In retrospect, I thank Mary Lou for her willingness to help a young person find herself in that huge city and for motivating me to move to the International House, located across from the old Juilliard site (now the Manhattan School of Music on Broadway). I stayed at the International House for three and a half wonderful years, enjoying my exposure to students from other countries. I practiced German, French, and Italian with many students and made lifelong friendships. I stopped clinging to a familiar home environment and began to experience the world.

IN SEPTEMBER 1955 I was twenty-four years old and more determined than ever to have a singing career. I sang an audition for the entire voice faculty and was immediately placed in the opera department. The adjustment to being a full-time student was surprisingly easy. In rapid succession, I was introduced to mezzo-soprano operatic literature, duets, and ensembles. I voraciously learned them all.

In October I took a train to Philadelphia, where the Marian Anderson Vocal Competition was being held in an auditorium on Rittenhouse Square. I shared a dressing room with several other female contestants. Although I recognized a few other Juilliard students whom I hadn't met formally, we just nodded politely to each other. Several of them were just singing away—up and down the scale, without a care. I remember not having a place to vocalize, and I had always been self-conscious about vocalizing before other people. So I warmed up by humming a series of scales or something.

My bravado all but vanished. Feeling very nervous because I hadn't really vocalized my entire voice, all I could think about was finishing, getting on the train, and going back to New York. To this day, I can barely remember what I sang. Peforming one or more of the songs was mandatory for all contestants in certain voice categories. I do remember that Marian Anderson wasn't there. Her sister was one of the judges. She, too, had a fabulous voice, I was told.

In those days, contestants were notified by telegram after the competition whether they had won or lost. Some of the Juilliard girls asked me at school if I had heard anything. A week or more passed and I tried to act nonchalant about the whole event but found myself subconsciously pacing the floor.

Then a telegram arrived. I had *won* the Marian Anderson Award! The final decision took a little longer than expected because the judges had declared a tie between a baritone and me. I told myself that it was sheer luck. Shirl, you better learn to vocalize in front of people, I thought. I never did, though. Even at the Met and other opera companies around the world, years later, I always vocalized at home.

I was incredibly happy and relieved to win the contest. The prize was only $500 but priceless for its prestige. Miss Anderson was such a famous name in the concert world that I knew it would advance my concert career. This proved to be true almost immediately. When I made a brief trip back to Los Angeles, I sang in a concert sponsored by the Young Musicians Foundation. The newspaper reviews praised the new young singer "Shirley Carter," who had won the Marian Anderson competition the previous October. Singing for the first time with an orchestra, I performed the *Samson* aria that I had done on the Godfrey show, because the foundation wanted to promote me for winning. I also sang the big aria from Donizetti's opera *La Favorita,* "O mio Fernando," which I had studied with Madame Freschl. The *Favorita* became my signature aria and remained in my repertory for over thirty-five years.

As excited as I was about getting this far, I was aiming for another league. I was impatient to get there and still had much to learn. Later in the spring of 1956, the president of Juilliard, William Schuman, and the dean of students, Mark Schubart, hosted a reception for new students, to see how we were coming along. My mouth got me in trouble again. The other students and I didn't feel that we were getting enough acting help in the opera program, and we agreed to voice our collective dissatisfaction to the president and dean at the reception. In the receiving line, guess who was the only one to speak up? I politely told the president and the dean about the problem. Their smiles turned to frowns. They were clearly not amused.

President Schuman said, "We seem to have done well by Leontyne Price and Gloria Davy." I assumed that he had mentioned those names because they are both African Americans. I had egg on my face but managed to respond, "I don't know what they received here, I'm just telling you what I'm not getting." I said this as I walked off, with my tail between my legs.

From that point on, I was under a magnifying glass at Juilliard. If that wasn't a lesson in being prepared to stand alone, I don't know what was. It sounded like the advice my father had given me years before. He'd say, "Shirl, never depend on what others do or promise to do. Just have the courage to stand alone. Have the courage of your convictions."

Not long after that incident, I met Leontyne Price, thanks to a poetry reading at International House given by my friend, the actor Roscoe Lee Browne. He had an incredibly cultivated speaking voice. His oratorical gifts notwithstanding, he could be chillingly frank. You did not want to cross him or get on his bad side, because he would let you have it. He could insult people and they wouldn't even know they'd been insulted. Fortunately, he and I liked each other.

After Roscoe heard me sing, he said, "You have to meet my friend Leontyne Price." Of course, that immediately caught my attention. She had appeared in an NBC televised production of Puccini's *Tosca*, a broadcast that several Southern cities blocked out because she sang opposite a white male singer. I am told that not even people in her hometown, Laurel, Mississippi, saw that broadcast.

As it turned out, Leontyne had also heard of me through her longtime accompanist David Garvey, a former Juilliard student. He accompanied me on a tape I made to enter a competition to debut at the Hollywood Bowl. Anyway, Leontyne knew me as Shirley Carter. Roscoe finally arranged for us to meet at International House at a reading, and we liked each other immediately.

"You are so pretty," she said when we were introduced.

I smiled and said, "So are you."

As the academic year drew to a close, I considered getting a summer job in New York. Mother, Dad, and James Carter expected that I would return to California. I dreaded it. I did not want to be around James Carter one second longer than necessary. I may have written Elvira at Oakwood College, telling her I might not be back that summer. A reprieve came when Leo van Witsen, the costume design head at Juilliard, heard me sing and suggested that I try out to spend the summer of 1956 in the Boris Goldovsky Opera Program at Tanglewood Music Camp in western Massachusetts. Fortunately, I won the audition. It meant that I stayed in California for only about two weeks after classes ended, before returning to the East Coast for the opera program.

It took many more years for me to call myself an opera singer. Because great singers like Marian Anderson and Dorothy Maynor sang primarily in recital and neither of them had careers in opera, the concert stage still seemed good enough to me. But the opera world was enticing.

Trying and failing to be a good Seventh-Day Adventist, I wrestled daily with the moral dilemma of singing opera despite my religion. Perhaps I had grown so accustomed to my parents punishing me for dancing and listening to jazz as a child that I was willing to take the punishment from God.

I respected the church's rule regarding smoking and drinking alcohol and even the prohibition on jazz, because it was performed in clubs where we were told foul language and other questionable activities took place, but I didn't feel the same about opera. Despite the violence and illicit activities of some of the characters, I knew I was singing great music. Yet when I performed, I also felt that I was compromising my parents' beliefs.

*   *   *

ONE THING I knew for sure: working with Boris Goldovsky that summer was fabulous. He was a great communicator and taught acting stagecraft. For example, he explained how to faint, walk, sit, and fall, depending on whether you were portraying a princess, a gypsy, or a pauper. He gave talks on what to do when you forgot a line and taught us how to memorize stage directions quickly, like stage right, left, upstage, downstage. He said that all these things would make it easy for other directors to work with his students, and those directors would be inclined to recommend us for other engagements.

I was also impressed by the director of lighting at Tanglewood, Tom De Gaetani, who happened to be the lighting director at Juilliard as well. He gave me some great advice that I pass on to my students today. Tom said I should always befriend the lighting people in a production, because they could make you look like hell. To demonstrate his point, he showed me that by adjusting the light just slightly, he could wash out people's faces, making it difficult to see what they were doing with their eyes, or he could even make them look grotesque by changing the color of the gel he put into the lamp. I was captivated and remembered these guidelines throughout my career.

As positive as the program was, it also taught us lessons in professional jealousy that nearly soured me on an opera career.

The trouble started subtly enough. The assignments I was offered included several scenes from *The Marriage of Figaro, Don Carlo,* and the Lukas Foss opera *Griffelkin.* I was also used in a number of demonstrations. A rival singer who auditioned for the roles I was offered dropped by my room to "pick my brain" about what I was working on. I apparently said something about being behind on some of the assigned music because the copies had arrived late at my home in California. The next thing I knew, one of the directors came into my coaching session, wanting to know why I was not working on the *Griffelkin* scene. I was surprised that he questioned me on that specific music, but just to prove I knew it, I sang the part on the spot, without looking in his direction, and immediately went back to coaching *Don Carlo*. When there was a break, he said that a "little birdie" had told him I didn't know my part, but I knew who the stool pigeon was. She had lied about me to get the part for herself.

This was a bad introduction to opera. At the end of the program, Goldovsky asked me why I seemed so unhappy. I told him that I was uncertain about an opera career because of the mean-spirited atmosphere at Tanglewood. As it turned out, I wasn't the only one who was put through it. Another African American singer, Annabelle Bernard, a soprano from New Orleans, was targeted as well. She had a beautiful voice and was one of the younger members of the class. She had a pronounced Southern drawl and, like me, said whatever was on her mind. Goldovsky assigned us a duet from Mozart's *Cosi fan tutte* and frequently used us to demonstrate the correct singing of Mozartean line. This created more envy among other students.

Once Annabelle walked by a group of students, and some of them imitated her singing in an unflattering way. I'm sure they didn't notice me watching them. The laugh was on them, though. Annabelle soon had a fine career in Europe, particularly in Germany. Most of her detractors had none at all.

MY ENTHUSIASM for the opera stage crystallized in the fall of 1956 when I went to see Maria Callas in her debut season at the Metropolitan Opera in a production of Bellini's *Norma*. New York was buzzing with excitement. Callas was singing all over the world, and it was the first *Norma* the Met had staged in over seventy years. It was an all-star cast, with Mario del Monaco as Pollione, Fedora Barbieri as Adalgisa, and Cesare Siepi as Oroveso. Jimmy McCracken was also in the opera in the small role of Flavio, the centurion.

I have to admit that when I first heard Callas on a recording, I didn't like her voice. I was a Renata Tebaldi fan at the time. When I heard Callas singing the *La Gioconda* aria, "Suicidio," I found a number of things she seemed to be doing "wrong." The arrogance of youth is something. But Callas *was* controversial. Even my teacher wasn't that impressed with Callas and thought she was old-fashioned, as far as her acting was concerned.

Fortunately, I didn't care too much about such opinions, including my own. When the opportunity came for me to see Callas in person, I took it. I had already determined not to criticize anyone without hearing or seeing that person in a live performance. Even now, I usually go to a performance hoping to have my soul enriched. That night I expected Maria Callas to give me a message.

Juilliard students received a discount for performances at the Met. We paid one dollar for "score desks," which meant that we could watch the performance and follow the score from a special section with desks, high up in the theater. I arrived at the theater early to get a good choice of desk.

There was a lot of excitement in the audience that evening and for good reason. Mario del Monaco's voice was like a clarion, strong and bright, right up to a brilliantly sung high C in his aria. He had wonderful stage presence. When the martial music and chorus announced the druid priestess Norma's arrival in the sacred forest, people sat up in their seats. All eyes, including mine, were glued to the stage.

When Callas appeared, the audience spontaneously applauded. She never blinked an eye of acknowledgment. It was powerful! There was a pregnant pause of a few seconds after the orchestra's last chord. Slowly, she looked around the stage once more and began, "Sediziose voci, voci di guerra . . ." (Seditious voices, voices of war . . .). I was mesmerized by her.

This was what opera could and should be. The smoothness of her singing in "Casta Diva" was incredible. There were moments of wobbling in the recitative but such commitment in how she communicated the words that I got over the wobble in about five minutes. What Callas did with her singing reminded me of how my parents taught me to stress certain words when I recited poems or sang songs as a child.

Callas was absolutely wedded to the words, and seemed to love them as much as I did. She understood every word, every nuance of idea and emotion. She sang with conviction, as if she had written the opera herself. The arias came out of her body, unhampered by technical bragging. In the trio where Norma confronts Pollione and Adalgisa, Callas was a firebrand. The conclusion of the opera was incredibly intense. I was moved to tears when she did the trio with chorus "Qual cor tradisti" (What a heart you betrayed).

Seeing that production was like discovering a whole new world. For the first time, I realized what I could do on an opera stage. If you were an opera singer, you didn't have to just come out and plant your feet on the floor. You could present an opera as if it had just been written.

I no longer disliked Callas's voice. Whatever she did that night, she touched me more than most other singers at the Metropolitan. I knew that this was what I wanted to do. I appreciated her art.

BEING ALL the way across the country from James Carter didn't help matters. He proposed to be my personal manager and produced a formal agreement, giving him 10 percent of what I earned. I told him that I wanted my dad to look it over but never showed it to my father. I thought to myself, I'll cut my finger off before I sign that. The next summer, 1957, out of James Carter's reach, I signed on with the Shakespeare under the Stars Lyric Drama Group, at Antioch College in Yellow Springs, Ohio. Dr. Benno Frank hired me for my first professional operatic engagement to sing Lucretia in Benjamin Britten's *The Rape of Lucretia.*

The next thing I knew, Benno asked if I would also consider the role of Linda, the cabaret singer, in a production of *Lost in the Stars,* the Kurt Weill/Maxwell Anderson adaptation of Alan Patton's novel *Cry the Beloved Country,* set in 1940s apartheid South Africa. It would be staged on alternating nights with the Britten opera.

Benno liked the idea of my being the virtuous Lucretia one night and the seductive Linda in the Weill the following night. Before committing myself to doing Linda, I asked to see the part. After I looked over the score, I accepted. It seemed like a golden opportunity. When the contract reached me in California, however, it mentioned only "Lucretia."

I contacted the Antioch business manager in New York and asked him why the Weill role wasn't in my contract. The business manager bristled at my questioning the integrity of "Dr. Frank," but Benno and I initialed a written adjustment to my contract, specifying the Weill part.

It was just as well that I insisted on the contract being amended, because when I arrived for rehearsals in Ohio, I found that Benno had promised the part of Linda to several other ladies before he heard me in New York. Because I was the only one with the forethought to have the change made in my contract, I was the only one who sang Linda in that summer's run of *Lost in the Stars*. Before the other singers realized that I had a contract for the role, the air was frosty, to say the least. Then they redirected their anger from me toward Dr. Frank.

I did not let that detour spoil my summer. This was my first opera performance for which I was paid a salary. I liked the chorus of "Cry the Beloved Country" so much, I asked if I could dash offstage in Linda's clothes, put on a long shawl, and sing the solo lines in the chorus. The director agreed. By the end of the summer, I made many new friends. And because I pitched in and helped with so many other aspects of the productions, such as sewing costumes and sweeping the stage, during the last night of performance, I was called onstage and given a bouquet of flowers for "collegiality."

I also sang a concert in Columbus, performing the Brahms *Four Serious Songs*. My friend from Israel, Ruth Mense, a talented pianist and fellow Juilliard student, who is now deceased, accompanied me. Ruth, Evelyn Greene (another talented African American student of Madame Freschl), and I roomed together that summer and had a great time hanging out.

BACK AT Juilliard with Madame Freschl that fall, I found myself at an open audition for Julius Rudel, director of the New York City Opera.

He was devoting the 1957–1958 season to staging several American operas. Beverly Sills was singing in a production of *The Ballad of Baby Doe* and Phyllis Curtin in *The Taming of the Shrew.* Maestro Rudel offered me the lead female role of Irina in *Lost in the Stars.* I loved the role from having heard it the summer before and was excited about doing it in New York.

I was not disappointed. Unlike the Antioch production, City Opera put together many big African American names for its run. Lawrence Winters, the celebrated baritone, played the lead, Stephen Kumalo. The cast also included Louis Gossett Jr., Geoffrey Cambridge, Rosetta Le Noire, Eva Jessye, Douglas Turner Ward, and Olga James singing my old role, Linda, the jazz singer. Olga had a name because she had appeared in the movie *Carmen Jones,* playing and singing the role of Cindy Lue. I also met my lifelong friend Margaret Tynes, who understudied Olga James as Linda. I thought that Margaret's seductive voice suited the role better. Some of the cast members from that production still call me "Miss Carter." I don't think that Louis Gossett and maybe some others even know me as "Verrett."

The performance ran for eight days straight in April, then was extended an extra week. I sang every night, with Julius Rudel at the podium. Jose Quintero, the first great director I worked with, staged the production. Quintero was a real method director, very impassioned about what he did. He aimed at getting under the skin of the spoken word. He said that acting was about listening and reacting to what you hear.

"When you ask the question, really *ask* the question from your soul," he said to me.

We received strong reviews in the *New York Times* and *Newsweek,* among other publications. The *New York Herald Tribune* described my singing as "operatic in caliber." When Julius Rudel asked me to record the Weill with him some years later, I said no, because the role just didn't feel right in my voice anymore. I was happy that he asked, though, because it meant he still had faith in my abilities.

*   *   *

WHILE ALL of this was taking place, Madame Freschl watched over me like a doe. Whenever I caught a cold, she took me home to her spacious apartment. Her housekeeper took care of me until I was better. Madame Freschl spoiled me in many other ways, too. We had one scheduled lesson a week, but if another student canceled, she gave me additional time. Our vocal exercises were the standard up and down the scale on the vowels, and a mixture of vowel and consonants. I learned a few exercises from Madame Freschl that I continue to use with my own students; these involve vocalizing on "ee, eh, ee eh ah, eh, ah eh, ah," on a five-note scale.

Madame Freschl routinely remarked, "There is only one star in this studio, and that's Shirley." This really was a bad thing to say to the other students. I'm sure that it fostered resentment toward me, even though the students did not show it. I felt sorry for them when she said things like that, and I went out of my way to be nice to them.

By the fall of 1958, I had accepted Madame Freschl's view of my destiny. As a result of winning the Walter W. Naumburg Foundation Award in the spring of 1958, my formal appearance in the concert world took place on November 4 of that year, at New York's Town Hall. The competition was held before the run of *Lost in the Stars,* and I was the voice category's winner. Like the Marian Anderson prize, the money was insignificant, but the winner was sponsored in a debut recital at Town Hall. For over thirty years, this recital had been the springboard for many successful artists.

November 4, 1958. That concert still resonates in my memory as if it were yesterday. The auditorium was filled with Juilliard students and International House residents. The tickets to the performance were free. Adele Addison, an established African American soprano and well-known name, insisted on paying for hers. She advised me to get people in the habit of paying to hear me perform.

I debuted as "Shirley Verrett-Carter" in a beautiful size-nine dress made by a seamstress named Renée, from Paris. I had developed a taste for designer clothes. Even then, I didn't want to risk seeing anyone in the audience wearing the same dress. Made from a gorgeous green and gold fabric Madame Freschl had given me, the dress was very French—that is, form-fitting and strapless.

I hummed to warm up because I didn't want to oversing by vocalizing too much. I was afraid I might tire myself out before completing the performance. As I walked onstage, very poised, and smiled graciously to the audience, my shoes felt a little tight, but after things were underway, I forgot all about my feet.

It was an ambitious program. I opened with the arias from Purcell's *Dido and Aeneas.* Although, at the end of the section, I felt I had sung them better in the past, I wanted to save my voice for the more demanding Brahms *Vier ernste Gesaenge* (Four Serious Songs) and the Mozart *La Clemenza di Tito* (Clemency of Titus) aria, "Parto, parto." Charles Wadsworth was my accompanist and played divinely.

I was satisfied. The *New York Times, New York Herald,* and a New York–based German paper, the *N.Y. Staats-Zeitung und Herold,* all reviewed me favorably. The night would have felt like a complete triumph except for the backstage drama. James Carter had flown in from California. When he saw "Verrett-Carter" on the program, he went ballistic. It was as if I were out to personally insult and belittle him as a man by not using my married name. My intention was more practical than that. I saw where our relationship was going and knew I had to drop the name "Carter." If I ever switched back to "Verrett," I wanted people to know I was the same person.

I sang all over the New York area after my debut. I did a Mozart *Requiem,* conducted by a fellow Juilliard student, Nathan Carter; Bach's *St. Matthew Passion* at the Juilliard School; and solo recitals here and there. If asked to sing, I generally did.

That season, I auditioned for various prizes and formed important new musical friendships. As the voice winner of the National Federation of Music Clubs contest, I earned a monetary prize and a concert at the National Gallery in Washington, D.C., where I repeated my Town Hall program. My alternate accompanist at the time, my good friend Warren Wilson, joined me later for a concert in Boston at the Isabella Stewart Gardner Museum. A gifted African American accompanist and a Juilliard graduate, Warren had allowed me to introduce him into Madame Freschl's studio. As it was the tercentenary of Henry Purcell's birth, we opened with a Purcell group, starting with "When I Am Laid in Earth" from *Dido and Aeneas.* I think being surrounded by the great works of art at the National Gallery and the Isabella Stewart Gardner Museum made me sing better. I felt inspired in the presence of greatness, as if we were contributing something beautiful to the atmosphere.

It was also during this time that I first met Martina Arroyo. She was still a student at Hunter College. We participated in a performance of Strauss's *Ariadne auf Naxos* at a music camp in upstate New York, although Martina and I sang from the orchestra pit. Her mother, a comedian like Martina, was a fabulous cook. We sat for hours on the park lawns laughing, gossiping, and eating her sandwiches, fried chicken, and deviled eggs during rehearsals.

My MARRIAGE to James Carter finally ended in 1959. I believe that even he saw the end coming. I'd gone back to California for a brief period. I woke up one morning and, while making up our bed, found a gun under his pillow. I don't know whether he intended to scare me, to send a message, or what, but I hid the gun where I knew he wouldn't find it.

He questioned me in a roundabout way as to whether I had come across anything while I was making up the bed. I responded with feigned innocence, "No. I didn't see a thing. What was it?" He surely knew I was lying.

Yet in 1959, when I finally demanded a divorce, he seemed stunned. He had arrived in New York to surprise me for my birthday, and I wasn't having it. It led to another all-too-familiar argument between us, but ended when I insisted that I wanted out—a divorce. He said he was returning to Los Angeles. I told him fine; I would call the airline to arrange his flight. He ended up staying at my apartment that night but slept on the sofa. He thought that I was acting in the heat of anger, but I was totally serious.

Before James Carter left, he agreed to write me a letter, stating that he would not contest the divorce. He said he wanted to wait until he got back to Los Angeles before writing it. I waited two weeks and there was no letter—no word from him at all. I finally called him.

"Do you still want to go through with this?" he asked me.

"Absolutely," I said quietly.

"Well, there is going to be a change in what I say. What you will have to do to get this divorce is sign over all of our property to me!" By that time, we had amassed quite a bit.

Without batting an eye, I said in a calm but determined voice, "Send the papers, I'll sign them."

There was a long pause, which seemed like an eternity. It undoubtedly shocked him that I would give away the considerable amount of property we held jointly. I had already suspected he might try something like this, but my feeling was that I had my whole life ahead of me. I could buy more property. I was young and didn't need or want to live a lie with a man with whom I was not compatible.

That summer I lived in Las Vegas on a shoestring budget. I was told by a lawyer at school that this was the easiest place for me to get a no-fault divorce. I cut costs by staying with a kind former client to whom I had sold some property in California years ago. I had to return to Las Vegas in November for a final court appearance. The divorce was granted on November 4, 1959, one year to the day after my Town Hall debut.

James Carter and I never met again. It has been over forty years. For a while I had nightmares, in which I saw him and had to cross the street to avoid him. To my knowledge, he still lives in the Los Angeles area. He would be in his mid-eighties. My brother Leon saw James Carter some years ago and said that he looked well for his age. He also remarried and, I understand, had a son.

James Carter and I never had children, and that was a blessing. God must have said, "You have made enough mistakes, Shirl, so I'm going to help you in this area."

Years later my sister, Elvira, told me that I had caused a real stir back home when people heard I was signing away everything. "I thought you were out of your mind. All that property?"

Later she understood and thought I was very brave. I valued my freedom more than houses and other material possessions. I never regretted that decision.

I resolved never to marry again. Instead, I thought I would just have great love affairs and when they broke up, that would be it; no signing papers, nothing official. When I informed Mother, she calmly said, "I hope you change your mind." I suspect that she thought I was overreacting, because romance is very important to me.

I have always been a romantic. I love romantic gestures: little presents, opening car doors, flowers, a kiss. I love being with a partner. Romantic love is the greatest thing. Yet there are times, many times, when I just like to be alone—alone with myself, alone with my thoughts. I'm very happy being in my own company. When it was time to end my marriage, I was ready. I felt perfectly happy being alone.

PART TWO

5

Hurry Slowly

M Y CAREER unfolded rapidly by strokes of luck, good fortune, and incredible blessings. Immediately after my Town
Hall debut, I began to receive calls from agents. I remember Thea Dispeka being interested in handling me. Her old school
strategy would have meant my going to Europe to affiliate with an
opera house. The idea was that after an American artist made a name
in Europe, that singer could come back to the United States to be promoted as a star. But the idea of needing to be validated by supposedly
more culturally enlightened Europeans did not appeal to me. I preferred
to be based in my own country, with the potential of then being invited to European houses as a guest. So I declined the Dispeka offer.

A stout, elderly Jewish man with graying hair, named Siegfried
Hearst, had heard me sing Mahler's *Kindertotenlieder* at Juilliard.
Suddenly, he was also interested in helping me. He spoke to Madame
Freschl before approaching me directly. Siegfried lived with his wife
in an apartment at Seventy-second and Riverside Drive. He began
our relationship by photographing me. I can only conclude that God

put him in my path. I am not aware of him managing any other singers, and I can't remember writing any checks to him.

Siegfried Hearst had recently left Columbia Artist Management, I believe, to form his own agency. When he departed from Columbia, he took with him all of the conductors whom he had managed as clients. These were names like Leopold Stokowski, Josef Krips, Georg Solti, Joseph Rosenstock, Franz Waxman, and, eventually, a young Zubin Mehta. He sent each one my picture and arranged my audition for most of them.

Almost immediately, extraordinary things began to happen. Siegfried Hearst arranged for me to sing for the great conductor Leopold Stokowski, who was then the principal conductor of the Houston Symphony Orchestra. We met at the beginning of the fall season in 1959 at his beautiful apartment in New York City. It was full of musical scores. There were symphonic scores, operas (which I was unaware of him conducting), and numerous piano and chamber music manuscripts. Other students at Juilliard would have died to spend a day in his apartment just looking at the music. I sang the "Habanera" from *Carmen* and a few other arias.

In those days, Stokowski recorded his observations in a large book. That book was considered quite powerful. Most aspiring musicians wanted to be mentioned favorably in it. A negative comment in "the Stokowski book" could injure a career, because other conductors, booking agents, and musical organizations frequently consulted him. It seemed that he liked my voice. A few weeks later, Stokowski contacted Siegfried Hearst and told him he had programmed Schönberg's "Gurrelieder" for the Houston Symphony, and he wanted to engage me to sing the Wood Dove in the work. I began learning the part.

But shortly afterward, Siegfried informed me that I wouldn't be singing with the symphony after all. He was vague about why. Stokowski himself would call me, was all he said.

Had I said or done something wrong? Perhaps I misinterpreted how much the maestro had liked my voice.

Maestro Stokowski called. He was embarrassed, but said that it would not be possible for me to sing with the Houston Symphony because the symphony board did not want to use a Negro singer. He said that he would have fought in the past, but he was now an old man and tired of fighting.

"This will not stop you and will not stop our relationship," he continued. "I would like you to know I *will* have you to sing with me."

All I could say was, "Yes, maestro. I understand, maestro. Thank you, maestro. I appreciate your confidence in me, maestro." What else could I have done? What could most black people do during that period? We could try to appear dignified and swallow our hurt and humiliation. I swallowed a lot, but not nearly as much as so many others had. I was in New York City and had lived in California, where things were only *slightly* better, or perhaps such feelings were covert. In the South, we suffered open racial insults and attacks. I was upset, almost to the point of crying, and then became angry about this kind of stupidity from supposedly cultured people.

Feelings of defiance I hadn't experienced in years rushed back. I determined now that despite blatant prejudice, I would still have a career.

Literally within a few weeks, Siegfried received a call from Joseph Rosenstock. He not only liked what he had heard and seen of me but had been engaged to conduct the newly revised opera of Nicholas Nabokov's *Der Tod des Grigori Rasputin* (The Death of Grigori Rasputin) in Cologne, Germany. Rosenstock had suggested to the composer that I play the role of the gypsy in his opera, and Nabokov had agreed.

As if this alone weren't enough to celebrate, I soon had the satisfaction of having the last laugh on the Houston Symphony board. Just before I left for Europe, Siegfried Hearst called to say that Stokowski wanted me to sing Manuel de Falla's *El Amor Brujo* with him, in his guest appearance with the Philadelphia Orchestra. I could learn the part while I was in Europe. This was to make up for the experience with the Houston Symphony.

True to his word, Maestro Stokowski came through for me in a big way, giving me hope for my country, after all. I am sure there are those who would not have remembered my singing the Schönberg, even if they had been at the concert in Houston. To this day, I could almost thank the Houston Symphony board, because the board members' racist stupidity catapulted my career in ways they could never have imagined.

IN NOVEMBER 1959 I left the United States for my European debut. Siegfried set up other engagements for me in Europe, and the Juilliard administration agreed to let me take a leave of absence. Although I was technically enrolled as a student, I would be away for almost three months.

The Cologne Opera began rehearsals without delay. The hotels were relatively expensive, compared to my earnings, and I was broke as it was. As a recent divorcée, I had no other means of support.

One of the dressers for the production, a Frau Grün, generously offered to let me stay at her home instead of my spending so much money in a hotel. Initially, I turned down the offer, but after a few days I accepted because she persuaded me it would be no inconvenience to her. She and her youngest daughter lived in an apartment together in a section of Cologne that had been badly bombed during World War II. Frau Grün never allowed me to pay her.

I settled down in the dining room, where there was a very comfortable sleep sofa, but I woke up one night a little disoriented. I didn't know where I was. When I came to myself, I thought, I am free! I am free! I could have gone out and danced in the streets. I guess the reality of the divorce had finally set in.

After I got my bearings, I was stunned to realize how American I was and how much I loved my country. During one rehearsal break, a group of cast members and I sat in the canteen, speaking in German (with some broken English). Someone was going on about how terribly America treated its black citizens. My stomach turned, even though the conversation was clearly intended to be sympathetic to me. Finally, I had to respond.

"What you say is true. It is absolutely correct, but we are trying to do something about it. But what about you and the six million Jews? What about your history? What about your Hitler?" The others shut up. An ex-soldier in the group said, "You are right." I thought to myself, People think the Nazis are out of Germany even today? That's a big joke.

I was surprised to find myself defending America, but I could not forget what the Nazis did to the Jews. While I lived at International House, I had been riveted by the news coming out of Europe about the Holocaust. I read everything I could about the Third Reich— how they manufactured weapons, how they thought of Jews as livestock. When I wanted to know more and asked my Jewish friends (such as Ruth Mense and Esther Admon), many of whom had relatives directly affected by the horrible events, most of them were embarrassed to talk about it. It was as if *they* had done something wrong. I couldn't grasp the shame and hurt it brought to them. I made a point of visiting several Holocaust memorials when I was in Israel in the 1960s.

The final irony in all of this was the use of my voice in the soundtrack of the 1998 Roberto Benigni film *La Vita e Bella* (Life Is Beautiful). With the horrors of the concentration camp being played out on screen, my recording of the "Barcarolle" duet from the *Tales of Hoffman* was used as a signal by Benigni's character to let his wife know he was still alive in the camp. When I saw the film, I fought to hold back my tears but lost the battle. I sobbed audibly. Memories of Ruth, who had passed by then, rushed to my mind. I believe she would have been proud of the filmmaker's use of my voice in such a dramatic context.

WHEN *Rasputin's Tod* opened, the review from *Das Rundschau Feulleton* described my performance as being "in a class by [itself]." The *Frankfurter Allegemeine Zeitung* said, "the pretty chocolate-skinned Shirley Carter (Gypsy) stood out of the ensemble . . . in an entirely different manner and upon the highest artistic level." Other articles equally complimentary followed. I felt vindicated. I think I really was as good as they said. When I read reviews, it can feel almost like hearing my own voice.

I know that some people say, "I don't care, I don't read reviews." I tended to disagree. I had a lot of confidence that I was doing well. But even if the reviews were not great, they still meant that someone else recognized what I was doing and believed it, too. Winning over the critics—like winning one music competition after the other, another kind of critical feedback—boosted my confidence. Reviews told me that I was doing well. When those German reviews came out, I really knew I was moving forward. As time went on, I developed more guarded feelings about critics.

ONE FREE afternoon, while taking a long walk, I noticed three people walking ahead of me, a black man and a German man and a German woman. The black man turned around and briefly stared at me. Every few minutes he turned again to look at me. Finally, he came back.

"I am so sorry to have stared at you, Miss, but you bear a striking resemblance to my daughter in London," he said in a pristine British accent.

He introduced himself as Mr. McNish and said he was from London, doing business in Germany. After exchanging pleasantries, he invited me for afternoon tea with his associates. Over the course of the tea, it came up that I would be in London in a few weeks to do a recording. He insisted that I stay with his family and wouldn't take no for an answer.

The day I arrived in London, his daughter Althea, who was about my age, met me at Heathrow Airport. We went to meet Mrs. McNish and they immediately accepted me into the family. Every day Althea took me to and from the recording sessions that were held in a large studio outside London. I had never been in a recording studio before. I practically had the mezzo part memorized the first day and tried not to let my nervousness show, as the legendary Josef Krips conducted Beethoven's *Ninth Symphony*. Althea brought me lunch each day. She was so thoughtful. It is amazing how kind strangers can be. Although Mr. and Mrs. McNish have passed, Althea and I remain friends today.

After the recording session, I returned to Germany to do a recital at the Kammerspiele in Cologne. This time, a reviewer commented on my "native musicality" as if to suggest that I didn't have to develop and refine my art. He also described me in very sensual terms. There were more references to my looks and physical appearance than there were to my musicality. It was a little insulting, but no one referred to it as sexist language in those days.

FEBRUARY 1960. Back in Philadelphia, I was approaching one of the defining moments of my career. Mrs. Gertrude Ely had graciously invited me to be a guest in her beautiful Main Line home. I was waited on hand and foot, in anticipation of my appearance with the Philadelphia Orchestra. Stokowski was returning, as a guest conductor, to the Philadelphia Orchestra after a nineteen-year absence. It was big news in the concert world. He had been responsible for building what has been called the "Philadelphia sound." He had conducted that orchestra from 1912 to 1941 and was still beloved by that city. Anything and anyone associated with that engagement would receive a good deal of attention. He had asked me, an unknown young black woman, to sing with him when he could have done the concert on his own. What stronger statement against racial prejudice could there be?

I'll always remember that concert. It was a Friday afternoon and the house was packed. When the maestro walked onstage, the applause was thunderous. He may have received a standing ovation before he started. He opened with Mozart's *Marriage of Figaro Overture* and then it was my turn to sing the Falla. Stokowski and the Philadelphia Orchestra had premiered *El Amor Brujo* in this country in 1922. The maestro had planned in advance that at a certain bar in the music, he would gesture (i.e., lower his head), which was my cue to slowly walk onstage.

I wore a red velvet dress, very form-fitting, with points at the wrist and a black chiffon train, attached to the shoulder. A friend had designed it for me in a Spanish style to complement what I sang. People commented that the red dress, followed by the black train, was very effective. I was nervous, but my backstage rituals—keeping very quiet and talking only to those I needed to speak to before going on-stage—helped to calm me. I also wanted, in those days, to be alone in my dressing room. No standing in the hall or speaking.

To the audience it seemed that I made eye contact, but in fact I looked over people's heads, because if you stare at someone too directly, that person may feel nervous. The other practice I had developed was to have the lights dimmed just enough so that the audience could read the program, and I could see faces in the front rows. I was, after all, singing to them.

For the balance of the performance, the orchestra played Respighi's *The Pines of Rome* and Shostakovich's *Symphony No. 5.*

Afterward, the reviewers raved about Stokowski's return and me as the featured artist. They affirmed all my hopes and more. One called me a specialist in Spanish song literature. That was somewhat amusing, because this was the first time I had ever sung anything in Spanish. To celebrate the evening, Mrs. Ely had a small dinner party in honor of Maestro Stokowski. There were so many flowers throughout the house.

Later, when "Stoki," as he was known by the concert community, did the same program at Carnegie Hall in New York, he forgot to cue me. But I went out anyway at the same spot in the music. The applause was, again, thunderous. It was a heady feeling.

Stoki apologized after the concert for his lapse and called me a "real professional." I hardly needed an apology from the maestro, although I did appreciate it. When I think about this phase of my career, it was as if God directed me. The right thing to do just came to me. For example, there were also some vocal executions in the Falla, which I quickly corrected after the New York performance. For example, that opening line, "Ay! Yo no se que siento" (Ay, I don't know what I feel), is very intense and I sang it in "open chest" voice. If I had continued that practice, I wouldn't have had a voice for long.

I recorded the Falla with Stoki and the Philadelphia Orchestra on Columbia Records. This was just one more act of generous support that I received from him. He invited me to a party at his home in New

York City, shortly after the success of the concert. I met many well-known New York–based musicians. And I collaborated one more time with Stoki. He recorded an all-Wagner concert, featuring the celebrated "Ride of the Valkyries" from the opera *Die Walküre*. I was one of the Valkyrie maidens. Martina Arroyo was also in that recording.

BACK IN California the following June, I debuted on a Friday night at the Los Angeles Music Festival. Franz Waxman, also a Hearst client and a composer of movie scores, conducted Karl Hartmann's *First Symphony* for contralto voice and orchestra. It was the American premiere of the work. The promoters played up the fact that I was from the Los Angeles area and a product of the Young Musicians Foundation. They also highlighted my having just sung with Leopold Stokowski and the Philadelphia Orchestra, as well as the London Symphony under Josef Krips.

I stayed with Mother and Dad at their new home in the Griffith Park area of Los Angeles, up in the hills. Of all their houses, this was the most serene. After climbing many steps, you arrived at the front door and entered a large foyer. To the left was a large dining room, and to the right an equally large living room. There was also a library in which Dad kept a small organ. They had a wonderful view of Los Angeles from their bedroom patio.

Yet Dad was anything but serene. He was still particularly incensed about the Houston Symphony incident and called the board a "bunch of crackers." When I received the call to sing with Stokowski in Philadelphia, it was almost as if Dad felt more vindicated than I did.

Unfortunately, he and Mother missed my concert with Waxman, because Friday evening was their Sabbath eve. Waxman, who was Jewish, apologized afterward and said he would be mindful of that in the future. When I performed with him again a few months later, he went out of his way to accommodate my parents. It was a lovely gesture from a lovely man.

*   *   *

THAT HOUSTON Symphony board denial made me identify with Marian Anderson's 1939 DAR incident as never before. In the same way that her artistry had been vindicated by singing to an audience of more than 75,000 from the steps of the Lincoln Memorial after the Daughters of the American Revolution had denied her the opportunity to perform in Constitution Hall, I, too, had reached a much larger audience when Stoki invited me to sing with him in Philadelphia after the Houston Symphony board fiasco.

I saw Marian Anderson as a musical icon and a symbol of resistance. The DAR incident seemed only to increase Miss Anderson's stature among African Americans, who poured out in large numbers any time she appeared in an area. Almost single-handedly, it seemed, she boosted African American attendance at concerts and recitals.

Miss Anderson always wished that opera had been a greater part of her life than it was. When she sang dramatic arias like "O mio Fernando," among others, on her programs, she acted with all her being—even to the point of kneeling when indicated or using dramatic hand gestures as her soul moved her into action. Many concertgoers went to see her glamorous gowns and jewelry.

Marian Anderson was a beacon to me. I thought that our paths were destined to cross, because she took some private voice lessons with Madame Freschl, but instead of bumping into her in New York, I met this great singer formally when I returned to Philadelphia to sing a Spanish program at Robin Hood Dell (now the Mann Center).

It was hard to imagine controversy surrounding this very dignified and elegant woman. Nothing had turned her bitter or hard; anger never showed in her public persona. What this woman endured amazed me. Although I had seen her perform several times before, I had never gone backstage to see her. I felt ennobled that we were meeting as musician to musician. For a moment, I mused on our encounter as a symbolic passing of the baton.

I reminded her about my winning the Anderson competition a few years before, but under the name Shirley Carter. She seemed to remember me by that name. We posed for a picture together, looking over the score of *El Amor Brujo*, which I sang at the concert. As I recall, though, she had a little more interest in the career of a white student in Freschl's studio, also a contralto, who later sang small roles at the Met. But our meeting was very cordial and Miss Anderson, very complimentary.

The community of African American musicians in the concert world was small but a force nonetheless. I went back and forth to California several times that summer of 1960 and in September met Henry Lewis, the young African American conductor. Henry was a talented bass player who had made the transition to the podium. Even as a young conductor, his directions were clear and his command of the orchestra impressive. Henry had a booming bass speaking voice and a hearty laugh. He and his future wife, Marilyn Horne, were both products of the Young Musicians Foundation.

When I made my debut at the Hollywood Bowl under the sponsorship of the Young Musicians Foundation, Henry replaced Miklos Rosza at the podium. I was one of three musicians who had received a cash award, along with the debut opportunity. The well-known soprano Dorothy Kirsten presented my award. I recall that she was not amused that I had won. In her view, by my having performed with Stoki and Krips and having participated in three commercial recordings, I was already a professional singer. I guess she thought a neophyte would have been a more appropriate winner. Her condescending comment, "I didn't know you had done so much, dear," seemed disingenuous, almost like a slight. I just kept quiet, feigned a smile, and attempted to look appreciative.

I remember with greater pleasure another engagement in Los Angeles that fall, to sing Beethoven's *Ninth Symphony*, with Georg Solti conducting the Los Angeles Philharmonic. Solti was also a Hearst client. I really appreciated the care that Solti took with regard to the quartet's balance. He was adamant that one singer not cover the others in the ensemble, and wouldn't you know, the singer who suffers the most in that work is the mezzo. David Poleri and Donald Gramm were the tenor and baritone soloists in the Beethoven. David Poleri was known for his temper, a real *primo uomo*. But on the few occasions we performed together, I never saw that side of him. He was a professional and a gentleman.

SPRING 1961. Graduating from Juilliard and quite confident of competing, I was accustomed to being in the winners' circle. I had entered every contest that came along. But when Madame Freschl urged me to compete in the Metropolitan Opera National Council Competition, I was skeptical, because if the Met wanted a certain voice, that's who won. Adding to my qualms, the Council insisted I do the "Habanera" from *Carmen*. I had never heard of anyone winning a major competition singing the "Habanera." It is a well-known work but doesn't show off the voice at either extreme. Maybe some singers have won contests with it, but it didn't feel right for me.

I wanted to compete with "O mio Fernando" from *La Favorita*, but the Council decided that a girl from California, who, ironically, had studied with Lotte Lehman, should sing that aria. It was pure politics. The girl did not sing the recitative, probably because she did not sing it well. To skip it was unheard of, as far as I was concerned. It sets up the aria. I had sung that aria in several places and had sung it well. The cabaletta was also a showstopper, with a climactic ending.

Ultimately, the top prize, a Metropolitan Opera contract, went to George Shirley. And I want to make it clear, he *should* have won. He sang "Nessun Dorma" (No one sleeps) from Puccini's *Turandot* and sang the hell out of it. I had known that aria for years because my brother Leon sang it powerfully. But George had catapulted it to another level that day. I was backstage and wholeheartedly applauded when he finished. I completely forgot that we were in competition with each other. The runner-up was a soprano, Francesca Roberto, who sang "Un bel di" (One fine day) from *Madame Butterfly*.

I ended up sharing the $1,000 Euclid W. McBride Memorial Scholarship with a soprano, Billie Lynn Daniel, also a Juilliard graduate. The late Sir Rudolf Bing, then general manager of the Metropolitan, in the audience as usual, undoubtedly noticed me. He was still at the Metropolitan several years later when I debuted with the company.

I learned something that day about the politics of judging vocal competitions. I also learned something about losing. I wasn't good at it. I was a real sourpuss that day, but, in a roundabout way, it was probably a good lesson. I had agreed to enter the competition. No one had forced me. I had to take responsibility for the outcome.

Fortunately, I was too busy to spend much time licking my imaginary wounds. Right after the Metropolitan competition, I was presented in Washington, D.C., in a recital with two other National Federation of Music Clubs audition winners—Terius Klausner, a violinist, and William Alton, a pianist. That July I had another engagement with Josef Krips. It was again a performance of the Beethoven *Ninth Symphony*, in Lewisohn Stadium in New York before a crowd of more than ten thousand. The soprano soloist was my friend Theresa Green. I would sing the Beethoven for the last time with Maestro Krips that December at Carnegie Hall. Twenty years passed before I sang it again. When I did, Leonard Bernstein was on the podium in Vienna, Austria.

I was about to perform Brahms's *Four Serious Songs* when the scheduled accompanist became ill and had to cancel. Charles Wadsworth, who had accompanied me for a few engagements before and after my Town Hall debut, stepped in at the last minute to play the concert for me.

From that point on, Charles became my official, but not exclusive, accompanist. It was meaningful to me that he was very active, musically, in the New York area, had great connections, and was a good organizer. In conjunction with Gian Carlo Menotti, the composer, Charles was the musical director of the noonday concerts in Spoleto, Italy, as part of the Festival of Two Worlds. Spoleto was a showcase for young artists. Charles invited the musicians to perform, accompanied most performers at the noon concerts, and gave short lectures before the selections.

That summer, Charles informed Menotti that if anyone went to

Spoleto, I had to go. I auditioned, and consequently, another exciting and crucial period of my early career began.

SPOLETO, 1961. I was singing Darius Milhaud's "Chansons des Negresses" when the lights in the auditorium went out! I didn't stop singing nor did Charles stop playing. Someone quickly brought out a candle and set it on the piano. It made a wonderful glow on my face, and the recital continued. Samuel Barber, the other eminent American composer in Spoleto with Menotti, who was there to oversee a production of his opera *Vanessa,* was in the audience when the lights went out. He told me later that he was impressed by my sangfroid (cold-bloodedness), a compliment in French that suggests that no matter what the adversity, one still delivers.

I was a real "Minute-lady" that summer. When someone didn't show up for the noonday recital, Gian Carlo sent for me, and I stood in and sang for the audience on very short notice. Spoleto showcased my versatility and professionalism as few experiences had before.

I noticed a man taking pictures of me during a few of my performances and assumed he was a photographer. He turned out to be John Ardoin, writer and critic for *Musical America* and *Opera News,* who really appreciated my talent. From that point on, my name began appearing in those and other journals on a routine basis. John became a dear friend, one of the few critics I ever allowed myself to become close to. We had a great rapport. I had many dinners at his home with his partner, Norman Fischer, who became one of my early dress designers. A few years ago John and I participated in a Maria Callas symposium in Washington, D.C. He was the world authority on her life and career. When he recently died, the musical world lost a major figure.

Several of my African American friends appeared at Spoleto that summer. Reri Grist sang in Charles's noonday festival. Margaret Tynes did a fantastic job singing the title role in Strauss's *Salome.* The Italian film director Luchino Visconti, who directed that production, really loved Margaret and her work. She was singing at the New York

City Opera and had several engagements in Europe at that time. Margaret and her late husband, Hans, were residents of Milan, and when I began singing at La Scala years later, I always saw them. We had some wonderful times together.

Friends are important to me. I still don't have many close ones, but I have many wonderful acquaintances. I'm a loner in many ways and will not let most people get terribly close. It's hard for me to trust people. But once I do, they have a friend for life. In my early career, I learned to protect myself by not trusting people too quickly. I had been burned a few times, enough times to know better. Whenever colleagues became envious of my success, what I saw bothered me—the cattiness and the backbiting. And my career was barely off the ground! So I built a shell around myself. I decided that I must be a very strong person. Intuitively, I didn't want my colleagues to see the soft part of me. I did not want them to see my vulnerabilities.

WHEN I returned to the United States, a friend named Louis LoMonaco met me at the airport. My boyfriend at the time, whom we will just call "Buddy," was away. Lou and I had met in November 1960 at a dinner at Buddy's apartment. Buddy wanted me to meet this talented young artist he had met studying in Europe on a Fulbright Fellowship. Louis LoMonaco, an Italian American, was tall and handsome and had chiseled dark features, beautiful eyes, a full head of hair, and a thick mustache. Unlike Buddy, Lou had no formal musical training but had always heard classical music at home while growing up, especially the Texaco Metropolitan Opera broadcasts. He, too, came from a close-knit family.

A short time later, he came to hear me sing at Juilliard. I think I sang Mahler's *Kindertotenlieder*. That night Buddy gave a party, and when Lou saw me, he just held out his arms.

"That was so beautiful. It brought tears to my eyes," he said. I already liked him, but I liked him even more when I felt his sincere love and appreciation of classical music. I sensed a hidden reserve of warmth and passion. We stayed in touch.

After I came back from Spoleto, Lou began taking me to lunch at small French restaurants or lovely delicatessens, and we gradually started seeing more of each other.

It was obviously not a happy situation when Buddy returned. Madame Freschl knew about Buddy but also knew I was developing feelings for Lou. She thought I was having fun, keeping these two young men interested in me. She reminded me of my promise to never marry again, which, according to her, would have been best for my career. At one point Lou told me I had to decide. Was it him or Buddy? I knew I would have to reach a decision, but things came to a head sooner than I expected.

One night Buddy arrived at my apartment while Lou was there. Because Buddy and I had keys to each other's places, I began to fasten the security latch on my door. He came one night unannounced and the latch was on. When I let him in, he realized what was going on and, suddenly, I was in the middle of a confrontation. After Buddy calmed down, I told him that I liked Lou an awful lot.

Lou looked him straight in the eyes and said, "I'm in love with her. Now it's up to her to decide what she's going to do about it."

Buddy left. Lou stayed.

It was impossible not to think about my romance with Lou during my next career move—a tour of the segregated South, where I'd spent my childhood. As I was about to graduate from Juilliard, a professor had asked me to consider a five-week recital tour of several Southern states, mostly at historically African American campuses.

Before agreeing to it, I set certain conditions. I insisted on being met at the airport and driven to the performance location. I wanted no part of any segregated traveling facilities. I knew in advance that hotels still did not accommodate blacks, so I wanted to be sure we stayed in very nice private homes. At that time in the South, blacks couldn't go to just any hall. If the white universities on the tour had segregated auditorium policies, I refused to show. Finally, although Charles Wadsworth was my official accompanist, for this tour I wanted Warren Wilson. I wanted to send a signal that as an African American singer and role model, I needed one of my *own* there.

We had between seven and ten dates altogether, including Bennett College in North Carolina, Spelman in Georgia, and Tuskegee Institute in Alabama. The civil rights movement was really picking up. I was proud to see many of the young ladies at Bennett and Spelman carry themselves with such dignity and grace. I also had appearances at a few white colleges. Some of the places weren't ready for "prime time." In one performance, the lighting person put a red light on me because not much was known about lighting black faces, even by other blacks, at least not in the arena of classical music. The justification was that the red light would create a nice effect for me onstage. It didn't work.

Mother had misgivings about the tour because she was worried that I would sit where I wasn't supposed to or would speak out about some injustice. Dad had a little more confidence that I wouldn't do anything to endanger my life.

I was well aware of racial protocol in the Deep South, but my parents should have worried about Warren. One day we were waiting to be met at the airport in Jackson, Mississippi, where I was to appear at Jackson State College. There were the standard "White" and "Colored" drinking fountains.

"I want to see what White water tastes like," Warren said, bending to take a drink. I told him to stop it. We were in lynching country.

I had my own incident within a few minutes. I saw an empty seat between two white women, who were apparently waiting for a flight. I went to sit down and before my buttocks hit the chair, they both got up and walked off. I could see their facial expressions out of the corner of my eye. They must have thought I was either a "Northern agitator" or some civil rights demonstrator. After they left, I said to myself, "Good! Now I have three seats." I calmly placed my bag in one of them.

NEW YORK CITY, September 1961. I believe that life is largely about being at the right place at the right time. There were many terrific singers in New York, yet in a relatively short time I had opportunities that more seasoned musicians would have died for. Doors kept opening for me.

You don't always know immediately that you've created an opportunity. For instance, Charles Wadsworth customarily took singers to perform at the home of Ellie Bernheimer, a wealthy arts patron in New York City. I sang at one of Ellie's parties and met Roger Hall, my future manager at RCA Records. Then at other times you see the opportunity right away. For example, Dorothy Rodgers, the wife of composer Richard Rodgers, introduced herself to me after I sang at a United Jewish Appeal fundraiser. She said, "You'll be hearing from me. I'd like for my husband to do something for you." I thought to myself, "That's nice," and thought no more of it.

A few days later I heard from Mr. Rodgers, who suggested I sing for him. I breezed through several arias at the audition, which he liked very much. He was casting his musical *No Strings,* which was to star Diahann Carroll and Richard Kiley. He called me back afterward and said, "What can I do for you? I'd like to help you. I can hire you as Diahann's understudy, but I can tell you, you'll never get onstage because she is as strong as a horse. She never gets sick. It'll just be $500 a week that you'll collect for showing up."

"Mr. Rodgers, may I think about it and get back to you?" I replied, even though I didn't have to think about it, really. I called him the following day and explained how I saw myself as a recitalist and, most likely, in opera, as opposed to musical theater. I had begun down a certain path and didn't want to detour in another direction. I thanked him very graciously and told him how honored I was to have the generous offer from him.

But he was tenacious. He said, "I've got to do something for you. My wife will be upset if I don't."

That's how it came about that he set up a scholarship fund in his name at the Juilliard School and said I could get up to $25,000 if I needed it. I told him I was about to sign with new management and needed $5,000 in start-up costs. I used some of the money for publicity brochures. The rest I used for a down payment on a co-op on the Upper East Side in Spanish Harlem. Dorothy Rodgers's niece told me about the place.

I never asked for another penny from the fund. Mr. Rodgers never forgot that. He said that anyone else would have used all the money allotted.

Somehow it got around in a gossip page that Rodgers had wanted me for Diahann Carroll's role in *No Strings*. A rumor circulated that I was trying to move in on her. But those stories were a complete fabrication. Richard Rodgers was just trying to do a favor for a young singer. Diahann Carroll was already a star and is still a fabulous singer and actress.

Diahann Carroll and I sang "Summertime" from *Porgy and Bess* together on a PBS television show in New York City in the 1970s, and we began to be friendly at that point. When she invited me to a party at her home, I casually asked her if she happened to remember that *No Strings* incident years before. She did, so I explained again that it had been blown out of proportion.

IT WAS time for me to move on to new management. For all practical purposes, I was a professional singer, having had major orchestral appearances and opera engagements since the late 1950s. Much of this resulted from Siegfried Hearst's efforts. Siegfried Hearst was a dear man, God rest his soul, and without question he delivered on his promise to help me. But he had a small setup, operating out of his hip pocket, so to speak. He worked out of his apartment, and I don't believe he even had a secretary. I talked to him about leaving, and he wanted to know why. He noted all the engagements he had gotten me, which was entirely true, but he finally accepted my decision to go. He had known that our relationship would be transitional, but he wanted me to go to Sol Hurok, the last of the great impresarios. It was not yet time for such a management. It hurt Siegfried when I didn't go to Hurok.

I felt that Hurok was too big and would push me along too fast. I recalled Hall Johnson's often-quoted dictum regarding my career, "Hurry slowly." I understood this to mean that I should be prepared when the opportunities presented themselves and not just jump at everything that came along. Even if Columbia had wanted me at that time, I would have thought it too big. I needed management, not a big organization. I had known a few young performers who had signed with Hurok, and it seemed as if they were performing everywhere for a period, and then they disappeared. I wanted a management in which I had a say in how my career was run—a management where I had time to grow a bit slower.

After I left Siegfried Hearst, I never saw him again. I think there were some bitter feelings on his part. It was understandable.

Herbert Barrett's management firm approached me before I went to Spoleto, and I auditioned for them. I liked what Barrett had to say and decided that his office should handle my career. Madame Freschl may have influenced my decision because she also knew him. Barrett understood that I was still primarily a recitalist. Although I had had a few successes as an opera singer, I did not consider myself one at the time. Recital work and orchestral appearances were the "bread and butter" of my career.

When I was about to sign the contract with Herbert Barrett Management, I asked Lou LoMonaco to do my publicity brochure. I told him I was tired of the standard black and white photograph on the cover of a brochure and wanted something original. I thought that an artist might be more creative. He finally agreed and designed a red and orange sunflower, with my face seeming to burst out of the middle of the flower when you held it up to the light. I didn't like the photograph he picked, but Lou didn't like glamour girl–type photographs. I thought it made me look older, but he argued that it made me look serious.

6

Turning Points

THERE WERE few who played the Brahms *Four Serious Songs* like Charles Wadsworth did. I felt that I had been *born* to sing those songs. With his accompaniment, I performed them, along with several French things, when I made my Chicago debut at the Studebaker Theater. The reviews in the *Chicago Daily News* and *Sun-Times* were very complimentary. However, one critic said the Brahms *Serious Songs* were still "beyond me," which, as far as I was concerned, was way off base. In 1959, when I performed them at a special recital in Cologne, the German audience applauded after each song instead of waiting until the end, as is customary. This was as strong a show of appreciation as any singer could ask for.

Hall Johnson had introduced those songs to me in 1955, and his understanding of Brahms and many other German lieder composers was nothing short of profound. Now, in 1962, I actually took offense at that one critic, because it was as if someone were criticizing Hall Johnson. As far as I was concerned, no one knew the German lieder repertoire better than he did. He could explain lieder to you in a way that touched your soul, and I always made the effort to sing them from my soul every time I performed them.

Dr. Johnson always started with the text, and I believe that is where I got the practice. For example, in the Brahms song "Die Mainacht" (The May night) he said that the interpreter must communicate the feeling of lost love from the very beginning. The first few bars of the piano accompaniment suggest the melancholia of the song, "Wann der silberne Mond durch die Gesträuche blinkt" (When the silver moon shines through the tangled trees). The mood changes quickly, "Überhüllet vom Laub, girret ein Taubenpaar sein Entzücken mir vor" (Hidden among the leaves, I hear two turtle doves softly cooing of their love), and ends with a held note on the word *Thränen* (tears), where the accompaniment takes over the expressiveness of the song. The words and the music are truly partners. If I didn't fully under-stand, Hall Johnson readily came up with an analogy or metaphor to drive home the point. His practices influenced me in other song lit-erature that I performed, and even in preparing for opera roles.

The other influential person in deepening my understanding of and affection for the lieder repertory was Jens Nygaard, a fellow Juil-liard student whom I also met at International House. He was an outstanding pianist and a sensitive conductor. My interpretation of the Brahms *Serious Songs* deepened considerably with Jens. He also exposed me to the lieder of Schubert and Hugo Wolf, among others. Sometimes after dinner at the International House, where he also lived, we worked for hours in a practice room there or across the street at Juilliard.

PERFORMING CONTEMPORARY music was my next major mu-sical challenge, starting with Igor Stravinsky's contemporary opera-oratorio *Oedipus Rex,* presented by the Opera Society of Washington in honor of Stravinsky's eightieth birthday. I studied the score my way, almost like learning and singing a Verdi aria. Robert Craft, the young assistant to Stravinsky, who worked with him on practically all his projects, led the first rehearsal. I told him how I had studied the *Oedipus* score. He liked my Verdi analogy.

The maestro was very cordial at our first meeting and also liked what I did musically. I was a little shy at first, but after the rehearsal was underway I was alright. In fact, he called me his "ideal Jocasta," a real compliment coming from a great living composer. On the night of the performance, there was such electricity in the atmosphere. Stravinsky was a composer I had studied at Juilliard in music history courses. Now I was singing his opera, with him conducting! My friend Bliss Herbert was the stage director. George Shirley sang the title role, and Donald Gramm, Creon.

After the live performances, we recorded *Oedipus* with the same cast. I recorded the aria in one take. We recorded another one just in case something went wrong with take one. Some years later I was asked to sing Jocasta at La Scala with Thomas Schippers conducting, but by that time it no longer felt right in my voice.

I performed and recorded again with Maestro Stravinsky later that spring. He was conducting the Canadian Broadcasting Corporation Symphony Orchestra in Toronto. I performed the American premiere of his work *A Sermon, a Narrative, and a Prayer.* At the rehearsal, Robert Craft thought he'd have to cue or whistle the pitches to me for certain difficult entrances. When he found that he didn't, he became very interested in me as a musician. He wanted me to become more involved with performing contemporary music, but I didn't.

I RETURNED to the classical tradition in a concert version of Rossini's comic opera *Il Conte Ory* at Carnegie Hall, with Thomas Schippers conducting. We performed Act I of the opera as part of a larger symphony concert. Judith Raskin, Helen Vanni, and Norman Treigle were also in the cast. The role of Isoliero is full of vibrant coloratura singing and I was happy to sing it.

I became better acquainted with Tommy Schippers in 1962, although we had met the previous summer at Spoleto. His musical directions were always clear, and he rehearsed the orchestra very well. In addition to that, he loved singers. He breathed with us every step of the way. It was the beginning of a very fruitful relationship.

Over time, I knew many conductors and their styles. Zubin Mehta, Claudio Abbado, Carlo Maria Giulini, and several others also had great communication with their singers. I liked Georges Prêtre very much as a conductor, when he stuck to what he initially set, but he could also be a little erratic. He would rehearse something one way and change it on the spur of the moment. He also wanted you to look at him all the time, which I was not trained to do. I was supposed to be communicating with the audience in a concert and with other singers onstage in an opera. As far as I was concerned, the eye contact with the conductor was supposed to be peripheral. Boris Goldovsky had taught me this at Tanglewood.

ALMOST FROM the beginning of my career, *Carmen* was grafted onto me. The production in Spoleto in the summer of 1962 gave me the chance to sing the full role for the first time. The production costs skyrocketed and the opera producers had run out of money, but they managed to pull it off somehow. In retrospect it was a splendid production, even though at the time I hated it.

Gian Carlo Menotti, the great composer, and now stage director, wanted Carmen to be mysterious. For example, instead of Carmen being showcased by entering the stage alone, as the score indicates, he had me enter with some friends (as part of the chorus), barely noticed and smoking a cigarette. When the music began, announcing Carmen's appearance, I was already onstage. As I stretched my arms and began rolling my shoulders with suggestive upper body movements, as if emerging from a cocoon, other activity on the stage was minimized. The audience's attention was *then* drawn to the otherwise anonymous girl factory worker on a smoking break with her other colleagues. I dropped my cigarette on the ground, put it out with my shoe, and began my line, "Quand je vous aimerai? Ma foi, je ne sais pas" (When will I love you? I have no idea).

It was an intriguing approach. As for me, I wanted Carmen to be daring, but also to have the quality of elegance. Playing down Carmen would not wash. In this opera, if anything should be played up, it should be played up to Carmen. The last act, of course, was powerful no matter what you did with it. I thought that it was written so well, theatrically, that nothing could go wrong. And nothing did.

From start to finish, it was terrific to work with George Shirley as Don Jose. When he portrayed a role, he did so wholeheartedly. He was an ideal colleague, always willing to work untiringly at attaining a certain nuance or effect or discussing it with me when there was a difference of opinion.

Several of my closest supporters joined me for the summer, knowing that *Carmen* would be a great landmark in my career. My friend Joanna Simon (Carly Simon's sister) was my cover. Mother and Dad came, making their first European trip. In order to see me perform, they were willing to break with the church's position. I was touched by their sacrifice. Dad told me that he and Mother got down on their knees and prayed to the Lord for forgiveness. "Oh, Lord," he said, "Please understand. She is our daughter. We don't make a habit of going, but you did give her this wonderful instrument."

Madame Freschl also came and stayed for the whole six-week run. She and I rented a large apartment from the family I had lived with the year before. This was the only time a voice teacher traveled with me. I do not believe that students should use teachers as crutches; I saw this kind of dependency too many times in my career. Some singers went so far as to fly a teacher in to "vocalize" them before a major performance.

Although I didn't know at the time, a certain Maestro Siciliani, one of the upper administrators at La Scala, also saw this production. He would have a significant influence on my career in Italy. In fact, it was on the strength of this Spoleto *Carmen* that La Scala and others became interested in me.

IN THE Friday, October 5th edition of the *New York Herald Tribune,* I had the following notice printed:

Shirley Verrett-Carter, young American mezzo-soprano, has dropped the
last part of her surname and will henceforth be known as Shirley Verrett.

Soon after, I was working with Leonard Bernstein in New York
City on one of his Young People's Concerts, later televised by CBS.
Bernstein, of course, was a gifted composer and conductor and a
world-famous personality by then. He had a strong commitment to
increasing children's awareness of concert music, without intimidating them. I think he also saw this as a means of cultivating the next
generation of concertgoers. Bernstein was also a musical maverick.
He routinely broke with established musical traditions set by earlier
conductors, and I liked that about him.

When Bernstein saw me at the concert, he jokingly called me a
"name-dropper." I can't remember if I laughed or groaned at his humor. With this notice, I not only erased the last vestige of my failed
marriage, I also made room for Lou LoMonaco to enter.

I tell people to this day, you never know who you are going to fall
in love with. I know it is kind of silly to say we don't think about race,
but there are days when I look at Lou and remind myself, "Yeah, he
is white," because I sometimes forget. He has been such a part of me,
such a part of my life. If that isn't a soulmate, I don't know what is.

In 1963, Lou was very involved in the civil rights movement, and
he drew me further into it. He had designed the official commemo-
rative souvenir for the 1963 March on Washington, a collage of men
with hoses and dogs attacking marchers in the South. He did another
work equally as provocative, which depicted Myrlie Evers (widow of
assassinated civil rights leader Medgar Evers) at the obelisk, with a
swastika creeping up on the American flag. He took this work to
Time, Esquire, Newsweek, and similar magazines where he had had
other works accepted, but none of them would touch the material
with a ten-foot pole.

As the march was in the planning stages, Lou felt that the organizers might want to use some of the material. He met with Bayard

Rustin, one of the planners, who was dealing with the internal squabbling that went on. Lou offered his work and Bayard put him in touch with Whitney Young, the late president of the Urban League, who then arranged a presentation to the entire planning committee. After Lou spoke, Whitney decided to move ahead on the project. The sale of Lou's design as a button and a flyer would help to defray part of the cost of putting on the march. Everyone felt that the historic event needed a memento. The official souvenir was a variation of the Michelangelo Sistine Chapel painting, where the finger of God is touching Adam's finger, giving him life. That scene is enclosed in a circle of black people holding hands, with the caption "We shall overcome" painted in red, white, and blue. It is a gripping piece of work, and Louis LoMonaco did it.

Forty thousand buttons sold like "hotcakes," for a dollar each. Lou told me that his pockets were bulging with one-dollar bills. I missed the historic march, because I was in Europe at the time, but having him there made me feel proud. The original poster on which the March on Washington memento was based was part of a major Whitney Museum exhibit, *American Century: Art and Culture 1900–2000*. This was a great honor for Lou, given his strong commitment to the civil rights movement.

His concern for civil rights issues and man's inhumanity to man extended further, and he became involved with other issues. For example, after John Lindsay became mayor of New York City in the mid-1960s, he appointed a black fire department chief. I remember Lou telling his family, "Well, we've got our first black fire chief." From the way he said it, you would have thought he was black and proud of such an achievement. He also made me get more involved in the movement. After a housing discrimination case that involved us, he suggested that I work with the National Committee Against Discrimination in Housing. I sang a benefit recital at Carnegie Hall to help raise funds for the organization.

If any members of his family were disturbed when Lou and I became a couple, they never said anything in my presence. Some may have been concerned that I was a divorcée, but my eyes were wide open to any racial slights. I have to say that I have always felt loved and welcomed. His mother was a little afraid that if we ever married, our children would feel out of place, but my feeling was that if Lou and I were okay with the situation, we would teach our values to our children.

The Verrett side was also gracious. Mother liked Lou a lot after the first meeting. I think anyone would have been better than my former husband, as far as she was concerned. Mother said, "All I'm going to say on the subject is that this is someone who I think is very decent and who I believe you will be happy with, whatever you decide to do." When Lou and my father met, it was very businesslike.

BESIDES MY love for him, there was another factor binding me to Lou. I relied on his advice for complex career and personal decisions, like those concerning the famed mezzo-soprano Grace Bumbry. Grace and I had had a unique relationship for some time. Louie helped me to address it early on.

Grace's career started before mine in a big way. In 1961 she was the first African American singer to appear at Bayreuth in a major role. The production of Wagner's *Tannhäuser* and the casting of Grace as the so-called *schwarze* (black) Venus made international headlines, clearly put Grace Bumbry's name on the opera and concert world map and gave her career a quantum leap. There are those who still remember it as a historic event. Sol Hurok immediately signed her to a much-publicized six-figure contract, with the idea of her carrying forth Marian Anderson's legacy.

Right after Grace's Bayreuth triumph, she returned to the United States and did a simply fabulous recital at Carnegie Hall. She sang so gloriously that I *had* to go backstage to congratulate her. Franz Rupp, who had been with the Hurok organization as Marian Anderson's accompanist, and who had played for me when I sang for Miss Anderson's manager a few years earlier, was Grace's accompanist for her recital. The room was full of well-wishers, reporters, and publicity people who were interested in seeing Grace after her Bayreuth success.

Franz Rupp saw me as I walked into the green room backstage and said in an audible voice, "Now *there's* a musician!" He gestured to me when he said it, so Grace obviously heard the remark and turned around to see who Franz was talking about. Others in the room did the same. I remember smiling with an awkward embarrassment. It was an innocent gesture on Franz's part, but definitely ill-timed. If I were in Grace's shoes, I, too, would have felt a little insulted by it. She had just given this beautiful recital and *her* accompanist (i.e., her partner in the performance) made a remark like that about another singer in her presence. It clearly had the effect of briefly diminishing her triumph.

This was the first time Grace and I had met, and in that moment, I believe, this so-called rivalry between us started.

Grace's success, to be brutally honest, made me feel insecure, perhaps even afraid. I feared that the "powers that be" would permit only one or two blacks at a time to emerge prominently. Leontyne Price was already a star and becoming a bigger one year by year. By the early 1960s, Marian Anderson, the great contralto, was near the end of her career. Grace seemed to have come out of nowhere, but maybe I just hadn't been paying attention to other emerging singers. I didn't have anything against her. She has a wonderful talent, but I thought, Here we are, essentially contemporaries (I am a few years older), with the same voice type. What is America going to do now? Trying to get my start, I felt that we would be treated like two black race horses and the one that ran (or sang) the fastest, in the figurative sense, would cross the finish line first.

I discussed my anxieties with Lou. He advised, "If you want to hold your ground, you need publicity. You need a public relations person." He asked me what I wanted in my career, and I said I wanted to do whatever my talent allowed. I had met Peter Gravina in Spoleto, who was a PR person and was interested in representing me. I called him and asked for an appointment. He became my public relations representative, as well as a friend. I began appearing in newspapers and magazines. Peter made me visible in a social way. John

Ardoin also helped me in this area, from a purely musical sense. My photographs and concerts began receiving notices in several papers around the country, mostly by way of wire service.

Meanwhile, it seemed that the music world conspired to create tension between Grace and me. Some people in the music business thrive on the hint of intrigue between two well-known singers of the same voice type. Marian Anderson also experienced something like this when Dorothy Maynor emerged, although they had different voice types. Maria Callas and Renata Tebaldi had their huge tensions. Beverly Sills, Joan Sutherland, and, eventually, Montserrat Caballé also had similar press rivalries, because they did many of the same kinds of roles. The public seems to love it.

Rightly or wrongly, I felt there was not much I could do but stay my course to focus on my own artistic growth.

IN OCTOBER 1963 I went to the Soviet Union at the invitation of the Soviet government. Some officials heard me sing at the Los Angeles Music Festival the year before. I sang for an attaché in New York and was hired on the spot to do ten recitals. I was also to appear as Carmen with the Kiev Opera and repeat the role with Moscow's Bolshoi Theater.

The U.S. State Department had its media apparatus in place and used it to publicize the upcoming engagements. In addition to its sponsorship, the State Department played up my being the first African American (back then, "Negro") to sing a major role at the Bolshoi Opera. As these things go, I am sure the State Department wanted to put its propaganda twist on an African American going to the Soviet Union, because the Russians had been critical of this country's ill treatment of black people. At the same time, the United States was calling itself the "land of the free and the home of the brave." Cold War politics infused the entire trip. It was kind of a cultural mission, part of an ongoing effort to smooth things over after the Bay of Pigs incident in Cuba.

It didn't take me long to see that this trip wouldn't be easy. Charles Wadsworth began having problems almost immediately after we got there. He was under a lot of stress and knocked on my door late at night because he couldn't sleep. I have always been a light sleeper and needed my rest. I was in a foreign country, so different from anything I had ever experienced. I didn't speak the language, except to say "nyet" and "da," so I didn't have any more of an advantage than he did. We were assigned an excellent interpreter, Marina, but when she went home, that was it. We were on our own. The food wasn't really good. The suites were gorgeous, but they were cold.

My first stop was in Kiev for a performance of *Carmen.* My costumes were designed in the United States by my good friend Norman Fischer and taken to the Soviet Union for the performances. I sang in French, but the rest of the cast sang in Russian. It was a little funny at first, but I adjusted and the cast was very supportive. We used a lot of smiles and gestures to communicate with each other. A few times, the Don Jose and I simultaneously broke out in laughter during rehearsal, reacting to this bilingual production. Were it not an opera role that I knew well, I wouldn't have done it, because I had very little rehearsal time with the cast and no time with the orchestra before the opening.

The first recital was at the University Hall in Riga. In Riga, so different from Moscow in those days, there were smiling faces on the streets, and the food was better. The audience was simply ecstatic. It took the audience three songs to realize I was a good singer. But from that point on, they kept up a rhythmic applause and would not let me continue the program until I had repeated the just-completed song. Because of the success of the Riga recital, all my future performances were broadcast live over the radio, and people mobbed us at the backstage door after each recital.

Unfortunately, I think the audience reception unnerved Charles, because he was still not well after having played two very excellent programs. I told him the best thing was for him to go back to the

United States because there was no point in both of us being stressed out, and his keeping me up at night had a negative effect on me.

After Charles left, the Russian government supplied me with another accompanist, Vilma Sirulez, from the Riga radio station. She was remarkable. Vilma could sight-read like no one I had ever met, and that was saying a lot because Charles was a first-rate sight reader. She also played the spirituals, after a short time, as if she had played them all her life.

In between recitals, I sang another *Carmen* at the Bolshoi Theater. Peter Gravina, I must say, did an excellent job of publicity, because my appearance at the Bolshoi was widely reported throughout the United States. It was mostly via the newswire service, but the story and my picture ran in papers in Wilmington (Delaware), Duluth (Minnesota), Milwaukee (Wisconsin), Huntington (West Virginia), Fort Worth (Texas), and Tampa (Florida), among many others. The good thing was that this further publicized my name, and I was subsequently invited to perform recitals or make orchestral appearances in many of those places.

A young singer named Elena was allowed backstage because she had already begun a promising career at the Bolshoi. Russian soprano Galina Vishnevskaya, the wife of conductor Mstislav Rostropovich, was her mentor at the Bolshoi Opera. Elena was very enthusiastic about my singing and asked me, through the interpreter, if she could look at my music. She was so polite, I offered to let her copy it, if she returned it promptly. She seemed startled at my offer, as if it were too generous. She was almost beaming when she rushed off with the music. We met again some years later in the United States.

But as rewarding as the Bolshoi was, I will never forget the recital in Leningrad. I could sense that many of the Russians were shy and afraid to speak to a foreigner, but once they were in the concert audience, it was another story. This audience was so fantastic that after I repeated a few works in the printed program, as was the custom, and about six encores, the stage managers had to move the piano off the stage and turn out the lights before people would leave. An incredible outpouring of gifts and flowers came from the audience. I have experienced that reaction only a few times in my career.

I have to underscore one thing about Soviet audiences. If they like something, they will keep applauding, which means you have to repeat the song. This literally wore me out. I wasn't getting my customary nutrients, like orange juice and fresh green vegetables. It was really a hit-or-miss situation as to whether you got a good meal in the Soviet Union at that time. Most of the food was canned. Although I didn't need to, other people stood in long lines to buy such basics as bread.

I continued the tour until I became so ill with a bad cold that I had to cancel the last three of the ten scheduled engagements, those in Odessa; Warsaw, Poland; and Sofia, Bulgaria. When I sang my last recital in Moscow, I looked at some of the faces in the audience. They were grateful and appreciative, but not as ecstatic as the audiences in Riga and Kiev.

I was happy to come home. Before I left the Soviet Union, the State Department offered me another tour, but I declined because I had other engagements to fulfill in the United States. Besides, I have to say that I didn't make a great deal of money on that State Department tour. In fact, I lost money by doing it. When I sat down with my manager after returning, we calculated that I had forgone several thousand dollars in fees that I would have made had I concertized in the United States over the same period. I was paid in Soviet rubles, but I couldn't take the money out of the country because of currency restrictions. So from that standpoint, the thing was a wash, except for my buying large quantities of caviar and a few beautiful signed lacquered boxes.

In my private life, I was happier with the outcome. Lou proposed to me by phone while I was in the Soviet Union. He had actually asked me the first time about six months after we met and started dating, but it took a lot of talking before I felt comfortable going down the aisle again, and there was the added problem of my career.

He asked, "Could you give up your career for me?" I answered, "No way. It's not fair." That's what kept us from marrying right away. I had not come this far, with all of the studying and commitment, just to give it up because a man asked me to, not even a man I dearly loved.

At the same time, I always felt that a career would not be enough. I wanted a family and a home, but marriage alone wouldn't do, either. Lou was very upset, but I couldn't lie and tell him I would give up my career for him. I asked him if he could give up his career as an artist for me. I believe that drove the point home to him. We could work something out. After God gave me this gift, there was no way I could promise anybody on this earth that I would take it and bury it.

Dad's primary concern was that Lou might impede my career. Lou was very blunt in saying he didn't like the idea of being married to a woman who would be traveling as much as I did, but he also realized that I was very talented and he would try not to stand in the way of it. I think part of his response had to do with his traditional Italian upbringing, where the wife stayed home or came home every night, even if she had a profession. In the end, Dad liked Lou because he appreciated Lou's honesty. He said that most people would have lied to curry favor, but Lou didn't.

In the black community some people became upset when they heard about Lou and me. They knew I had been married to a black man and thought I had divorced him as my career was taking off, in order to marry a white one. I suppose, from the outside, that's how it might have appeared. The late African American choir director Eva Jessye (who was a major presence in the black community) was somewhat bitter about this, but she didn't know that I wanted to divorce shortly after the ceremony the man I had married. She could only go on appearances. I know that black men and women have experienced a history of oppression together, but who can say how love is supposed to work?

I RETURNED to the United States in time to recuperate for an important recital I had coming up at Philharmonic Hall (now Avery Fisher Hall) in New York that November. Charles Wadsworth accompanied me at the recital, but within a year or so, I made a transition to Warren Wilson as my official accompanist. Charles and I have remained friends all of these years, though.

My arrival from the Soviet Union was widely reported around the country. As a result of Peter Gravina's work, I appeared on *The Ed Sullivan Show*. Sullivan played up my having sung Carmen in the Soviet Union. I, of course, sang the "Habanera" on the show.

On November 22, 1963, President John F. Kennedy was assassinated. I was in the Midwest and scheduled to do a recital that evening. When the news came from Dallas, I felt an immediate shudder of fear rush over my entire body. President Kennedy and his wife had ushered in an unprecedented focus on culture and elegance in the White House. Mrs. Kennedy had redecorated the White House in a way befitting American prominence as a world power. They were a special inspiration to the youth in America, as it was a time signifying that the "pioneer stage" of this country had ended. Kennedy had also become a symbol of civil rights in the United States, and now he was dead. My scheduled concert was canceled. I mourned with the country, and especially my people, who, I was sure, felt as deeply about his death as I did.

The president of Kapp records, a relatively small label, had heard me on *The Ed Sullivan Show*. He somehow found out about my religious background and asked if I would do a recording of religious works. I made it in President Kennedy's memory. I also wanted to make it for Mother and Dad and readily agreed to do the project. I did hymns and spirituals, including "How Great Thou Art," "Let Us Break Bread Together," "The Old Rugged Cross," "When Jesus Beckons Me Home," "His Eye Is on the Sparrow," and "I Hear a Forest Praying," among other selections. I was accompanied by piano, harp, and organ. Although the recording didn't remain in circulation very long, it gave me reason to remember to rejoice in my blessings.

WHEN LOU and I were finally married on December 10, 1963, we were ready for a life together. We made our vows to each other in one of the private rooms of the fabulous Four Seasons restaurant in Manhattan. Lou's brother Leon and his wife, Terry, paid for the ceremony and the small reception. Lou's family, my voice teacher, Marion Freschl, and Peter Gravina attended. Peter took photos of the wedding. A Presbyterian minister presided. Because I was a divorcée, we couldn't get married in the Seventh-Day Adventist Church, but I really didn't have much interest in that since I no longer claimed membership. Lou had grown up in the Catholic Church, but left it as a teenager.

After the wedding, we flew to Los Angeles, where my parents had a reception for us at their home during the Christmas holiday. My parents really made it into a grand occasion. They invited friends whom I had not seen in years, and we received many lovely gifts.

I did not rush into marriage with Lou. You know the saying, "Once burned . . ." I think that people should take a little more time to decide to get married. Oftentimes we're swept away by the passion of the moment. Some probing questions need to be asked before you jump into marriage, especially for the second time. Lou and I finally agreed that I could be on the road no more than six months out of the year, and the summers and in-between dates were largely to be "family time." Of course, I wasn't able to stick to this schedule as rigorously as I would have liked, but this was the framework for it. I did give up some opportunities that would have kept me in Europe, away from home and Lou, including an Easter festival and a summer festival that Maestro Herbert von Karajan had routinely invited me to participate in. I wanted to maintain as much peace at home as a career like mine allowed.

In the early days, Lou was very involved in the inner workings of my career. He tried to protect me from some of the vulgarities of the business, the "Who bit John?" intrigue that seems to follow celebrity. I never made an important decision without him.

During those early years, Lou helped me develop a serious interest in art and we loved going to galleries and exhibitions. We also began to collect American and English antique furniture. At times, we might be sitting together, reading the paper, and, at the same time, would spot an advertisement for an antique furniture sale. Without saying a word, we would look at each other as if we couldn't wait to get there. Of course, we had some of the tensions present in any marriage, but ultimately, we respected each other's careers. I relied on his counsel for most things.

7

From Covent Garden
to La Scala to the Met

S EVERAL RCA executives had invited me to a luncheon after my recital at Philharmonic Hall. George Marek, Richard Mohr, Roger Hall, and the soprano Anna Moffo were there. So was Lou. He always attended my important meetings. Richard Mohr had been to the recital and was very complimentary. He spoke about expanding the label and its growth potential.

Finally, I asked, "What does all of this mean?"

"Well," said George Marek, "We want you to sign with RCA as an exclusive artist." When I asked what that entailed, he said it would involve recording a minimum of three works a year, a combination of operas, recitals, and works that required a mezzo soloist. I was offered a three-year contract, with an option to renew. Roger Hall, who I am sure was responsible for the label's interest in me, had proposed the idea of putting together a strong group of core singers for RCA—that is, a soprano, mezzo, tenor, and baritone quartet.

The reigning label sopranos were Leontyne Price and Anna Moffo. Eventually, Montserrat Caballé was signed. I was to be the label's mezzo (possibly along with Rosalind Elias, who was not, I believe, under exclusive contract). The tenors were Carlo Bergonzi, Richard Tucker, and, eventually, Plácido Domingo. The baritones were Robert Merrill and later Sherrill Milnes. It was a great idea.

ROME, 1964. Rome was a superb place to sing, particularly in the summertime. The air was so good for the voice in those days. I always thought I could sing anything when I was in Rome.

I had gotten closer to being able to do 100 percent of what I wanted with my voice. Madame Freschl had given me a good basic foundation from which to move forward, but I finally realized that it was up to me to arrive at the point at which I could do what I wanted with my voice. At first, I searched for a new voice teacher. I tried a lesson here and there, but mostly I prayed to God to give me guidance to do it myself. Taking my time, I was really beginning to understand my throat and my vocal cords. And Madame Freschl and I remained in touch.

First, I recorded a recital of Spanish songs, including Falla's *Seven Popular Songs,* in May. I didn't get much of a break because the following month I recorded my first opera, Verdi's *Luisa Miller.* Anna Moffo and Carlo Bergonzi were in that cast. Everyone used scores, because it was impossible to learn the music for the recordings, as well as learn new recital and opera repertory for the fall season.

In July and August I was in the studio again to record Preziosilla in *La Forza del Destino.* That project involved an all-star cast with Leontyne Price, Richard Tucker, Robert Merrill, Giorgio Tozzi, and Ezio Flagello, with Tommy Schippers conducting. I sang several interpolated high Cs, and Tommy was as happy as I was about the way they flew out of my throat.

Roscoe Lee Browne sat in on some of the *Forza* recording sessions. Afterward, we strolled around the city, reminiscing about our International House days when he had introduced me to Leontyne. Her singing in the *Forza* recording was superb. I had finished my session for the day but stayed behind to hear her. Her high notes in "Pace, pace, mio Dio" (Peace, peace, my God) were so soft and glorious, I didn't know where the voice was coming from. Leontyne was *the* prima donna on the RCA label. There was no question about it. She even maintained an apartment in Rome and used to invite Lou and me over, or we went out to dinner when our recording schedules overlapped.

Lou eventually suggested that we also find an apartment to rent in Rome, instead of paying expensive hotel bills. We found a one-bedroom place in the Parioli district that we rented each summer. The Parioli was a chic area at the time, with nice restaurants and movie theaters. I saw many American movie-types there, including Orson Welles.

Lou and I traveled the Italian countryside after the recordings ended. We rented a car and drove around to our hearts' content. We visited friends and Lou's family near Naples, did sightseeing, and then found places to stay when sundown approached. We would wake up early the next day and do it again. It was a great and exciting time.

I SIGNED on to premiere an original role in February 1964. The composer Hugo Weisgall, who introduced me to the great acting coach Stella Adler, had approached me about participating in an operatic version of the biblical story of the Queen of Judah, Athaliah. I vaguely remembered her name from bible study, when I was young, as the wicked daughter of Ahab and Jezebel. Yet there was something tantalizing in the character, as Weisgall described her to me. Others in the cast were John Reardon, Raymond Michalski, and William Lewis. It was a twelve-tone opera, so I applied the same discipline to it that I had to learn Stravinsky's *Oedipus Rex*. I immersed myself in the character of Athaliah's wickedness but attempted to bring out another side of this complex woman.

The semi-staged production benefited from the fiery red gown that I wore, and I used some of the most stylized hand and arm gestures while onstage, to convey her stature. The music director, Thomas Scherman, did a lot to help us in rehearsal because some cast members took to the work better than others did. I later commissioned Weisgall to write a song cycle for me. I think it hurt his feelings when

other engagements interfered with our learning the music. I did perform several songs of my fellow Juilliard graduate, Thomas Pasatieri,
who dedicated several of his works to me.

By the time I sang Carmen at the New York City Opera that fall, I
had become quite celebrated in that role. There was a demand for me
to sing it. Of course, much of that had to do with my being a shapely
black woman (i.e., the Carmen type). The *New York Herald Tribune*
hailed me as one of the "greatest Carmens in a generation."

The summer before the City Opera opening, Julius Rudel invited
me to do a concert version at Lewisohn Stadium. But the debut at
City Opera had come out of my having sung *Carmen* at Spoleto with
George Shirley two years earlier. Julius Rudel, who attended a few
performances there, was very impatient to have George and me repeat our Spoleto success at City Opera. It was my first appearance
with the company since singing Irina in *Lost in the Stars* in 1958.
Though I still worked primarily as a recitalist, I was a proper prima
donna now, with ideas about everything. George had an idea of how
he wanted to kill me in the opera's death scene, and we worked that
out to a tee. We rehearsed and rehearsed. We even worked out the
very chord at which the knife would strike me.

Meeting Beverly Sills, then a star at City Opera, I complained to
her about the terrible wigs in the *Carmen* production. Sitting in the
costume shop, she looked at me.

"You've got to have patience. Things move very slowly here. Don't
let it get under your skin." She said it like a real pro. Her advice was
comforting, although it didn't help me get anything done about
my wig.

AROUND THIS time, Lou and I attended a cocktail party at the
beautiful New York City townhouse of Franz Waxman. I didn't feel
like being in a crowd that evening, but Lou thought it was important.
As we walked in the door, and Franz and his lovely wife greeted us, I
immediately noticed a very handsome man wearing a bow tie. He
was seated next to the British conductor John Pritchard, on a sofa

across the room from where I stood. Tall, pale, and thin, with a long nose and laugh lines around his eyes, this stranger was the archetypal British gentleman.

We exchanged glances several times that evening before he asked someone to introduce us. His name was Basil Horsfield. He had been a British intelligence officer during World War II and had excellent people skills. We exchanged some pleasantries, but, sensing some kind of agenda, I came straight to the point.

"What do you do?"

"I am a manager, and I hear that you are a really gifted singer," he replied. He had worked with George Shirley, among many other opera stars, to help establish them in Europe. Lou nudged me as if to discourage the discussion, but I kept talking. Before the evening was over, Basil and I scheduled a time to meet again at a friend's apartment. He wanted to hear me in person, but I said no. I knew I could sing. Instead, when we met a few days later, I played the recording of *El Amor Brujo,* with Stoki conducting. As it turned out, the disk was flawed, so it made my voice sound distorted. At the time, I thought it was the equipment, but I was wrong. Even so, Basil asked me to join his management.

That is how I came under European management, as a separate arrangement from my North American agreement with Herbert Barrett's management company, which handled my recitals and orchestral appearances in the United States and Canada. Basil took over my entire European career and handled it brilliantly. He never pushed me to perform, which is part of what I was looking for in management.

At the same time, I could not accept 90 percent of the work he contracted for me, because I had promised Lou I would sing only six months of the year. If I went over my six-month limit, Lou inevitably had a talk with me about our agreement. He used to keep a big board listing all the places where I was singing. This became one reason why I never sang often at the same opera houses.

THAT SUMMER, in addition to recording Gluck's *Orfeo ed Euridice* with Anna Moffo and Judith Raskin, with Renato Fasano conducting the Virtuosi di Roma Orchestra, I experimented with Roger Hall's brainchild entitled *Singin' in the Storm.* He felt that I could do "crossover" material if it were handled the right way. We chose a collection of songs with peace, freedom, or struggle themes, including "Where Have All the Flowers Gone?," "If I Had a Hammer," "Oh Freedom," "When Johnny Comes Marching Home," and the song "Cry the Beloved Country" from *Lost in the Stars.* I also sang "Strange Fruit," the lynching song made popular by Billie Holiday back in the late 1930s. In all honesty, her version was better. Still, I am very proud of that effort. Best of all, it gave me the opportunity to work with the late, great Army choir director Leonard DePaur. He had parlayed his musical military success into a professional conducting career. When I was young, I had seen him conduct the all-black chorus of men dressed in uniform, singing spirituals and work songs.

I MADE a vow to God that if he let me have success with my next project, singing the role of Ulrica in *Un Ballo in Maschera,* I would never sing it again. Ulrica, the mysterious elderly soothsayer, definitely wasn't the role I would have liked for my Covent Garden debut, but Basil thought it was a good beginning. Coincidentally, I was going to record Ulrica for RCA in Rome that summer with Leontyne Price and Carlo Bergonzi, with Erich Leinsdorf conducting. Basil apparently made the Covent Garden management aware of the upcoming recording.

I questioned the role, mainly because I had concerns about how low it lay in my voice. Yet when I talked to Madame Freschl about the part, she thought I could do it. My ear heard a much darker voice singing the role. Freschl said I just shouldn't push too hard at the bottom of my voice. We decided that it was time for me to make my debut at a major opera house in Europe. It turned out that I would sing more in London at the Royal Opera House than at any other opera house during this significant period of my life, because I generally tried out new roles there. It became my "home house," before the Met.

In rehearsals at Covent Garden I was fighting a cold, but the energy of a new beginning gave me an extra boost. Now I would finally get a chance to use some of Grandma Verrett's swaying movements and stylized hand gestures that I remembered and had practiced for hours as a child. In my mind, I envisioned her with her white headdress and her all-too-familiar hum. If there had been some way for me to incorporate the hum into the production, I would have. At one point I put my arms out like Christ's on the cross, as I had seen Grandma do so often. The director asked what my motivation was for the gestures, but I came up with something vague. In any event, I persuaded him of its effectiveness. It was a legitimate outgrowth of a very real experience. It was beautiful.

The cast included Amy Shuard as Amelia and Jon Vickers singing Riccardo. This was the first time Jon and I had worked together in an opera. He was much better in the French repertory, to my mind, and was also a good colleague. Somehow, he seemed to have thought I was nervous about the debut. He kept checking on me. I assured him that everything was okay, but I appreciated his support. It was Jon who also warned me of the overuse of nasal inhalers. He said that the medicine in the spray could adversely affect the cilia in the nostrils. I became careful from that time on.

The following month, I was in Rome for the RCA recording. Leontyne Price and Carlo Bergonzi were the ill-fated lovers. I was to sing Ulrica and Reri Grist was to do Oscar. This was the first time, to my knowledge, that a major label had cast three African American women in lead roles. I was told that when Leontyne was consulted about the casting, she commented about the three of us together, "They are the best, aren't they? Then that's who should be there."

After the recording, I kept my vow.

DONIZETTI's *Lucrezia Borgia* in the summer of 1966 was my first recording with my friend Montserrat Caballé. Montserrat had scored a big success in a concert version of that opera, when she did it for the American Opera Society at Carnegie Hall, which was under the direction of Allen Oxenburg.

Unfortunately, I remember the occasion so well because Grace Bumbry and I had another encounter, adding to the legend that we disliked each other. At the opera, Grace and I sat in adjacent boxes. I recall her deliberately ignoring me when I tried to get her attention to say hello. Instead of turning the other cheek or giving her the benefit of the doubt that perhaps she didn't even see me, I took offense and began to deliberately ignore her. That, of course, was wrong. Even during the intermission, when we were both in the upstairs lobby, neither of us looked in the other's direction. I must admit that the situation was less embarrassing than when we had first met a few years before, when Franz Rupp made that ill-timed remark after her recital. I should have just gone over and said hello, but instead turned my nose up, as I had perceived her doing. People in the lobby recognized both of us and fueled gossip about our mutual dislike of each other.

After the performance, I attended a party at Allen Oxenburg's house. I'm not sure if Grace was invited or not. A photographer took pictures of Montserrat and me cooking paella. After a while, Grace's escort from that evening came to me and said, "Grace wants to know what she has done to you." I told him my side of the events. It was most probably an imagined slight that took on greater significance than it ever deserved. I relate that story with some shame, because I was probably being too sensitive. A couple of years went by before we finally resolved that episode.

As for recording *Lucrezia Borgia,* I enjoyed everyone in that cast, including my dear friend and colleague Alfredo Kraus, who recently died. This was the first time I had heard of him and heard his singing. He looked very youthful, but was actually older than I was. The character I sang in that opera, Maffio Orsini, a trouser role, is one I never would have sung onstage. It was fun, because I worked out the cadenzas in the drinking song with Bliss Herbert, which others have borrowed when singing that aria. Interestingly, Orfeo and Ulrica were the only opera roles I recorded for RCA that I ever sang onstage.

*   *   *

BY THIS time, I had gone to the Sol Hurok organization, which took over managing my North American recital and orchestral appearances. I had worked with the Barrett agency for three years, until the mid-1960s, before things became strained. I wanted bigger dates in larger auditoriums and wanted to move outside performing in the university circuit. When the agency couldn't deliver, I left. Joe Lippman was the top person there, after Barrett himself, and I think my departure upset him more than it did Mr. Barrett. Lippman thought I was ungrateful, but I had given the office three years and several opportunities to improve things for me. John Browning, the pianist, was also a Barrett client who thought I was being uppity, but years later he said he understood why I had left.

Barrett was a total gentleman and asked if there was anything he could do to change things. When I told him it was time for me to move on, he accepted it graciously. He and I had developed a personal rapport. I even sang at the wedding of one of his daughters.

Lou had helped persuade me to make the move by arguing that Barrett was not really helping my career grow to its full potential. Lou felt that after all the great reviews, my fee should increase each time so I could always be competitive. That should have been the role of the management. I believe that the Barrett management was a bit afraid of such a move because of my color. By that time, Columbia, along with other big management companies, had approached me about representation. But Lou and I reasoned that there was something special about seeing "S. Hurok Presents . . ." printed on a billboard. People all over the world recognized that name. Lou was correct, as he was about so many other things.

Sol Hurok was an elegant man. He was not tall and was a bit stout, but he carried his weight well. He dressed impeccably—always with a hat and cane. Mr. Hurok did not require a formal contract, simply a letter of agreement. He felt that if an artist and he were good for each other, that was fine. If not, the artist could get out of the agreement, as could he. It was a smooth operation.

Hurok really *managed* a career. He was inventive and creative. I, of course, had known of him for many years. He had been Marian Anderson's manager, and that was a factor in my switching over to him. He had a keen sense of showmanship and stayed on top of the business, because he always had his associates out looking for new talent. He was also not afraid to manage African American artists or those of other races. The person assigned to me was Sheldon "Shelly" Gold.

Basil Horsfield still did everything for me outside the United States. For example, he had received several offers from German opera houses. I still had some misgivings about performing in that country because of its treatment of Jews under the Nazi regime. Eventually, I had to come to terms with those feelings, but it took time. All the people couldn't be entirely to blame for what the leaders had done. After all, I was going there to sing, not to make a political statement. There was enough for me to do in that area in the United States. When I did perform in Germany, I was always received very well.

LOU AND I invited Leontyne Price over for dinner at our apartment in New York City one evening before my upcoming engagement at La Scala. I was going there to perform the mezzo part in Verdi's *Messa da Requiem,* to benefit UNESCO. Basil had secured the engagement, with Herbert von Karajan conducting. There would be several performances, one of which was to be televised throughout Europe via satellite. The other soloists were Leontyne; a young and upcoming tenor, Luciano Pavarotti; and bass Nicolai Ghiaurov.

After dinner, Leontyne looked at Lou and said, "Lou, you've got to go to Italy with Shirley."

Lou protested that it would be difficult. He had art deadlines to meet. As if she hadn't heard a thing he said, Leontyne looked at him again and said, "Lou, you've got to go."

This time he looked at her seriously and responded, "Really? You're trying to tell me something, aren't you?"

She nodded her head and said, "Just go."

When we arrived in Italy, we found a whole "can of worms." I had understood that I was supposed to do all the performances but learned that Fiorenza Cossotto was also scheduled to do several.

When I think back on it, I must have made a terrible impression on Maestro von Karajan. Here I was acting as the archetypal difficult-to-get-along-with prima donna, but I felt I had good cause. The contract had been written in an underhanded way. I had understood that my performance was to be recorded and televised, but to my surprise, Fiorenza Cossotto would appear in the televised performance! When I looked at it in a clear light, it made sense for the La Scala management to have her sing the televised performance. She was a very established artist and I was a relative newcomer. We can be so arrogant in our youth.

She was the reigning mezzo at La Scala in the dramatic mezzo repertory. Before her, the big name had been the great singer Giulietta Simionato, whom I found to be a very lovely lady and new friend-to-be. Whoever became top dog at that house didn't want another singer in his or her place. Cossotto didn't like me or anyone else who appeared on the scene whom she considered a threat. It was silly because she had a huge voice, was singing all over Europe, and unquestionably was *the* big name in Italy. I was told that she commuted between Milan and Bologna, where she was singing in an opera, just to get those performances and prevent me from gaining a foothold or invading her turf.

When I learned the conditions of the contract, I contacted Basil, who flew in from London. We set up a meeting with the *sovrintendente,* or general manager, Antonio Ghiringhelli, and his assistant Dottore Oldani, but we met with Oldani first. We asked questions and he "talked around Jack's barn." I wasn't fluent in Italian but could hold my own. Lou was much better. At the end of the meeting, I asked who would sing the televised performance. Dottore Oldani paused and said, "Madame Cossotto." At that point I took my bag, slammed it on my lap, stood up, said, "Thank you very much," and left with Lou.

For the next two days, no one could reach me. I wouldn't go to re-hearsals or take any phone calls. What made matters worse was that Maestro von Karajan must surely have been annoyed at this little up-start from New York, who refused to show up until they changed the casting for the broadcast. But it *wasn't* changed.

Basil finally caught up with me and said, "Shirley, you have to grin and bear it this time. Von Karajan likes you a lot and can be very im-portant to your career. Let's not cause any more friction."

Leontyne was quite gracious during all of this. After I went back to rehearsals, she made herself available to work with me, when she could have been resting. A colleague like that is worth more than gold. The performances were successful. This was the first time that I had met and performed with Luciano Pavarotti and Nicolai Ghiau-rov. Both were very fine singers, and, of course, Leontyne was first-rate. In all honesty, Fiorenza Cossotto also did a splendid job. After the performances, Antonio Ghiringhelli wanted to see these "Ameri-cans" who were causing all the trouble. He took Lou and me to din-ner to make amends for the misunderstanding.

While we were eating, Ghiringhelli looked at Lou and said in broken English, "You Americans are like cowboys. You shoot from the hip."

Lou lived up to that reputation by saying very bluntly, "We just don't like how business was done here. We had a contract that said one thing and arrived to find something else." I am glad that Ghir-inghelli did not hold this first encounter against me, because it was he who signed me to a contract two years later.

I HAD to get an Italian manager. Basil still had overall control of Eu-rope but usually had an associate in various countries with whom he worked. In Italy it became Simonetta Lippi. She came to visit me in Rome while I was recording *Lucrezia Borgia*. She produced a contract for me to begin work with Radio Italiana (RAI). Simonetta had known me years earlier at Spoleto, when she was Tommy Schippers's personal secretary. Simonetta was very inventive and not afraid to tackle any problem. She is a fine businesswoman from a renowned

Italian family in Lucca. Lou and I decided that she should handle everything in Italy, and she, too, did a superb job for me. We have remained good friends.

Simonetta introduced me to Maestro Francesco Siciliani, the director of RAI. When we first met, he had held a high-level position at La Scala and a few other prestigious posts. Through him and Simonetta, I began doing recitals and concerts throughout the country. I sang Bach cantatas and several operas over the air. Those were glorious times. After hearing me in recital in Florence, the managers of the Maggio Musicale proposed to mount a production of Donizetti's *Maria Stuarda* the following May. They wanted me to sing the role of Queen Elizabeth I of England. Before committing, I informed Simonetta that I wanted to look at the score.

I kept waiting and no score arrived, but they wanted an answer about whether I would sing the role. I knew it was a soprano role, but I had already begun to sing what I thought was good for my voice, without regard to the mezzo or soprano label. Finally, Lou said, "Shirley, let's just take a trip to Florence." He had lived in Florence while on a Fulbright Fellowship and still had friends there.

We drove from Rome to the opera house in Florence, with no appointment (typical Americans), and asked to see Dottor Luciano Alberti, the sovrintendente of the Comunale. Simonetta had told me that he was the one who wanted me to do the role, because he had been impressed by one of my recordings. When we arrived at Alberti's office, we were given the runaround. Finally, Lou told the person to whom we had been referred, "If she doesn't get the score, you can count on someone else singing the part, because she will not do it." The man we were speaking to looked at us as if to say, "Who the hell are these cheeky Americans?" During those days, I *was* cheeky, but I didn't get the score either, at least not *that* day. The man gave some excuse about it still being printed or copied or something.

In July 1966, as I performed the mezzo part in a Verdi *Requiem* in the Piazza at Spoleto, with Tommy Schippers conducting and Gundula Janowitz the soprano, there, sitting in the very front row, was none other than Dottor Alberti from Maggio Musicale. Simonetta saw him and pointed him out to me before the start of the performance, because we hadn't formally met at that point. When I sang my opening line of the *Requiem,* "Kyrie eleison . . . ," which comes in very strong after the tenor's entrance, I noticed Alberti's face light up as if to say, "She really *can* sing." He was staring right into my mouth. After the performance, he came backstage, very enthusiastic and apologetic.

"Signora, signora, you will have the score tomorrow. I am so sorry about the delay." We became friends from that day on. I believe he wanted to hear me live and see this woman who had made a scene in his office.

MARIA STUARDA in the Maggio Musicale production marked the beginning of my Italian career as a major artist. I was a young singer with a good voice and growing stage skills, and people were talking about me even during the rehearsals. Leyla Gencer, who sang the title role, was a *real* prima donna and could have easily taught me a thing or two about being one. She was an established artist. I believe that she was afraid and felt, "Here is a new singer on the scene. What's going to happen to me?"

Leyla had a strikingly beautiful face, with a well-chiseled jaw line. She appeared almost regal on the stage because of her looks alone. Her complexion was somewhat olive, suggesting someone of Mediterranean background.

We were rather formal, perhaps even distant, toward each other during the rehearsals. Perhaps if I had been more deferential toward her, it might have eased the discomfort between us, but I didn't think about it at the time. I was concentrating on doing a good job, reminding myself that this would be my major Italian operatic debut. The director, the late Giorgio de Lullo, was fantastic, as was the conductor, Maestro Francesco Molinari-Pradelli. He was another of those singer's conductors who was a joy to work with, even though he could, as I found out later, be a pill.

Opening night arrived. The costumers had me in white face

makeup, because I was playing the British queen. It was a joke. Because one of the costumes I wore showed some cleavage, they had to put the makeup quite far down on my chest. It was hard to get out of that grease paint. My first aria, "Ah, quando all' ara scorgemi" (Ah! When at the altar of love), received long applause. I believe this made Leyla more nervous. In retrospect, I know it did. The performance itself was strong because her first aria, "O nube, che lieve per l'aria ti aggiri" (Oh cloud! that wanders light upon the breeze), also received sustained applause, especially after she sang the cabaletta "Nella pace, nel mesto riposo" (In the peace of sad seclusion). At one point in the drama, Elizabeth uses her riding crop to lift Mary's chin up in a mocking gesture. Fireworks really start flying between the two queens when Mary denounces her as the "Figlia impura di Bolena" (Impure daughter of [Anne] Boleyn). Provoked further by Elizabeth's taunting, Mary ultimately says to her, "Profanato e il soglio inglese, vil bastarda, dal tuo pie!" (The English throne is sullied, vile bastard, by your foot). Leyla did that line with incredible power and conviction. All the other characters onstage were frozen, while attention focused on the two queens. This was a stirring piece of staging, enhanced by lighting that centered on us. I still remember de Lullo's directions.

When the cast came out to take bows at the end of the first act, we lined up backstage, which was the custom. It was also the custom for Leyla Gencer, who sang the lead, to go out first. She grabbed me by the hand—I suppose, to prevent me from usurping her position. That kind of thing was known to happen in opera theaters all over the world, especially in Italy. I didn't perceive it as a friendly grab, because she wasn't smiling. As she took my hand, she squeezed it very tightly. I felt my back stiffen and my eyes widen at the pain of her strong grip, with rings on her finger that cut into my skin. My immediate reaction was to return the same to her, but in that split second, thank God, I realized that she was nervous. I could feel her trembling. We were in front of the curtain by that time. I just took my free hand and covered her hand and rubbed it as if to assure her that it was okay. I felt her hand relax, and she gave me a look as we went offstage. She still made sure that I didn't upstage her, though, by pulling me off the stage after her. The important thing was that we became friends from that moment on. I could see the look in her otherwise piercing eyes. They softened when she looked at me after that.

Leyla and I both had towering success in that production. After the "hand" incident, she knew I wouldn't try to upstage her or engage in any other silly antics. Had I played into that, I have a feeling that we would have been enemies to this day.

Years later, she did an interview in San Francisco and couldn't say enough good things about me. She always invited me to parties at her home in Milan, where, after dinner, we talked and, depending on who the other guests were, sang. Once with Plácido Domingo and Claudio Abbado, we did excerpts from *Aida.* Leyla performed at several opera houses in this country but never became the big name she should have. This was a shame, because she could sing high pianissimi with seemingly no effort at all and in the next instance become very dramatic. She once stepped in at the last minute to replace Beverly Sills in a Dallas Opera production of *Lucrezia Borgia.* She should have had a much bigger recording career. Whatever the case, the Italians loved her, and she was a success in South America as well. I never met anyone who had sung as many different types of opera roles as she had.

Leyla and I appeared together several times after that. She was a true woman of the stage. I remember that during one of our performances of *Don Carlo,* hecklers from the audience started screaming, "Voce, voce," which meant she wasn't singing loud enough for them. Leyla left her position, walked downstage, stared the hecklers down, calmly walked back to her spot, and signaled to the conductor to start again. She had an old-fashioned singer's stance. It was a powerful lesson in being in command of a situation.

IN THE world of opera, temperaments have a way of determining the mood of every project. After Leyla and I sang *Maria Stuarda* in Florence, I went to Rome to record my first solo opera album, *Verrett in Opera.* Georges Prêtre stepped up to the podium with authority.

Since I was singing several Italian arias, Prêtre wanted to check several Italian stylistic performance practices with Maestro Luigi Ricci, whom RCA had hired for such purposes. That was okay with me. Luigi Ricci was also my Italian opera coach in Italy. He had coached Leontyne Price and Anna Moffo, among others.

Unfortunately, Prêtre, a former prizefighter, couldn't always articulate what he wanted from the orchestra. He almost came to blows with one of the orchestra members during the recording session. During our recording of Donizetti's *La Favorita* aria, he yelled at the female harpist playing the introduction to "O mio Fernando." The orchestra did about four takes and Prêtre wasn't satisfied with any of them. He yelled at the poor woman each time. Finally, her husband, also a member of the orchestra, spoke up about Georges picking on his wife. Prêtre came down from the podium and stood in front of the man, yelling at him. Obviously, the rehearsal stopped. I quietly excused myself and went to my dressing room until things cooled down. I was glad I wasn't the one in the middle of that ruckus.

The recording finished without any more tirades. I was particularly pleased with the *Orfeo* aria from that album, "Amour, viens rendre a mon ame" (Love, come to restore my soul), because I had the opportunity to put in ornaments I had borrowed from the nineteenth-century singer Pauline Viardot. I couldn't use them when I recorded the entire role. I was also proud of "O ma lyre immortelle" (O my immortal lyre) from Charles Gounod's *Sapho*.

BY THE end of 1967, the offers were coming fast and I turned down many engagements. I sang another *Maria Stuarda,* this time in a concert version at Carnegie Hall, with Montserrat Caballé singing Mary, Queen of Scots. Sol Hurok came backstage after I finished my final scene. Then he realized that Monserrat had much of the final act to sing.

"This opera will not do. She is still out there singing and you're finished for tonight? Not good," he said. He was always on top of such details.

*   *   *

THE YEAR 1968 started off with one of the best productions of *Car-men* I ever performed in. I had been engaged to sing *Carmen* in Florence at the Teatro Comunale. Maestro Francesco Molinari-Pradelli was in charge, and the director was the late Franco Enriquez.

Despite being fraught with controversy, this turned out to be the definitive Carmen for me. When Maestro Molinari-Pradelli asked me to do the role, I said I would, but in French, even though the practice at that time in Italy was to perform all operas in Italian. Franco Corelli, who was a renowned singer and equally celebrated for being difficult, was singing Don José. I believe that he suffered from stage fright. Living up to his reputation, Franco came to rehearsals when he felt like it. I arrived in Italy, recovering from a bout of the flu. As I came to rehearsals from my sickbed, he would be leaving. That really annoyed me. Trying to preserve my voice, I showed up for rehearsals but mouthed the words. In a few instances, I sang an octave lower.

The maestro knew about my condition in advance, because I had told him, but he still put me on the spot in front of the chorus and other musicians.

"Signora, why aren't you singing?"

"Maestro, you know why," I said, and he moved on. At another point in the rehearsal, he asked again.

"Maestro, I am trying to get well. I came here for the benefit of the chorus so they will know where I am onstage at each moment. As soon as we are finished with this rehearsal, I am going back to bed." I could sense that he was becoming angry, but I stood my ground. I wasn't trying to be temperamental.

The third time he asked me (as if I hadn't said a thing before), Lou, who was sitting in the audience, spoke up.

"She said she's not singing!"

Silence followed.

Someone in the chorus called out, "Chi parla?" (Who speaks?)

Another chorus member said, "Il Marito!" (The husband!)

I admit, I wanted to laugh but didn't dare. The maestro left the podium, ending the rehearsal early. Italians really love such rehearsal antics, but that incident was mild compared to the opening night performance.

When the papers reported that this production of *Carmen* would be done in French instead of Italian, they also wrote that I had insisted on it. I assumed that someone from the theater leaked it to the press to heighten the intrigue. Despite a slight cough, I was ready to sing on opening night. The performance started out smoothly. The "Habanera" received enthusiastic applause. Corelli had sung in French up to that point, got to Jose's "Flower Song" in the next act, and sang it in Italian! When he began the aria, I lost concentration for a moment because I knew the aria in French. I thought, Oh, my God! He's forgotten the words. I soon realized that this had been his intention all along, to sing the aria in the "home" language. I was shocked, but then became angry. I could see the defiance in his eyes as he looked at me. But the joke was on him.

The audience let him finish. Half of the people cheered. Half jeered. Some audience members came prepared for Corelli, because many screamed and yelled. I saw one sign that read, "Vada a Berlitz" (Go to Berlitz), as if to tell Corelli to learn French at a Berlitz language school. Some people threw vegetables on the stage, bringing the performance to a halt. This commotion made me nervous, and I began coughing. Fortunately, while all that was going on, I could turn my head from the audience.

I said to myself, "Dear Lord Jesus, help me, because this audience is out for blood!" Stirred up about Corelli, they would let me have it, too, if I sang badly.

Corelli's experience was nothing compared to that of the baritone singing Escamillo. His name was Vladimiro Ganzarolli. A critic reviewing the performance later wrote, "his insecure performance had incurred the audience's displeasure." I didn't agree with the critic's assessment of the quality of Vladimiro's performance, but that comment about incurring the audience's displeasure was a dramatic understatement. When he reached the last high note of the "Toreador's Song," he cracked. He was having some trouble and was clearly nervous after what had happened to Corelli. The audience booed him! Some threw tomatoes and onions onstage at this poor man. The opera stopped for another five minutes. I started coughing again, because Carmen is also onstage for this aria. When Vladimiro sang the reprise of the "Toreador's Song" in the third act, after the Don José and Escamillo duel, his voice cracked again on his exit. The audience started back with the tomatoes and onions. He had a very good voice and an exceptional stage presence. This was a terrible thing to happen.

Lou, who was in the audience, became worried about me after the Corelli "Flower Song" demonstration and went backstage. After Ganzarolli's second crack, Lou overheard one of the managers on the phone, calling around to find another baritone to replace Ganzarolli, even before he was off the stage! He was dropped from the run of the production.

His replacement was Piero Cappuccilli, whom I met for the first time and who continues to be a wonderful colleague and dear friend to this day. He had to sing the opera in Italian, because he knew it only in that language. It really turned into another bilingual production of *Carmen*. I believe that another baritone replaced him after a few performances, because he had a scheduling conflict.

The following day the papers ripped Corelli apart for having sung the aria in Italian, while the rest of us were singing in French. Some reviewers said that he was rude and discourteous to "Madame Verrett" to do something like that. Corelli had recently sung a performance in Parma, where he had also been booed. He didn't try that nonsense again during the run of the opera.

Franco Corelli and I were on strained terms throughout that production. As if that wasn't enough, our respective spouses were drawn into the fracas. Corelli's wife, Loretta, told my manager, Simonetta, that Lou had given her the finger or some other lewd gesture. Of course, Lou would never have done such a thing, but I believe that she said this to deflect attention from her husband's bad behavior. Simonetta came to our hotel and told us. It had more to do with the bad blood between Franco and me. Even Simonetta knew it was a lie but wanted to avoid the bad press something like this could generate. In the end, she asked Lou to send Loretta some flowers as a peace gesture.

That's what Italy was all about in those days. You did not want to go there and sing badly, because they would have you off the stage before the end of the opera's run.

Even with all of those mishaps, it was the definitive *Carmen* for me because of the late director Franco Enriquez. He was with us every step of the production. Even though we were performing in a large theater, he wanted our eyes to communicate. He explained that although the majority of the audience might not see our eyes, our colleagues onstage would, and that helped to make the drama more powerful. I also liked his ideas about movement. He didn't want us to look affected, so he worked with our natural styles (e.g., walking, waving, and gesturing) and attempted to enlarge them. The overall result was an intimate and, yes, mysterious Carmen.

I very much wanted to create this Carmen. I had a more mature understanding of the part now. I realized that it could not be done properly with broad strokes, except for the expansive *Toreador* scene and its dramatic crowds. Carmen is composed of little vignettes, little glimpses, little slices of life. I never liked how they did it at the Met or La Scala. They blew it way out of proportion. Franco envisioned a *Carmen* that was like chamber music, the way I believe Bizet intended his opera to be. The audience had to look for her when she first came onstage. At first, I did not like this approach. I felt that I got lost in the scene. But in the end, this approach was right.

I captured Carmen's mystery by not flaunting her. In most productions, everyone onstage circles around Carmen. She is the center of attention. In this production, I positioned myself off in a corner. I spoke with a veiled quality to my voice—a quality achieved by lowering my voice, dropping my shoulders and body, or lowering my head. I turned my body away from the audience. Carmen was calmer, more human and down to earth, more attainable. The audience could truly relate to her.

I loved this version of Carmen, because it was not a giant production, but more *musica da camera* (chamber music). These things required a strong director, and whoever did the lighting also did a superb job. The opening night ruckus aside, praise should also go to the audience in Florence. The audience members understood everything we attempted to do onstage and showed their appreciation by their thunderous applause.

BY 1968, the Royal Opera House at Covent Garden was truly my home house. I was on good terms with the management and, most important, felt at home. The audiences in London adored my work, and the British can be die-hard loyalists where an admired singer is concerned.

As to my living arrangements while performing in London, Lou again suggested that I rent an apartment. Basil and his partner, John Davern, always found me a lovely place with many conveniences, a good location near major shopping areas.

Basil had me scheduled for three appearances at Covent Garden, starting with *Aida* in March. It was a glorious production, with stunning sets and costumes, Jon Vickers singing Radames, with Edward Downes leading us. Martina Arroyo sang the title role. This was the first time Martina and I performed in an opera together onstage. In our earlier appearance in Strauss's *Ariadne auf Naxos,* where we were nymphs, we sang from the pit.

Martina and Jon sang and acted so honestly that after the opening, a young girl came backstage and burst into tears because of the opera's sad ending. I put my arms around her and told her that it was all right, it was only a story.

Shortly afterward, I went to Rome to do a concert version of Rossini's *Mosé.* Wolfgang Sawallisch led the cast, which included Nicolai Ghiaurov as Mosé and Teresa Zylis-Gara as Anaide. Teresa and I had performed Rossini's *Stabat Mater* the year before, also in Rome.

As recorded and broadcast by RAI, we now performed in a large church with wonderful acoustics, but it was so cold we had heaters all around and wore warm underwear under our concert clothes. It was worth the trouble. I really enjoyed having coloratura opportunities, especially in the cabaletta of my big aria at the end of Act Two.

I returned to London for my first Brangane opposite Birgit Nilsson in *Tristan und Isolde* at Covent Garden that May, but Birgit became ill and had to withdraw from the performance. Instead of hiring another singer, the management decided to cancel the production. I believe Basil insisted that I be paid, because I had learned the role. I remember the process of working on that role. My voice seemed to acquire a weight and coloration unusual for me. It actually scared me a bit. I think my voice took on more heft because of the language and the music of Wagner. I never performed that role anywhere, although I would have liked to. I have often thought about the heft I felt coming into my voice and wondered where it would have taken me. Most certainly, I would not have retained my coloratura facility.

In June of 1968 I scored a major success in the Covent Garden's production of *Don Carlo*. It was my first time singing Princess Eboli, which became another signature role for me. Gwyneth Jones was Elisabeth de Valois, and Peter Glossop was superb as Rodrigo. David Ward, as King Philip, did a masterful job. Claudio Abbado conducted. By this time, we had a long-standing knowledge of each other. When he had won first prize in the Mitropolous Conducting Competition in New York City years ago, a gala reception was given at Tavern on the Green in Central Park. I was one of the invited guests. Claudio found out that I was a singer and he remained interested in me after that.

IN THE summer of 1968, my career was flying high. I was in demand on both the opera and the recital stages. I had a highly successful career in Europe that was still growing. I was one of the most sought-after Carmens in the opera world. I had just signed my second three-year contract with RCA the year before, and I was recording during the summers.

I suppose I felt a little too invincible.

I wanted to record *Carmen,* but the RCA label didn't want me to. I indicated my dissatisfaction to Roger Hall. Lou and I were in Saratoga, New York, where I was to sing a concert version of *Carmen* with Plácido Domingo, when Roger came to see me. He carefully explained that RCA had recorded *Carmen* a few years earlier with Leontyne Price and Franco Corelli. Another version coming so soon would have bumped heads with that recording.

I did not hear a thing he said. I just knew that I had sung the role enough to justify putting it on disk. Lou finally threw down the gauntlet by telling Roger, "If you don't do this for her, we are out of here."

The RCA executives didn't agree, so I left the label. It was a terrible mistake. I had clearly overestimated my influence and marketability.

If I had it all to do over again, I would have handled it quite differently. It is much better to be an exclusive artist with a label backing you, because the label will promote and advertise your recordings, no matter what. As a result of my leaving, I missed out on several important recording opportunities. At the end of the 1960s and early 1970s, RCA recorded *Il Trovatore* and *Aida,* both with Leontyne Price, Plácido Domingo, and Sherrill Milnes. I would have sung both Azucena and Amneris in those recordings, but after I told them I would leave, RCA asked Fiorenza Cossotto to sing Azucena and Grace Bumbry to sing Amneris.

Thankfully, that wasn't the end of my commercial recording career, but after leaving RCA, I became a freelancer. Under those circumstances, a label doesn't have the same commitment to you. The wisest thing for me to do after leaving RCA would have been for my management to approach another label. I believe that Columbia was interested and even began preliminary discussions. My reason for not proceeding with the discussions was that my career was on a roll. I could have done many more recordings and had a larger recorded legacy, but, frankly, my attitude and ego got in the way.

Technically, I had two years to finish before completing my second three-year contract with RCA, which ended in 1970. The highlight was the opera duet recording with Montserrat Caballé. That recording was made in London in the summer of 1969. I know that my recordings for RCA continue to sell, because they are still being advertised more than thirty years later. My other royalty payments have come from Deutsche Grammophon, Decca, and EMI.

I WAS in high demand and re-engaged, and my fee was steadily increasing. I just wasn't thinking about the future or my legacy as a singer as much as I should have. Besides, another milestone, my Metropolitan Opera debut, was coming up that fall season of 1968.

As a result of having placed in the national audition in 1961, I had been offered small roles like the Priestess in *Aida* and Erda in *Gotterdammerung*. I didn't want to sing those roles, especially the Wagner, under those circumstances. Neither role was prominent enough. And I was afraid that Wagner was not good for my voice at the time. Another offer came in 1966. I was asked to sing Carmen, but I remember that the terms didn't appeal to me.

The third time around, Howard Hook, who was on the Met board, advised me to accept the offer. He spoke very frankly to me.

"Look, Shirley, they are offering you two good roles, Carmen and Eboli. My advice is not to say 'no.' If you don't take it this time, it may be a while before they come to you again."

My first response was, "Who wants to do Carmen? It isn't my favorite role, especially not in that production." The Met had wanted me to alternate performances with Grace Bumbry singing Carmen. I sensed a little of that "black race horse mentality" in such a suggestion and told them to let her do the entire engagement since it was her production—that is, she opened in it. But in the end, I agreed that after her run, I would take over the role. Basil handled the negotiations, as he then managed all of my operatic appearances in the United States, as well as my European recitals and opera performances.

Jon Vickers, now acclaimed internationally for his interpretation of Don José, among other roles, was also in the production. Mirella

Freni sang Micaela, and Justino Diaz sang Escamillo. He had made a sensation at the opening of the new Met, singing Anthony in Samuel Barber's *Anthony and Cleopatra,* opposite Leontyne Price.

You would think that with such a combination of singers and conductor Zubin Mehta, we would produce a stellar run of the opera. Instead, the performances were just okay, and what's worse, Jon Vickers and I came out of the experience on very bad terms. Jon had been very supportive of me when we had performed together before. We had sung together at Covent Garden in *Un Ballo in Maschera* and *Aida,* and, as I said, he was always a helpful colleague. He even teased me when I debuted at Covent Garden as Ulrica.

"What are you doing, getting all of that applause, and you are just starting in this company?" he said jokingly then. Well, the dress rehearsal for *Carmen* at the Met set a whole different tone for our relationship.

I always made slight stage changes as I grew into a character or a production. That was especially true of Carmen. In one scene in the third act, where the gypsies are in the mountains, José throws Carmen to the ground. According to the stage directions, I was supposed to stay down, but something told me at the last minute, "Carmen wouldn't stay on the ground. In her defiance, she would get up, or sit up, turn around, and face José to let him know she was not afraid of him."

When I tried this, it threw Jon, who was expecting me to be down on the ground, instead of looking at him defiantly, eye to eye. He stopped singing and lambasted me, "Alright! You start improvising now, and I'll improvise opening night!" Jon is a nice man but could also be a bully. He was very pugnacious and had almost come to blows with critics who wrote unflattering comments about him. He himself had related such stories to me, but I had never experienced his anger before, because he had always been very kind and supportive. In any event, he now turned his temper on me.

Instead of responding in kind by saying, "Idiot! Don't you see I'm trying something? I would have explained it if you had given me the chance," I just walked off the stage. A *true* Carmen would have responded to embarrass him, just as he had embarrassed me, but it was a dress rehearsal, which meant that people were in the audience. I had to think about being a lady, as well as an African American making my debut at the Metropolitan Opera. I did not want to be an embarrassment to my race on the stage. All of these thoughts rushed to my mind seconds before I left the stage.

Jon followed me backstage to apologize for the outburst, and I then let him have it.

"Don't you *ever* do that to me again!" I screamed. People in the audience may have heard me, given my decibel level. "This *is* a rehearsal, *not* the opening! I don't ever want to be onstage with you again!" I stormed off to my dressing room.

Rudolf Bing, the Met's general manager, came to me and tried to smooth things over. I told him to get someone else for the opera. He was wonderful and had obviously had a lot of experience in dealing with such tense situations, because he managed to get me back to the rehearsal after forty-five minutes. If it had not been my debut, I believe I would have withdrawn. I was that angry. No colleague had ever spoken to me like that, nor had I ever felt compelled to address one in the manner I addressed Jon. I knew I had to sing the performances with Vickers, but it remained tense between us from that point on. If he had just waited until we were offstage to say something to me, I could have swallowed that better, but in front of an audience, no way! He had known me as a true professional.

I held on to that anger at Jon for nearly five years. When approached about singing in an opera for which he was even mentioned as a possibility, I said, "Thanks, but no thanks." Not until we performed *Les Troyens* at the Met in 1973 did we finally resolve that conflict. I was told of a written account of that 1968 incident. The writer merely referred to Jon having spoken rudely to the "singer" doing Carmen, and omitted my name. I suppose this was gallant, but *I* was the mentioned "singer."

In those days it seemed that many productions of *Carmen* were trying to rename the opera *Don José*. The Met production had a spotlight on José during the card scene, of all places. This is supposed to be the pivotal scene of the opera. I didn't even know I wasn't being properly lighted until Lou told me later. I just assumed that because we were in the mountains and it was night, the lighting director was going after that effect. After that, I made sure I watched the lighting when I suspected funny stuff. Jon Vickers was also "light savvy" and knew when he wasn't being properly lit. I thought I knew something about it, but that *Carmen* production taught me a few lessons.

NONE OF this dimmed the public's satisfaction. As with my Bolshoi Opera appearance, pictures of me appeared in newspapers throughout the country. The African American media, like the *Afro-American,* the *Chicago Defender,* and *Jet,* paid special attention. Eventually, *Ebony* magazine sent a reporter to my home in New York and followed me for a day for a feature story. With that level of national attention, I was invited once more to appear on *The Ed Sullivan Show.* I had appeared on the program several times since I first sang on it in 1963. This 1968 appearance, however, turned out to be my last.

Shortly before the Sullivan show, I visited Hall Johnson. I had often been to his Harlem apartment. It was a labyrinth of books. Hall Johnson read incessantly and also listened to the radio a great deal. He was a die-hard grammarian. When he heard someone make a grammatical error on the air, he promptly wrote to the station to point it out.

We talked about so many things, but the conversation ultimately came back to musical interpretations and what I was doing. He had suffered a mild stroke by then; his speech was labored and difficult. His movement was also a little more stilted. After we listened to a few of his recordings, he provided me with an arrangement of the spiritual "Oh, Glory," which I was to perform on *Ed Sullivan.*

Just before I left, he restated his familiar dictum, "Hurry slowly." It was, sadly, the last time I saw him. I may have spoken to him on the telephone after that, but he died in 1970. Hall Johnson was a great teacher. I valued his advice, his wisdom, and, above all else, his friendship. I will forever hold him dear in my heart. In his honor, I continued singing that arrangement of "Oh, Glory" for another thirty years.

I STILL wasn't thinking about another recording contract or the future. Within a month of the *Carmen* opening, I sang Eboli in *Don Carlo* at the Met, and Claudio Abbado led the orchestra. This was yet another big opening in a very long and fruitful relationship that continues today. In November, *Musical America* named me "Musician of the Month" because of my Metropolitan debut. Patrick Smith interviewed me for the article. I talked so much, he hardly got a word in. I guess I was just excited about the honor and the roles I was studying to perform the following year.

In December of 1968 I went back to Italy to do *Maria Stuarda* again with Leyla Gencer. It was the same production we had premiered the year before in Florence, but this time we performed in Naples. I had more engagement offers than I could possibly handle. Even with all of that going on, I was still, status-wise, a notch below where I thought I was.

IN 1969 I had several important opera dates, including two productions of *Aida*. The first was at the Maggio Musicale Festival in Florence. Tucked in my schedule that same month was the Radio Italiana broadcast of *Les Troyens* in Rome. The performance was on two successive nights. Marilyn Horne sang Cassandra, the prophetess, in *Le Prise de Troie* the first night, and I sang Didon in *Les Troyens a Carthage* the following night. Marilyn was just establishing herself in Italy then. Nicolai Gedda sang Aeneas, with Georges Prêtre in command of the forces.

Although we used scores for that broadcast, I tried not to stay glued to the music. I wanted to use as many facial expressions as possible. I remember my entrance when I sang Didon's opening phrase, "Nous avons vu finir sept ans a peine" (We have been finished nearly seven years). Prêtre looked at me and stiffened, as if surprised by the strength with which I sang that line. From that point on, he and I were in almost perfect unison by way of eye contact. He could have put his baton down and I would have still been able to follow him. It was as if we anticipated each other's next move. That is a strange and wonderful feeling for a singer to have. The chorus was glorious, and several members came up to me after the performance to thank me, as I had thanked them.

Berlioz's Didon touched a deep cord in my being. The love duet with Gedda, "Nuit d'ivresse et d'extase infinie" (Night of intoxication and infinite ecstasy), was almost magical. Our voices blended incredibly, especially at the end of the duet in the line "Souriez a l'amour . . . ," where we ask the gods to "Smile on our love." Gedda could bring his voice to a near pianissimo throughout his entire range. I never performed with another singer, male or female, who had such sensitive control over his or her voice, particularly in the French repertory.

I came back home to sing several recitals, which kept me on the straight path of not oversinging. It was a great vocal discipline for me. In August and September I went back to Europe to do *Maria Stuarda* once again with Leyla. This time the production went to Edinburgh. Following the performance, I appeared with the Philadelphia Orchestra and Eugene Ormandy. Ormandy was a great orchestra conductor but not a singer's conductor, in my view. We did Brahms's *Alto Rhapsody,* Ralph Vaughan Williams's *Magnificat,* and Max Reger's *Requiem.* Unlike conductors such as Schippers, Abbado, Mehta, and Leinsdorf, Ormandy didn't pay as much attention to the balance between voice and orchestra. With him, it was the singer's job to measure up, which usually meant singing louder.

After the Philadelphia appearance, I was off to the Dallas Civic Opera to begin rehearsals for the second *Aida,* which Nicola Rescigno conducted. My friend John Ardoin reviewed the production for *Opera News* and said that it "sailed down the Nile and sank." He thought the costumes were wrong and didn't like the chorus. But he was very complimentary of Elena Suliotis and me, as Aida and Amneris, respectively. Suliotis didn't sing that well at the opening and didn't want to take a bow at the end of the opera. Because she decided not to take a bow, I thought that I shouldn't either. I was trying to be a good colleague, but it probably wasn't a nice thing to do where the Dallas audience was concerned. I think I took being a good colleague too far that time. People were very enthusiastic about my portrayal of Amneris that evening.

I was supposed to sing my first Adalgisa in *Norma,* with the Dallas Civic Opera, around the same time, but I believe the performances were canceled. I know my contract was stamped "void." The important thing to me was that my La Scala debut was just around the corner.

THE LA Scala management first approached me to be in a new production of Rossini's *L'Assedio di Corinto* (Siege of Corinth) during the 1969–1970 season, with Tommy Schippers conducting. He undoubtedly suggested me. The production was also to feature Renata Scotto as the lead, but she withdrew from it. After I looked over the part of Neocle, I didn't feel it was substantial enough, so I, too, said "no." (I will come back to this performance later in the book because it did take place after all, but with an entirely different cast and stellar results.) The management then suggested my reprising my role in Stravinsky's *Oedipus Rex.* By then, I felt that the role was too low for my voice, so La Scala offered it to Marilyn Horne. Finally, an offer came of a new production of *Samson et Dalila,* with Georges Prêtre conducting. Basil and I agreed that this was an appropriate role for a La Scala debut, even though Dalila was also very low for my voice. I must say, however, that I loved the character much more than I liked Carmen, and it was an opportunity to finally portray the infamous biblical temptress.

There was a slight complication with the timing. Basil had already committed me to sing Azucena in a Covent Garden production of *Il Trovatore* in London, which overlapped with the performances of

Samson in Milan. After the opening of *Samson,* I had to commute between London and Milan. That was a rough experience, and I believe the first and only time in my career I commuted like that.

The costume designer of the *Samson et Dalila* production wanted to explore the "sensuality" of Dalila, which, in layman's terms, meant that they wanted to exploit my shapely physique. Tito Capobianco, the stage director, had his wife Gigi, a dancer, teach me dance steps in the opening scene and in the final act, Bachanal. The costumer wanted me in a sheer, see-through body stocking. I said, "I don't think so." Call me a prude, but I wasn't going to appear onstage like that. I ended up wearing a very form-fitting flesh-colored body stocking that suggested the nudity. I also wore two diamond-shaped silver breast plates, with nipples in the center of each plate. And that wasn't the worst of it. The headgear looked like something a space alien would have worn in a 1950s B movie. From the top of the cap came a long ponytail that reached down to my hips.

During the opening night performance, in the scene where I sing "Mon coeur s'ouvre a ta voix" (My heart opens to your voice), I was reclining on the floor with Samson, my fellow American Richard Cassilly. His hand was resting on my hair when the wig and cap started to give. For several nerve-wracking minutes I had to hold them on with my left hand, while I sang and expressed my desire with my right. At one point I attempted to swirl the ponytail around my shoulder suggestively, but this didn't work for long. If Richard had laughed or even smirked, I would have understood. I am sure the audience saw what was happening. I know that Lou realized something was wrong and held his breath, hoping for the best.

Maestro Prêtre was in the pit, completely oblivious to the comedy taking place onstage. Miraculously, the opening was a resounding success. The Italian papers dubbed me "'La Nera Callas [The Black Callas],' who can eat the stage." This was an incredible compliment from some of the most discriminating operagoers in the world.

*   *   *

AFTER THE Scala opening I had to begin rehearsals at Covent Garden for my first Azucena. Martina Arroyo and I were teamed up once more. Jimmy McCracken was cast as Manrico. We had never met before, but I knew he had risen through the ranks at the Metropolitan Opera, starting off in small roles back in the 1950s. I remembered him there with Maria Callas in *Norma.* By 1970, he was an opera star because of his performances of Otello. A previous engagement prevented him from arriving for rehearsals until later, so the Covent Garden management hired a stand-in until he showed up.

The stand-in was a young tenor named Ermano Mauro. He had a very beautiful voice, but when we were onstage rehearsing the Act II scene where Azucena tells Manrico the story of how she came to be his "mother," his face was blank.

"Don't just stand there, give me something!" I finally said to him.

Here was this woman revealing a horrendous secret she had never told another human being and which had most certainly driven her half-mad (at least, as I interpreted the character); Manrico couldn't just act as if none of this affected him. Ermano's wife overheard my remark. Some years later she confided to me, "What you told him that day was the best thing that anyone could have said."

That Covent Garden *Trovatore* had a great impact. From that point on, Azucena became yet another signature role. I grew to love the tormented gypsy. Martina also sang like an angel. She was especially moving in the last act, floating high notes so beautifully. True to his reputation, Jimmy McCracken, too, was outstanding.

I REALIZE, as I'm telling this story, that everything sounds rosy even though it wasn't always so. Perhaps I can be forgiven for trying to forget that those years also marked the beginning of a long and serious condition I battled for much of my career. The truth is that during the late 1960s, I experienced the onset of an allergy, resulting in vocal troubles so serious that at one point I thought this would end my career.

Around 1966, the year I left Madame Freschl and began teaching myself, I noticed signs of a problem. As it turns out, the condition dated back to my student days at Juilliard. The effect was that I sometimes did a concert in one state, felt just fine, and sang well. I then flew to another concert and suddenly my breathing was awkward and labored. I got good reviews, nonetheless, but I knew something wasn't quite right.

I explained my symptoms to a specialist, who found nothing wrong. He speculated that my breathing problems might be psychological in origin. I explained that I was particularly concerned because I had a recital coming up at Hunter College in New York City, where I was to do Schumann's *Frauenlieben und Leben,* among other challenging works. This physician sent me on my merry way, with some antibiotics and the assurance that things would be all right. He even promised to attend the recital to hear for himself.

The recital took place, but I didn't feel that it went well. I was taking breaths in places where I would never have taken them under ordinary circumstances. The antibiotics weren't helping matters.

After the performance, the doctor came backstage and said, "See there, you sang just beautifully." I could have slapped him, because he had no idea how hard it had been to sing.

It took me close to ten years to have my allergic condition properly diagnosed. At times the allergies would be so bad, I wanted to give up singing. The cause turned out to be candida albicans, a yeast infection. That diagnosis wasn't made until 1978.

Grace Bumbry was also at the recital and greeted me graciously afterward. If she heard anything awkward, she never said it.

A FEW years after this Hunter College recital, I ran into Grace in my neighborhood on the Upper West Side of Manhattan. It had to have been at the end of the 1960s. I asked her what she was doing in that part of town. As it turned out, she was seeing the same doctor I saw at the time (who also gave me the first dose of antibiotics, I must add).

We started to chitchat and, to make a long story short, I invited her to my house for cocktails with a few other people. It really was time to bury the hatchet, if there was one. The gathering was very small and intimate. She was delightful. That's when she first suggested that we sing together.

I said, "Sounds okay to me." It took some years before we were able to pull off that concert, in 1982. But that's another story.

Joseph and Mary Lee Verrett, my Grandpa and Grandma Verrett, in the 1920s.

At five, I was a flower girl at Aunt Noella's wedding in New Orleans. The date was August 1, 1936. I recall being pleased with my outfit, but I was a little cranky by the end of the day. My dad, Leon Verrett, Sr., is standing in the center.

Dad posed for this portrait in California, where he had taken us to begin a new life in the 1940s.

Elvira Augustine Verrett, my mother, had this picture taken in the late 1940s.

With my teacher at Juilliard, Madame Freschl. I had just won the 1958 Naumberg Competition.

Meeting the legendary Marian Anderson for the first time at Robin Hood Dell in the early 1960s was an incomparable thrill. I keep this picture in my studio.

Composer Richard Rogers and his wife, Dorothy, were generous patrons.

As Carmen in my Metropolitan Opera debut, with Jon
Vickers (seated, front) as Don José, 1968.

In Tel Aviv in 1967 singing
the mezzo part in Verdi's
Requiem with (left to right)
Martina Arroyo, Richard
Tucker, and Bonaldo
Giaiotti. Zubin Mehta
is conducting.

In London to sing another new role, Azucena in *Il Trovatore,* at Covent Garden, I strolled through the city with my husband, Lou.

The LoMonaco family joined us at the French Consulate in New York in 1970 when I received the Chevalier de l'Ordre des Arts et des Lettres. Lou is standing top left. My mother-and-father-in-law are seated next to me.

As Didon in *Les Troyens,*
1973.

As Dido with Jon Vickers as Aeneas and Judith Blegen
as Ascanius in *Les Troyens,* 1973.

As Azucena in
Il Trovatore, 1976.

As Floria Tosca with
Luciano Pavarotti as
Cavarodossi, 1978.

As Lady Macbeth at La Scala, 1975.

The opera *Fidelio* is about a woman named Leonora who disguises herself as a man in order to rescue her husband from prison. Here I am in my costume as Fidelio with Edward Sooter as Florestan, and John Macurdy as Rocco, 1979.

As the druid priestess in the finale of *Norma*, 1979.

As Aida in the Opera Company of Boston's *Aida,* 1980.

James McCracken was my Radames in the Opera Company of Boston's *Aida,* 1980.

Shirley Verrett by Louis LoMonaco. This is the image that Lou created for the NAACP's benefit concert, *An Evening with Shirley Verrett,* at Carnegie Hall, April 1980.

As Desdemona with James McCracken playing Otello in the
Opera Company of Boston's *Otello,* 1981.

As Norma with Joseph
Evans in the role of
Pollione in the Opera
Company of Boston's
Norma, 1983.

As Eboli in *Don Carlo* at the Metropolitan Opera House, 1986.

There's nothing as exhilarating as an opening night. Here I am at the opening of my second *L'Africaine* with the San Francisco Opera, September 9, 1988. (From left to right) Plácido Domingo, Ruth Ann Swenson, Justino Diaz, and general manager Lotfi Mansouri share the limelight.

As Dalila with Plácido Domingo, a great Samson, at the
Metropolitan Opera House, 1990.

After a concert in Rome in 1992, my longtime friend and accompanist Warren Wilson savors the moment.

Greeting President Jimmy Carter at the White House in 1977.

In 1993, I had a ball singing with a galaxy of opera, jazz, and popular music stars in "First Ladies of Song." Here I am with (from left to right) Barbara Cook, Marilyn Horne, First Lady Hillary Rodham Clinton, and Judy Collins.

With Marian Anderson and Grace Bumbry in 1982.

At a rehearsal for the 1994 revival of *Carousel* on Broadway, with Sally Murphy, director Nicholas Hytner, and Audra MacDonald.

My daughter, Francesca LoMonaco, photographed at the Juilliard commencement, May 24, 2002. I received an honorary doctorate from my alma mater that day.

Addressing students at the University of Michigan, fall 1997. "Professor" is a title that I wear proudly. Teaching and college life suit me, even as I remain passionate about acting.

8

Transfigurations

M Y FATHER drummed the idea of the recital into my head. Recitals for me are small operas, little opuses. Each one is a fraction of an opera, which makes the recital very challenging and often more difficult to pull off. In interpreting an opera, I need to find the composer's secrets in the words and notes, but in the recital I have to jumble many operatic stories and secrets. I don't have the external elements of the opera to fall back on—the other singers, the stage sets, the costumes. I am out there all alone, with nothing to hide behind, barefaced in front of the audience. As much as I love it, the recital has always been, as Callas would say, a straitjacket. But doing recitals kept me honest with my art and my singing.

By the late 1960s, however, it was clear to me that the music world thought of me more as an opera singer than as a recitalist. Seventy percent of my singing was on the opera stage. Recitals and orchestral appearances had become second tier, although I started the 1970s, the biggest decade of my professional career, with an active recital schedule of about forty to fifty dates a year. Honoring my commitment to Lou meant that I had turned down many engagements.

While I enjoyed presenting songs, I began to relish interpreting my opera roles. I felt passionate about the roles to which my voice was uniquely suited. Any lingering confusion in my mind about my commitment to opera simply vanished.

I gave up organized religion, although my spiritual beliefs remained rooted in the teachings of my parents. They taught me about God, about the goodness of man, about the need to be interdependent, that we're not just dependent upon ourselves. I never let go of the idea that there was something higher than myself.

On the day of a performance, I used to put my hand on the score and first say a prayer that I would discover more about the role and would find everything the score had to say to me.

I remain a spiritual person. Whenever I am in nature, I look at every plant, the beauty of the hills and streams, and think that something did this. Some people call this force God, and so do I. I latched on to this idea early, and it has helped me my whole life. I still pray every day, sometimes four or five times a day. It just depends upon the situation at that particular moment. I never leave the house without a prayer. Never.

THE EXPERIENCE of recording the duet "Mira, o Norma" (See, oh Norma) with Montserrat Caballé had convinced me that Adalgisa was a role that suited my voice. I had my second chance to sing the role of Adalgisa in *Norma* in a concert version at the Champs Elysees Theater in Paris. I anticipated the engagement eagerly, especially since I had learned the role already for the canceled Dallas production.

I was cast opposite Montserrat. She had already had success singing the druid priestess in her native Barcelona and was beginning to gain recognition in this role.

The rehearsals were finally in sight, and I had been in Paris a while when Maria Callas, whose legendary Norma had so impressed me when I was a student at Juilliard, invited me to dinner. Actually, Callas invited Montserrat and her husband, Bernabe Marti, to a dinner party in her apartment. John Ardoin and the pianist Ivan Davis were also invited. They suggested to Callas that she invite me to dinner, too. When she told John she didn't know me, John reminded her that she didn't know Montserrat Caballé either. John was, of course, the world's authority on the life and career of Maria Callas and might have been there to interview her for a book.

That's how I came to be in the apartment of "La Divina." She was my inspiration as an opera singer. She sparked my imagination to the possibilities of the genre. It was a special moment to be her guest when I was preparing to perform Adalgisa in the only opera that I had seen her in.

Callas's apartment was beautifully decorated. When she finally entered the room, she looked like a million dollars. She wore a very elegant floor-length dress. Actually, it may have been palazzo pants. In any event, she really looked great. She kept a little poodle nearby that she swore could sing. As it turned out, she was aware of who I was and had even heard a few of my recordings.

Maria Callas was very gracious that evening. As one of the reigning interpreters of the role, she offered Montserrat some advice about Norma. In fact, Callas had sung one of her last Normas in Paris about five years prior. She told Montserrat to "pay close attention to Norma. Don't oversing it." She recalled her performance of Norma in Paris in the mid-1960s with Fiorenza Cossotto. Callas didn't like Fiorenza, because she felt that Fiorenza tried to steal scenes. I could relate to her comment after my experience with Cossotto. I wondered how Montserrat took Callas's advice about Norma, because over the course of her career, Montserrat may have sung the role more times than Callas had.

I told this story to a writer from *Opera News* who interviewed me, and he mixed things up, implying that Callas had given the advice about singing Norma to me. When I saw that in print, I was a little disturbed, because he made it seem more plausible that Maria Callas would have admonished Shirley Verrett about singing Norma than she would Montserrat Caballé. I wasn't even singing the role at that time, although I knew then that the role was in my voice. It was while learning Adalgisa that I got the idea of singing Norma. I had to know both parts for the duets and ensembles. I just didn't tell anyone of my interest in singing the title role at the time. What Maria Callas *did* say to me at the dinner party was that she admired my talent and hoped we could become friends. I remember her asking if I had an issue about my age. The question seemed a little odd, but when she asked how old I was, I responded, "How old do you think I am?" We both laughed. I have never had an issue about my age.

After dinner, her butler came in carrying a silver platter with some pictures of her on it. Callas simply said to each of us, "Choose." Montserrat wanted two. Callas signed the photograph I chose "To Shirley Verrett. May she shine always." It is hanging in my studio at the University of Michigan.

I took Maria Callas's offer of friendship as a gesture, like someone else might say, "Let's have lunch." In other words, I felt that she was being kind but didn't really want me as a friend. She had just met me. What basis could there be for a friendship? I have regretted coming to that conclusion, because I believe that she may have been reaching out. I had assumed, "Here is the great Maria Callas, choosing to be a recluse," when it seems that she was actually lonely. When I think about it, Callas's situation reminded me of Madame Freschl. She was also lonely when her students weren't around.

Unfortunately, a choral strike erupted in Paris. *Norma* is an opera that depends heavily on the chorus, so the performance was canceled. In fact, it was Callas who informed Montserrat and me that that performance wouldn't go on, after all. This was my second near-miss with singing Adalgisa, but my evening with Callas was worth the trip to Paris.

If PEOPLE ever ask me to describe a totally wonderful recording experience, I'll tell them about recording *Don Carlo* that summer. Angel/EMI had assembled a stellar cast that included Montserrat Caballé, Plácido Domingo, Sherrill Milnes, and Ruggiero Raimondi.

Most were RCA artists, but I suppose the label lent them out for this recording. We also were lucky to get Simon Estes at the last minute. That's when he and I first met. Lou and I invited him over to the apartment we rented in London and talked to him a long time. Simon was at the beginning of a big career in Europe; he still sings beautifully.

Carlo Maria Giulini conducted the *Don Carlo* recording. If there is such a thing, Giulini was a conducting god. He was one of my favorites. We had performed several works together. His explanations helped me interpret Princess Eboli, especially when performing the veil song. For every subsequent success I had with that role, I thank him for his insight. He discussed his interpretation of Eboli with me and also listened to my thoughts about her. He believed that she was more than a jilted woman but was most probably intrigued that Carlo was more attracted to Elisabeth than to her, especially when Eboli believed herself to be more desirable. No one knew or had a better understanding of that opera than Maestro Giulini.

Maestro Giulini rehearsed an orchestra in the same way Schippers did. When the singers arrived at the studio, you could bet the orchestra was ready. There were few retakes and splicing, because everyone in the orchestra was so prepared. We rehearsed for three or four days, even before we began recording in the studio. Giulini was such a riveting conductor, even I didn't want to take my eyes off him.

I am very proud of that recording. It was some of the best singing I had done on disk up to that time, and it established me as a world-renowned interpreter of Eboli.

The following October, I made my Vienna Staatsoper debut as Eboli in *Don Carlo*. This time Horst Stein was in the orchestra pit. Franco Corelli sang Don Carlo. He and I had gotten over that strained relationship from the Florence *Carmen* a few years before. He was a good colleague and, on this occasion, even friendly. He was very much loved in Vienna and could do no wrong there. He was also a celebrated Don Carlo of the time. I watched him do calisthenics before going onstage, and he was remarkably poised. Gundula Janowitz, playing Elisabeth, and I had become good colleagues from having performed in Spoleto a few years before. After a few performances, Marti Talvela took over the role of Philip and was every bit as impressive as Nicolai Ghiaurov.

The stage director, Otto Schenk, did some very clever staging for Eboli in that production. That opera really does belong to her.

The Vienna Staatsoper management was somewhat cold—maybe *businesslike* is a better word—but the audience, on the other hand, was incredible. On opening night, after I sang Eboli's marvelously familiar aria "O don fatale" (Oh fatal gift), the roar from the audience almost unnerved me because it was delayed. Eboli can steal the show with that one scene, except when there is a singer like Caballé, whose high floating notes could be pure heaven.

When the performance ended, I found myself in the backstage area, boxed into a corner by fans. I was afraid for a moment that the audience would mob me, because people were so excited. Some of the stagehands had to shield me from well-wishers. I wasn't entirely well and didn't want to risk catching anyone's germs, so, for the next few performances, I took a back way out of the theater. Then I thought that my leaving like this was a little discourteous. The people were, after all, coming back to express their appreciation for my art and their love of the music. I asked the theater management if some of the stage people could stay a little longer, so that I could meet the fans.

WHILE I was in Vienna, I rented my friend Reri Grist's house. It was small, but just what I needed. Her housekeeper, Marie, stayed on to take care of me. She took me to rehearsals and gave me my first riding lesson. Some of Marie's relatives were "veddy, veddy" upper class, which I found out when she took me to one of their castles for a hunt, with all the ceremony that attended it.

Perhaps I had made my peace with the memory of World War II. I sang several recitals in the Musikverein, with a wonderful reception from the fans. It was also a great hall to sing in. I enjoyed singing lieder to a German-speaking audience. Many reviewers complimented me on my handling of the language and commented on my nuance, as if I were a native speaker. I took such reactions as credit to my late friend Hall Johnson and to my mother's love of words.

WORDS ARE important to me as a singer, of course, whatever the language. Yes, I want the voice to be beautiful—well, that's the first thing. But then comes the importance of the word. If you're looking for some kind of transfiguration, you can't have just a beautiful sound. You've got to have the word. The words have to mean something. It can't be just rote.

If I'm singing something in French, German, or English, I always read the libretto as poetry first, rather than going ahead and learning the notes. If the composer is great—and I usually sing the music of great composers—you already know the music. Even the sound of the word is an important part of the equation. When you're trying to say something that is "sweet" you say, "Swweeeet." If you have, in French, "douce," you wouldn't just say, "DOUCE!" That would not make sense. You've got to caress the word because of what it is. And you don't go overboard. You must not overdo it. For me, every single word is important. I must read each word and each sentence and ask myself, "What does this all mean? What is important here?"

ONE MONTH before I left for Milan to rehearse for a new production of *Maria Stuarda* at La Scala, I followed Lili Chookasian as Azucena in *Il Trovatore* at the Met. I believe this was the occasion of my Texaco Metropolitan Opera broadcast debut. Richard Tucker sang Manrico and Martina Arroyo was Leonora. Mario Sereni sang Di Luna and Zubin Mehta conducted. Martina and I regarded ourselves as old pros in that opera by that time.

By 1971 I had sung the role of Elizabeth I several times, so I was more than a little daring in my singing and interpretation in the La Scala production. I had even done the opera in a concert version with Montserrat at Carnegie Hall a few years earlier. She and I were good friends by then, and the opera world was accustomed to seeing us onstage together.

Montserrat was a different Mary Stuart than Leyla Gencer was, but her performance was every bit as valid. Gencer was more of a lioness in the role. Her style resembled Callas's in many ways. By comparison, the Verrett/Gencer match-up in Florence was dramatically stronger in the pivotal scene where Mary and Elizabeth confront each other. I think our temperaments were similar. Caballé didn't move on the stage as aggressively as Gencer did, but her singing was nothing short of gorgeous. I knew there was a special reason for Montserrat's quieter movements onstage during that production: she was several months pregnant.

Carlo Felice Cillario conducted the La Scala production. He was a character, but Montserrat used to love working with him. I liked him, too, as a person, but Molinari-Pradelli was a stronger conductor, for my taste, because he really took charge of the performance and was always faithful to the music. The stage designer, Nicola Benois, had the stage framed like a sixteenth-century Tudor-era painting, with period columns, trees, and plants. The opera took place inside this frame. The costumes were also very beautiful. My costume in the hunt scene was modeled on the black knit knickers I wore to rehearsal. The costumers added a fabulous dress, open in the front over the pants, which was very impressive. The production was a success for all of us. Having grown into the role over a four-year period, since I first sang it in 1967, I did more elaborate interpolations and cadenzas than before. My high notes were just flying out in that Scala production. In fact, one of the first notes I sang as I entered the scene was an interpolated high C, much stronger than ever before.

This was the last time I sang Elizabeth I. I sometimes wonder how the role would have developed if I had continued to sing it as a more mature singer. So many things are impossible to know.

MONTSERRAT KNEW I was trying to become pregnant, so while we were working on *Maria Stuarda,* she took me to the physician who had helped her. This man gave me male hormones, testosterone mixed with something else. My speaking voice, which is already relatively deep, became deeper, almost as deep as a man's. I took the medication for three months before I had to stop. That was some powerful stuff. It nearly ruined my middle voice. Even today, that is the weakest part of my voice. I had to vocalize constantly to warm up and continue to vocalize when I was not onstage during a performance, which I had never had to do before.

Before Lou and I were married in 1963, we had talked extensively about when and how we would start a family. When Lou and I *were* ready, I couldn't become pregnant. We did all kinds of things. I didn't ovulate every month, so when I was with him, the timing was wrong. We tried artificial insemination. With today's technology, Lou and I would have had no problem conceiving a child naturally. But in those days, I felt helpless.

I REMAINED in Italy after the *Maria Stuarda* engagement. After a few recitals and a Bach cantata, I went to Turin to do a concert performance of Purcell's *Dido and Aeneas* for Radio Italiano. That performance was unforgettable in more ways than one and eclipsed everything else in my life. I wish I could say that the memorable part of that performance was the musical event. The celebrated British conductor Raymond Leppard led it. Dan Iordachescu, a Romanian baritone, sang Aeneas. Helen Donath was Belinda and Oralia Dominguez was the sorceress. Maestro Leppard gave us carte blanche when it came to inserting appoggiature and period embellishments, within reason. I was more than willing to embellish Dido.

I became so ill, I hardly made it through the evening. By the time I reached Dido's second aria, "When I am laid in earth," my hands trembled and I had a sharp pain in my right side. After I finished the aria, the audience started yelling, "Bis, bis, bis!" (Again, again, etc.). I sang it again but noticed my hands trembling even more. Those in the audience sitting in the front rows surely thought that nervousness caused my hands to tremble. I eventually clasped them to make my stance look more dramatic, but there was a very functional reason for doing so.

I flew back to the United States the next day, feeling so bad that someone from the hotel staff had to pack my bags for me. I could only sit in a chair and watch. By the time I was on the flight, my ribs were aching. I'm not sure how I made it back home without passing out.

My doctor immediately diagnosed hepatitis. Fortunately, I did not have infectious hepatitis. It must have come from something I ate, or possibly from receiving B12 injections. What I did *not* do for the next five months or so was sing. I canceled all of my performances to just rest, because I was tired all the time. Among the cancellations were performances of *Don Carlo* and *Aida* at the Teatro Colon in Buenos Aires, Argentina. Publicity went out that I was there, but I wasn't. After a month of rest, I vocalized lightly, but there were no concert engagements. I stayed close to home and just enjoyed resting there.

I am sure Lou liked this, because I was a model wife at home, though unexpectedly. We began shopping around for houses and going to open houses in various neighborhoods. Lou and I were still living in a co-op on Riverside Drive and Ninetieth Street. I was also looking at renovated brownstones and townhouses. By the end of the year we bought property upstate in the Catskills and eventually built a country home that we stayed in for years during the summers and over long autumn weekends.

BY OCTOBER 1971 I was well enough to fulfill a Dallas engagement of Donizetti's *La Favorita,* which they were mounting especially for me. I had known the big aria, "O mio Fernando," since my days at Juilliard but had always wanted to essay the entire opera role. The Italian conductor Nicola Rescigno was the music director of the Dallas Civic Opera. We had been in contact before I arrived for rehearsals. I wrote to Maria Callas to get her ideas on interpreting the role of Leonora and to stay in touch after our meeting the previous year. It was the first time I had made such a request. The suggestion to do so may have come from Maestro Rescigno, because he and Maria Callas were such good friends. I don't remember if she replied, but apparently she saved the letter, because it was one of Callas's artifacts on display in 1997, marking the twentieth anniversary of her death.

Maestro Rescigno told me that the baritone scheduled to sing Don Alfonso had withdrawn because of illness. Without hesitation, I suggested Dan Iordachescu, with whom I had recently sung *Dido and Aeneas* in Turin. He had a wonderful voice and sang the Purcell with passion. The opera company engaged him and he learned the role quickly. He was less than wonderful in the Donizetti, though. For some reason he was stiff as wood onstage and generally unhappy because the director had expressed exasperation with him about his movement in the production. I wasn't quite as quick to make casting suggestions after that and learned to give them more thought.

Ruggiero Raimondi, on the other hand, was fantastic as Baldassare. He sang even better than when we did the Verdi *Requiem* together a few years earlier. Lella Terrell, a young Texan, sang Ines. She later went to Europe and became better known as Lella Cuberli. Peter Hall designed the beautiful costumes.

By this time, I had firmly grasped the advantages of understanding something about my colleagues' roles, as well as my own. In this production, the tenor Giorgio Merighi was Fernando. He and I had sung together in Rome. His sound in that role was robust but too strident for my ear. I envisioned Fernando in *La Favorita* as a study in innocence lost and betrayed, much like that of Leonora, the "favorite." I believe that she was attracted to him because he reminded her of her own innocence, lost as a result of her more infamous status. Fernando is a young novice who has been protected from the world by the monastery. With little preparation, he leaves this sheltered environment to pursue a woman whom he believes to be the personification of innocence and purity. She has come to the monastery to pray on a regular basis, which is where he first sees her. He is then told in a very blunt manner that his beloved Leonora is the king's mistress. This is too much for the naïve young novice to endure.

Merighi didn't communicate any of this in the performance, but he seemed to want to make Fernando more heroic (especially in the sound) and caught up in intrigue than to portray a vulnerable soul. I enjoyed singing this opera much more with Alfredo Kraus and Luciano Pavarotti. Pavarotti's phrasing and overall interpretation were very strong. Kraus's approach was more reserved and intellectual, but he had the boyish looks of a young novice. Both approaches were valid.

FROM DALLAS I returned to Europe, where I made my debut as Eboli at the Teatro del Liceo in Barcelona in a new production of *Don Carlo*. The production opened the day after Christmas. Katia Ricciarelli, scheduled to sing Elisabeth, had to cancel because of illness, so Montserrat Caballé stepped in and sang gloriously as usual. Teatro del Liceo was her home house, and she was known as the local girl who became an international opera star. Bruno Prevedi sang Don Carlo, Bonaldo Giaiotti sang Philip, and Vincente Sardinero sang Posa. Maestro Anton Guadagno conducted. It was a gratifying reunion for him, Montserrat, and me, our first performance since we recorded the opera duet album for RCA.

Giuseppe de Tomasi was always telling us jokes and infusing playful staging gestures into the opera. For example, in the scene where Eboli is flirting with Posa, he had us sitting at a huge chessboard. Posa would make a move and then Eboli would make one. The symbolism added a very clever twist to the staging, although Giuseppe had to tell me which pieces to move. I didn't have a clue.

9

And Baby Makes Three

WHEN I was a child, I told my mother that I never wanted children. I don't even know why I said this. But when I met Lou, I knew I had changed my mind. I became obsessive about babies. Every time I saw someone with an infant, I stopped and asked questions and admired the child. Lou sat me down and told me to be realistic. Adoption was the only feasible alternative left. Still, I hesitated until one day when I found myself "oohing" and "aahing" over the child of a couple we'd just met.

We were selling our co-op, and a couple with a new baby came to look at it. I told this mother the baby looked just like her. She glanced at her husband, and they smiled at each other. They let me go on babbling for a while, then said, "Can we tell you something? This is an adopted child." I appreciated their patience with me and found myself expressing my deepest fears about adoption. The new parents were very open in their responses.

That's how Lou and I ended up at the Louise Wise Agency in Manhattan and began the adoption process. As we were being screened, the agency wanted to know about my active performing schedule and expressed concern about my being away so much of the time. I explained my home arrangement with Lou. I also said that in the early years I would take the child with me. The agency confirmed that we were financially solid and had a stable marriage. I suggested that the child be biracial, because Lou and I were an interracial couple, and that's what our child would have been, had we had one naturally. The adoption agents made several site visits to see what our living situation was like. They ran a background check to be sure that neither of us had police records. I wasn't concerned about being rejected.

Less than a month after we had completed the screening process, Lou called me in the Midwest, where I was singing a recital.

"Shirl, the agency called and they think they have a child for us."

Oh God! This is sooner than I expected, I thought to myself. As it turned out, our baby was born on August 30, 1972. The agents had been watching us and her, without saying anything. Of course, they didn't want to tell us about the possibility until we were screened. By this time she was three months old.

"Well," Lou said, "I thought you might want to contact them to let them know we are interested in seeing the child."

"Oh? Why me?"

"Because you are the mother."

"But this is a decision both of us are making!" I said.

We got into a huge argument. I thought he was now trying to put all of the responsibility on me, and we ended the conversation in a huff. I wasn't feeling very well after I hung up, and on top of that, I had to sing the next day. I was ready to chew anybody's head off.

You better think about this, I thought. The idea itself came out of nowhere. I asked myself, Why did you react that way with Lou? Why are you so upset?

I fell asleep that night with this on my mind. The resolution came to me in a dream. A voice told me, "You are scared." I answered back, "No! I am not." The voice came again, "YOU ARE SCARED!"

That was it. I *was* scared. You know, Geminis can be stubborn. We can also change our minds in a matter of minutes. We ask for an answer, the answer comes, and we still don't accept it. Once I was able to deal with my fear of the unknown, I could move forward.

The next day I called my sister-in-law Terry in New York. I told her that I was scared to death about this adoption. I was going to be responsible for a new life. Terry said that for the entire nine months of each pregnancy, she had been scared. Yet she had had plenty of time to worry and be scared. We were given only seven days to decide. Terry said, "You have every reason to be scared." This conversation put things in a better perspective.

Lou and I ironed things out and went to see our baby at the agency. She was part African American and part Chinese. To keep her from crying, her foster mother held her. This child was so sensitive that going down an elevator caused her to cry. She wouldn't stop crying until she felt the elevator ascending. In the hush, I finally said, "We won't know anything until I hold her." I believe that when you touch a child a certain way, the child can feel whether it is out of love or duty. I wanted to know how this child felt about me.

When I held her, I started to talk to her and asked her if she wanted to come home with us. She looked right up at me. I'll never forget that moment. She wore a pink crocheted hat and matching dress. Her beautiful wide eyes seemed to see through to my soul. She stared right into my eyes and never murmured. When Lou took her, she started to whimper a little. I think it was because of his mustache. He played with her a little and let her touch his face, and she settled down. There was no question. She *was* ours.

When we took her home, her eyes darted everywhere. She was alert and active and soon began crawling around. She explored every room in that co-op. We named her Francesca, a feminization of Lou's middle name, "Frank." We were going to make it Francesca Louisa LoMonaco, but decided to just leave it as Francesca. I also noticed that she made very elegant, stylized gestures with her hands. In retrospect, I think all babies do this when they begin to discover things.

Cessie was an easy, relatively quiet child once she settled in with us.

I always said that she must have known she was coming to middle-aged parents. I hired a nurse to help me with the adjustment, but after a short time with Cessie I decided that Lou and I would do the work. I wanted her to be used to our hands and our voices; I wanted us to bond. This experience made her ours more than ever. Lou learned how to change diapers, feed, burp, and rock Cessie to sleep as well as any nurse.

We were so excited that we were always playing with her. Once, she wouldn't stop crying, and one of the Dr. Spock books I had bought said we had exhausted her with all of the playing.

We kept an intercom system in her nursery, and, although she rarely got sick, Lou was out of bed to check on her if the least thing went wrong. Louis was and is still a heavy sleeper. Whenever I wanted to wake him in a hurry, or when I was tired, I'd shake him and say, "Lou, did I hear Cessie?" Up he would jump and run to her room. The LoMonaco household was, at last, complete.

IT HADN'T quite hit me yet that freelancing wasn't the right way to have a recording career, but the companies asked for me, so I concluded that there was still a demand for me. The recording of Donizetti's *Anna Bolena* took place that August in London. The conductor Julius Rudel had asked me to do it. This was my first complete commercial opera recording since *Don Carlo* with Giulini. In 1966 I had intended to sing the role of Jane Seymour onstage in a production of *Anna Bolena* in Los Angeles with Montserrat Caballé, and Zubin Mehta conducting, but it didn't take place. I had recorded the big duet with Montserrat (with cuts) and, from my solo album *Verrett in Opera,* did Jane's big scene for RCA. The ABC recording of the Donizetti had no cuts. This was my first recorded performance with Beverly Sills. Rudel did that opera with all the repeats. I enjoyed working with Stuart Burrows, Paul Plishka, and Beverly. After Beverly became director of the New York City Opera, she asked me to sing the title role there, but we couldn't work out the details. I never sang either of the major roles of *Anna Bolena* onstage.

*　　*　　*

BACK IN the United States, I avoided the Met by focusing on other major opera companies. The big one was San Francisco. This debut, too, was a long time in coming. My relationship with then general manager Maestro Kurt Herbert Adler dated back to the 1950s. I had sung for him in San Francisco, when I was a student at Juilliard. As I recall, I was on my way home for summer vacation. He had kept his eyes on my career from that point on. We met again in Cologne, when I performed *Rasputin's Tod.* He had called on me during the 1960s to sing with the company, but at the time I didn't feel it was an appropriate offer. I don't remember the roles, but Adler kept track of my rise.

He got my attention when he proposed Meyerbeer's *L'Africaine* for the 1972–1973 season. This staging, he said, would be done in grand style. He told me the opera hadn't been staged in this country since 1933, when it was done by the Metropolitan Opera. This production would be an extravaganza. It was scheduled to open in November 1972. I committed. Sometime afterward, I received a call from Maestro Adler and he asked me if I would sing Amneris in a single performance of *Aida* the month before my scheduled debut. The acclaimed Russian mezzo Irina Archipova, scheduled to sing Amneris in the production, had a conflict and would not be available on a particular date. Archipova and I had met in the Soviet Union years before. So my technical debut was October 14 as Amneris in *Aida,* as a replacement for Archipova. Maestro Adler gave me plenty of notice for the *Aida,* so it was announced to the press as my debut. We had already begun musical rehearsals for *L'Africaine* by then.

The *L'Africaine* cast included Plácido Domingo as the explorer Vasco da Gama, Evelyn Mandac as Ines, Norman Mittelman as Nelusko, and Simon Estes as Don Pedro. I sang the heroine, Selika. It was a tour de force. The disappointment in that production came from the conducting of the young hotshot French conductor Jean Perrison. He did not know the opera well enough to be conducting it. He spent time in our musical rehearsals correcting our pronunciation, telling us when to use the opened and closed "e" in French. Any half-wit musical coach could have done that. I was angry, because he wasted our time. He made mistakes in our entrances, and several of the orchestra members became frustrated. If the cast hadn't known that score well, we would have been in trouble. I didn't even call him "Maitre," as was the practice for French conductors, but "Mister" Perrison.

During the performance, he made elaborate conducting gestures, the kind that give the audience the impression the conductor knows what he is doing and is involved in leading the orchestra. He still made errors. As the leading lady, I was supposed to call him out for his curtain call at the end of the performance, but I was so disturbed I didn't take his hand, as is the custom. I am sure he saw the disdain in my eyes. What really took the cake was that when the reviews of the opening performance came out, *he* received accolades for having carried this show! I guess this was because he is French, and the opera is in French. Years later he came to my dressing room at the Paris Opera and said, "Please forgive me, Madame. You were right." It took him all of those years to confess that he didn't know the score, but at least he was big enough to admit it.

The singers made those performances of *L'Africaine* worthwhile. By then, Plácido had been a wonderful colleague for some time. He sang "O Paradis" so beautifully, I have never heard it sung better. I believe this was the first time I had performed a live opera with Simon Estes, Norman Mittelman, and Evelyn Mandac. Also a Juilliard graduate, Mandac had a 100-percent well-placed voice. Most of us come with 75 or 85 percent of the voice in place, which then must be refined, but she had it all. There was no perceptible break throughout her entire range. It was a seamlessly marvelous instrument.

The last thing I recall about the opening is a bomb threat right after the first act. Maestro Adler announced a short delay because of a technical difficulty, but a bomb squad came in to search. We resumed after they gave us clearance. As far as I know, it had nothing to do with any of us in the cast.

*   *   *

I TOOK Francesca with me to Europe for the first time in April 1973, when I sang Azucena in a new production of *Il Trovatore* with the Paris Opera. Lou couldn't go, because he was teaching and still renovating the townhouse we had bought. My French agent, Michel Glotz, hired a pediatric nurse from a local hospital to help me with Cessie. She was eight months old at the time.

Cessie cried a lot at first in Paris, because I had to be away all day in rehearsals. She finally adjusted to the nurse, who was very gentle with her. She stayed in the dressing room when I was in rehearsal because the nurse wanted to see the opera. Before one performance, I was made up as Azucena, snaggle tooth, hooked nose, and all. Cessie was in her playpen in the dressing room. When I leaned over to look at her, I saw her eyes widen and she sat up as if startled. I immediately said, "This is Mommy, Cessie," and she calmed down. Later that night, though, it gave her a nightmare. She cried almost all night. I finally had to put her in bed with me, and she settled down. After that, I didn't let her see me in costume until she was much older.

That performance of *Il Trovatore* was a smashing success for me, though the production was a revolving door with several cast changes. Riccardo Muti was supposed to have conducted it, but he had a dispute with the stage director, Tito Capobianco, and the management let Muti go. Muti was fairly young at the time and did not have the name recognition he later won in the music world. I hated to see him leave, though, because he was very musical and a gifted conductor. The official reason given was that he withdrew for health reasons. Sir Charles Mackerras took over the performances. There were several cast changes. Piero Cappuccilli sang Count Di Luna in a few performances, and Renata Scotto sang Leonora in my last one or two performances. Mignon Dunn sang Azucena after my run ended.

Verdi wrote a French version of the opera, *Le Trouvere,* which premiered at the Paris Opera in 1857. He expanded the final scene with additional music for Azucena. This was the version used for this production. In the 1857 *Trovatore,* after Leonora dies, the "Miserere" is heard again in the background. Manrico is executed onstage, instead of being dragged off, which is how Verdi originally composed it. This altered version expanded what I sang as well. I actually prefer that ending because it is more dramatic, but this production was the only time I did it. This version gives Manrico a few more lines to sing and Azucena more time to react to his impending execution. She is torn between saving her "son" or allowing the evil Count Di Luna's brother to die. Of course, they are one and the same. In her crazed state, she decides on the latter. The stage director, Tito Capobianco, was wonderful. He had Azucena in a state of madness, as she laughs at the execution of Manrico and exults that she has at last avenged her mother. I really felt this role. It is little wonder that Verdi considered naming this opera *La Zingara* (The Gypsy). Azucena is the most developed character in the work.

David Mitchell came up with some elaborate sets for this production. I didn't like them overall, but there were some exceptions. For example, he had Azucena and Manrico in a dungeon that gave the appearance of a cage. I objected to the bars, but on another level, it made my portrayal of Azucena even more convincing. This character was accustomed to being outdoors, in tune with nature, and was now caged like an animal. It was a powerful set for me to do the role in. It was all very dark and drab, and the steel bars were unsettling. In the scene where Azucena is captured and imprisoned, I played her like a crazed woman, even allowing my eyes to go blank at one point. It was as if she were hallucinating toward the end. The audience applauded for three minutes after this scene.

BACK IN London, Covent Garden's *Carmen* was in the making. Everyone wanted a big production and talked about a stellar cast, director, costumes, the whole works. I was consulted on every aspect of the show. As it turned out, though, a good production of *Carmen* had been done recently at the London Coliseum. I saw it. It was performed in English, but it was still good. I couldn't understand the logic of Covent Garden doing the opera so close on the heels of the

Coliseum production. It was like RCA recording me in *Carmen*, when they had recently done one with Leontyne Price.

These discussions involved the movie director John Schlesinger, who was originally scheduled to direct the opera. I told him my views of *Carmen* and how many different productions I had been in since first performing the work onstage in 1962. I told him my feelings about the importance of the chorus to the drama and how each chorus member should be involved, instead of just standing around, waiting for Carmen to show up. This was my view of a total production. It was not supposed to be another *Carmen* with a star. After Schlesinger and the Covent Garden general manager John Tulley met, Schlesinger decided to withdraw. He agreed with my concept but felt that he could do nothing to outshine the recent Coliseum production.

Covent Garden then engaged Franco Zeffirelli, the highly regarded movie director. For some reason that I don't know, he also withdrew from the production. That made me a little nervous. I then wanted it specified in my contract that if I was not satisfied with how things went, I could withdraw from the second run of the opera.

The third director, Michael Geliot, took over the production, which finally opened on July 4, 1973. Sir Georg Solti led the cast, with me as Carmen, Plácido Domingo as Don José, Kiri Te Kanawa as Micaela, and José van Dam as Escamillo. A young lady named Jenny Beavan designed the costumes. The directors at Covent Garden decided to give her a chance, because she was the daughter of someone prominent. She did a great job. Some of my costumes were really lovely. I liked Jenny's idea of having Carmen wear white in the final scene, instead of red or black, as she is traditionally dressed.

To add to my misgivings, I had nasal troubles. I had a deviated septum and let a physician in London cauterize it. I went through with the performances, but I felt that they were just okay, despite some good moments. I withdrew from the second run, as I thought I might, and Covent Garden booked Tatiana Troyanos to sing Carmen. She made the commercial recording of the opera with the same cast. It was probably a mistake for me to withdraw, because that would have been my opportunity to finally record the opera commercially, which I never did. Highlights of that Covent Garden production became available on compact disk recently. When I heard it, it wasn't as bad as I recalled. I can be my worst critic sometimes.

MY FAMILY provided much-needed peace and light. Basil had arranged for Cessie and me to have an apartment in London with a piano. Since we were going to be there a while, I was concerned that she would forget her father, so I put a big picture of Lou on the piano. Twice a day we kissed the picture, and I said, "There's Da Da. Let's kiss Da Da." When Lou met us in London, Cessie was in her playpen. She looked at him and looked at the picture; she gazed back and forth, from him to the picture; then she smiled. I could not have staged such a touching scene if I had tried.

With Cessie settled into a comfortable routine, I continued with other engagements. My recording that summer of Bellini's *Norma* for ABC had been planned for about three years. Beverly Sills really wanted to record it. The two of us were signed early on in the project. After two near misses, this would be my first Adalgisa.

When the time came for us to be in the studio, I tried but failed to get out of the recording date, because I had come down with a cold. Jimmy Levine was the conductor, and a little tension started between us then, which I recognize in hindsight. I put in certain kinds of ornaments that he didn't agree with, but he let me do them anyway. We also had a few musical disagreements over some interpolated notes I inserted. It was difficult, to be sure, because I didn't know if I would be able to make it through the recording. Little did I know that he would become the Met's artistic director. I suggested to Levine that he get another singer, but he ignored the comment and persuaded me to do it. Levine wanted the orginal keys, which meant that "Casta Diva" and "Mira O Norma" were sung as Bellini had originally composed them and not transposed down, as is the tradition. He also reinstalled many sections traditionally left out.

My old Juilliard colleague Enrico DiGiuseppe was cast as Pollione for the recording. I was actually surprised by that choice of casting. DiGuiseppe's voice seemed a bit lightweight for that role. I felt that a fuller voice was more appropriate, but I didn't worry about it too much because I was more concerned with how well *I* would sing. The cold lay mostly in my head and I was trying to keep it there, because if it had gone to my chest, it would have been impossible for me to finish the recording session.

I have always respected Jimmy Levine as a conductor and musician. We enjoyed many memorable musical moments together. But the *Norma* recording seems to have started us down a rocky road, which may have been the basis of our later difficulties.

PART THREE

10

"Troy Meets Shirl"

"TROY MEETS Shirl" was the caption from the November 5, 1973, *Newsweek* magazine story about the Metropolitan Opera's production of *Les Troyens* (The Trojans). I had been away from the Met for two seasons before returning to sing in *Les Troyens*. That October 22nd opening night performance marked the turning point of my career. It also changed my life and put me in a different category, professionally. I was already a high-fee artist in Europe, but after the Trojans episode, I could get $35,000 per recital in this country. The Met also looked at me very differently from that point on.

Sir Rudolf Bing stepped down as general manager of the Met in 1972. Although he and I had a history that dated back to the early 1960s, we were on no more than cordial terms and had a few conflicts during those years. The roles he had initially offered, I could not accept, and when I sang Carmen as my debut, it was less than spectacular, from my point of view. I had better success when I did Azucena with the company in 1971, but I still didn't feel embraced by the Bing administration. I was away in Europe for the big Bing gala marking his departure. Many stars of the opera world came out to sing. At seventy-five years old, the great contralto Marian Anderson came out of retirement to return to the Met stage and perform "Auld Lang Syne" for Bing during the final Texaco Metropolitan Opera broadcast under his administration. I do give him credit for having the courage to finally open the doors of the Met to African American singers. Although Marian Anderson went there late in her career, Robert McFerrin, Leontyne Price, and several others were there in their prime.

As for me—I wasn't one of his preferred singers. Certain Met executive board members had something to do with this as well, because, according to an internal source, I was too aloof and not a team player. Whatever the case, it all changed after Bing left.

Goeran Gentele, the incoming general manager, was very different. He was from Sweden and had directed the Royal Opera House there. What is more important, he had seen me in performance in Europe and loved my work. I liked him very much. Through Basil Horsfield, Gentele let me know he wanted me to be on the Met's roster during his first season as general manager. There was an instant rapport when we met. I liked him so much, I was prepared to break my vow to never sing Ulrica in *Un Ballo in Maschera* again. He asked me to do it, but made it clear that this was only the beginning of a series of roles I would be offered. Then came the news of the terrible tragedy in Sardinia: Goeran Gentele was killed in an automobile accident. My heart sank when I heard about it. He had such big plans for the Metropolitan. There's no telling what he could have achieved had he lived.

Gentele's successor as general manager, Schuyler Chapin, was equally complimentary of my work. Chapin had come to see me after the opening of *L'Africaine* in San Francisco the year before. Even before that, he had made overtures about my returning to the Met. He told me how he wanted it to be a company where I felt comfortable and happy, and he may have said something about the planned production of *Les Troyens*. In any event, he had my attention. I had been away for two seasons.

When the discussions of mounting *Les Troyens* began properly, I was offered the role of Cassandra. I had sung Didon in 1969 in a RAI concert version with Georges Prêtre, but because I sang with the score in that performance, I had not memorized the role. Didon is the role I really wanted to sing, but it had already been offered to and accepted by Christa Ludwig. Before committing to Cassandra, however, I asked to look at the score. I had barely remembered Marilyn Horne's performance when we did it in Rome for RAI. The Radio Italiana performance was done with many cuts, but after I looked at the score, I said yes.

The driving force behind the Met's production of *Les Troyens* was Maestro Rafael Kubelik. I am not overstating things when I say, even Hector Berlioz would have agreed that, other than himself, no one knew the opera as well. I would argue that Kubelik knew it better, because although Berlioz composed the work, he had never heard Part One, *La Prise de Troie* (The Capture of Troy). Kubelik had a long history with the work. He knew and loved every note in that score. He had conducted productions in Europe as far back as the early 1940s. The 1957 Covent Garden production, which he also conducted, was done with heavy cuts. The proposed Metropolitan Opera production was to be the biggest one ever mounted in the opera's history, and the cuts would total no more than ten minutes, with most of those coming from the ballet music. Kubelik had been appointed the new music director when he joined the Met administration. He proposed *Les Troyens* for his conducting debut with the company.

The complication with my accepting this role was that Jon Vickers, the reigning interpreter of Aeneas, was to sing the part. I literally hadn't seen him since my Met debut in 1968, when he insulted me during the dress rehearsal of *Carmen*. Once we began rehearsals, I had intended to ignore him, since the characters of Cassandra and Aeneas do not cross paths as such in the opera. I was sitting alone in the Met auditorium when Jon walked up to my seat, put his hand on my shoulder, and asked, "Can we be friends again?" I have to give him credit, because the anger in me seemed to melt away. I responded, "Okay, we can be friends again." I am very sensitive, but I am also very softhearted. I have come to realize that holding on to anger does neither person any good, and yet we do it. It is truly a waste of energy. My peace with Jon lifted a burden from me, so that I could really become involved in my portrayal of Cassandra instead of wondering how I would avoid Aeneas onstage.

I didn't do a whole lot of background preparation, like read Virgil's classic *Aeneid,* but I wanted to have greater insight into the role. My interest in seeing the story as an opera led me to read as much about Berlioz as I could, including his letters and his celebrated lament that he would never see his "noble" Cassandra performed live onstage. Having grown up in the Seventh-Day Adventist Church, we didn't study Greek mythology or other standard literary classics, and as a result, I felt a gap in my exposure to such works. I tried to catch up by reading the mythology. In fact, at Juilliard, I tried to catch up on many of the classics and even bought the *Harvard Classics* for research.

Cassandra is a tragic heroine to whom the god Apollo has given the ability to forecast the future. This gift is also her curse, because no one believes her prophecies. She is seen as mentally unstable, because some of her predictions appear to be so outrageous and contrary to the people's beliefs. When she tells the Trojans to burn the horse left outside the gates of Troy by the Greeks as a peace offering, no one believes her. Even her betrothed Corebus, who is more sympathetic than anyone else, questions her sanity. Only at the end of Part One of the opera, when she convinces the Trojan women to commit suicide rather than submit to the hated Greeks, does she at last emerge as noble. One of opera's most dramatic moments is reached when, after driving off the maidens, Cassandra stabs herself and dies uttering the word *Italy!* It was a powerful and challenging role. I had no idea I would become as involved with it, after having previously fallen in love with the role of Didon.

Several music magazines heralded my return to the Met. ABC/Dunhill records ran an advertisement in *Opera News,* saluting me on the success of the Covent Garden *Carmen* and my return to the Met as Cassandra. My return to the Met seemed to take on a life of its own in the media.

During several of the stage rehearsals, another singer stood in for Christa Ludwig, who sang Didon in Part Two. This was not uncommon for an active singer like her, who was most likely engaged elsewhere. Then word came in that she wasn't well and, even though she was in town, had still missed rehearsals. It was getting close to opening night. She and I had several publicity photos taken together in our respective costumes, so I didn't think much of the rumors about her being ill. Apart from that, I didn't run into her, because *Les Troyens,* Parts One and Two, was like two separate operas, with different rehearsal schedules.

Since this was the biggest production ever mounted in the ninety-year history of the company, there was a symposium on the opera at the New York Opera Club. Maestro Kubelik; Peter Wexler, the lighting designer; Nathaniel Merrill, the stage director; and I were there, among others. At some point in the symposium, I said I was singing the role of Cassandra, but the role I really wanted was Didon. I think I even said that I wouldn't mind doing both roles in the same performance. After the symposium, Maestro Kubelik said, "We would love for you to learn the role," and that was that.

Nathaniel Merrill, undoubtedly persuaded by my statement at the symposium, approached me next.

"Shirley, why don't you learn the role?" he said. I asked, "Why? Ludwig is singing it."

Louise Sherman Merrill, Nathaniel's wife and our rehearsal pianist, also pushed me. She was a tiny woman who played the piano like an orchestra. She coached me on Cassandra but said, "Shirley, learn Didon, because Ludwig is not well. I don't know if she will be ready to sing on opening night."

Even Warren Wilson had gotten wind of something. "V! Learn the part." I asked Warren, "Why should I learn this long role when on opening night Ludwig will feel well enough to go onstage?"

"I think you will be making a big mistake if you don't learn it," he said.

It was as if everybody knew something I didn't. I called Basil in

London. He echoed what everyone else had said. He planned to be in New York for the opening anyway and decided to come earlier. I told him the same thing I had told Warren, about Ludwig's emerging at the last minute, and added that I didn't wish her any ill.

"When I get there, perhaps we can talk to the management and do something about this situation," Basil said.

"If I learn the part, I have to be sure I will get to sing it. I have to have at least one performance," I said.

No one at the Met administration was willing to commit to anything beyond "We would love for you to learn it." Everyone kept saying that it was a delicate situation with Ludwig. Although I received a tentative "We will see what happens," there was nothing firm about my singing the part. Yet God was working with me, because I went ahead and memorized most of the role within a week, a record for me. I had a memory slip here and there, but I learned all the arias and duets. Merrill began rehearsing me in the Part Two staging of the opera, but there was still no commitment to a performance. At one rehearsal, Christa Ludwig actually walked across the stage while I was working on Didon. It was very embarrassing. She was still not well. I understand that she was going through menopausal changes. I came to sympathize with her just ten years later, when I experienced the same thing. I knew something big was about to happen, because at the first stage rehearsal, where I sing a high B-natural toward the end of the Cassandra/Corebus duet, the chorus and stagehands stopped and began applauding. That was always a good sign.

October 19 arrived—the Friday afternoon dress rehearsal, three days before the opening. No one had given me the word. I was fully costumed as Cassandra. Basil and my PR person, Edgar Vincent, were in my dressing room.

"You will be doing the dress rehearsal of Didon, but they should give you word about opening night," Edgar said. Basil agreed but said, "Edgar and I have pushed as far as we can. You will have to take it from this point."

I went in costume to Schuyler Chapin, who directed me to Maestro Kubelik, who was already in the orchestra pit. I walked into the main auditorium and leaned over the guardrail.

"Maestro, I need to speak to you. Am I going to sing Didon on opening night if I sing this dress rehearsal?"

He hedged a little. I said, "It is not fair to me. If I tire myself from singing both roles in this dress rehearsal and don't do my very best on opening night, no one is going to feel sorry for me. I would rather not sing this dress rehearsal." He looked at me and I think he appreciated my honesty. Our eyes never moved from one another.

After a pause, he said, "I give you my word. If you sing this dress rehearsal, you will sing both roles opening night." He reached out and offered me his hand. We shook hands on the deal and the dress rehearsal began.

Part of me didn't realize what I had asked to do. A nearly five-hour performance was daunting. When I stepped onstage in the dress rehearsal as Didon, after having sung Cassandra in Part One, I could hear spontaneous applause from the audience. This dress rehearsal attracted a larger than average number of people. I could tell from the audience's reaction that something special was shaping up.

Almost immediately, Schuyler Chapin announced to the public that I would sing both Cassandra and Didon, because Christa Ludwig was indisposed. Believe it or not, rumors started to go around that I had *usurped* the role of Didon from Ludwig and had demanded that either the Met management allow me to sing both roles, or I would walk out of the production. This music business is really not for the fainthearted.

At the end of the dress rehearsal, several colleagues and well-wishers, including several singers, came backstage to see me. Among them was Grace Bumbry, who complimented me on my performance. She said I was wonderful but added, "Be careful not to raise your gown up too high because we can see too much of your legs as you are going up those stairs." I didn't have any idea what she was talking about. I looked at her in disbelief and said half seriously, "Honey, as hard as I have been working to get through all this, they can see my *thighs* if they want to! I'm just happy to get up those stairs."

The October 21 *New York Times,* which featured the head shots of Christa Ludwig and me in costume, ran a story about the historical significance of the opera. The following day, the paper announced that I would do both roles and listed my name in the cast for Cassandra in Part One and Didon in Part Two.

When that Monday arrived, I tried to keep as quiet as a church mouse. Lou was extra solicitous. It seemed that even Cessie, then only one year old, was no problem at all that day. I think we all sensed that the evening's performance would be a defining event in my career. Because of the length of the opera, I vocalized more lightly than usual before leaving home. When I arrived at the theater, it seems as if people were ready for me. Someone took my bag and my dress for the reception. All I had to do was walk to the dressing room. I smile as I remember this, because everyone was so attentive that had I stumbled while walking, I am sure someone would have carried me.

Well-wishers had sent so many flowers and cards, some had to be removed from the dressing room. The makeup head, Victor Callegari, put on my makeup in complete silence, which was unusual, because there was usually a lot of chatter. Everyone was being as quiet as possible. When I broke the ice by humming, speaking, or doing something, I heard the dresser's audible sigh of relief. It was tense.

When the wig person finished styling my hair, I began mentally transforming myself into Cassandra's character. As I walked up to the stage, I turned my head from left to right to loosen my neck and sang light scales. Every now and then I released a fuller sound, just so I knew the voice was there. Suddenly, it occurred to me that I had not seen the flowers Lou and Cessie sent, but in my heart, I knew they were there among the others.

When I reached the stage, chorus members and stagehands who might otherwise have come up to wish me well stayed clear of me. I was curious about this, but maybe something in my face or eyes communicated, "Keep your distance." I stood by myself, listening to the orchestra warm up. If an orchestra member warmed up with a melody in Part One that I sang, I hummed along for a minute or so.

I was standing backstage when Schuyler Chapin approached, kissed me on both cheeks, and looked at me for a moment as if to say, "This show is yours!" He then went before the curtain to announce that I would sing both parts and that this performance of *Les Troyens* marked the exact ninetieth anniversary of the company. When Schuyler made the announcement, the audience applauded. This heightened the excitement for everyone onstage. I was already in character by that point and never blinked an eye.

I still remember the staging well, although it has been thirty years. Cassandra makes her first appearance within five minutes of the start of the opera. Almost immediately, she begins to forecast tragedy for Troy. The directions called for me to raise my left arm in a pointing, trembling motion. Cassandra has seen the ghost of her dead brother, Hector, roaming the area. As if in a trance, she stares straight ahead and has a premonition of doom about the sudden departure of the Greeks. There is something foreboding about it. Toward the end of her premonition, her eyes widen in terror. She raises her left and right arms in a blocking motion in front of her face, as if to shield herself from some horrible event. This all seems to occur spontaneously in her head and Cassandra reacts, regardless of whether others are present or not. These gestures clearly contribute to the sense that she is emotionally unbalanced.

When the first chords of her dramatic aria, "Malheureux roi!" (Ill-fated king!), sound, the audience has a relatively clear picture of Cassandra, the prophetess of doom. It was an acting challenge, to be sure, because I had no more than a few minutes onstage to create this portrayal before the aria began.

One of the most stirring moments in Part One of *Les Troyens* is the magnificent octet with double chorus "Chatiment effroyable!" (Terrible punishment!), where Aeneas describes a horrible scene he has just witnessed. Laocoon, a priest, also suspicious about the huge horse outside the gates of the city, throws a javelin into it, whereupon a sea serpent comes out of the ocean and swallows him.

The music for this ensemble is some of the most beautiful and gripping ever written. Cassandra sings over the entire chorus and orchestra, "O peuple deplorable! Mysterieuse horreur!" (Oh pitiable people! Mysterious horror!). I was positioned so that I could project well, but I was also physically separated from the others onstage, on a large overhang, as if to heighten the character's symbolic distance from the others who refuse to believe her prophecies. Cassandra is ultimately believed, although she takes her own life and persuades a majority of other Trojan women to do the same, rather than submit to the hated Greeks. She is one of opera's ultimate tragic heroines. By the end of Part One, I should have been exhausted, but I knew the evening was just beginning.

For the opening night performance, the Met extended the intermission to forty minutes to accommodate me. The director let me get out of my Cassandra costume (and mode), breathe, and get ready for Didon in Part Two. The costumers altered my makeup to highlight my cheeks and eyes for the Didon portrayal.

I changed characters in my mind by envisioning Didon in *Les Troyens à Carthage* as a reincarnation of Cassandra, of sorts. Like Cassandra, Didon is also a prophetess, but that's about where the similarity ends. She is a woman less tormented, who seeks fulfillment in a love relationship. She has known the love of a man because of a previous marriage. She has proved herself a strong ruler to her people, but romance is missing from her life.

When the martial music of Part Two began, I was nearing the stage. When the audience saw me walk on as Didon, there was sustained spontaneous applause, similar to that during the dress rehearsal. It was as if people were asking, "Will she really do it?" It was a wonderful moment in hindsight, but all I could think of at the time was to pace myself and not overdo it.

As I said, one of the highlights in Part Two of the opera is the love duet "Nuit d'ivresse." Once again, it was a magical moment. Jon and

I were in lockstep with each other in a musical union. Someone had taken a picture of that scene during the dress rehearsal. It was beautiful. The Met continued to use it for years to advertise various events, like the live radio broadcast.

The ultimate test for me as an actress and a singer came during Didon's death scene. Her poignant aria "Adieu, fiere cité, qu'un generaux effort" (Farewell, proud city) was another high point, especially where she recalls the passion of Aeneas's touch of love in the passage "Aux nuits d'ivresse et d'extase infinie" (On those nights of boundless ecstasy and rapture). I put emphasis on the "s" of "ivresse" and saw a woman in the audience slump forward, weeping as I sang that line. She obviously understood French and must have identified with what I was singing. To touch someone at that level in a performance is a high compliment for an artist, because I was so deeply involved in the moment of Didon's despair. I had to see the ultimate fall of Carthage in a premonition and crawl several feet in my death throes. Didon dies abandoned and defeated.

My colleagues were more than supportive that evening. It seems they knew something special was taking place. At the end of the performance, the audience enthusiastically applauded its approval. Most had been in the theater for over five hours! I kept getting called back onstage for curtain calls. Each time the audience roared as I came out again. This was clearly the performance of my life up until then.

The next day, news accounts from all over the world reported the feat. I hit superstar status with that one performance in October 1973. Things like that can happen in the concert world. I sang both roles only on opening night, but it was enough to secure my place in the Met's history. I wasn't the first singer to do both roles, of course. Regine Crespin had done both at Covent Garden, but Part One in that production was dramatically cut. I sang both with virtually no cuts. Jessye Norman did it in the same Met production ten years after I did. Grace Bumbry and I did *Les Troyens* in a Paris production some years later. She did both roles when I had a scheduling conflict and had to miss a performance because of a prior engagement.

Sir Rudolf Bing said that he'd never considered mounting *Les Troyens* at the Met because he thought the work was boring. With such an attitude, it was a good thing he didn't attempt to do it. He would have failed. It is an epic opera, requiring enormous performing and technical resources. It is, above all, a great work! I considered it a double honor to have worked on this opera with Maestro Kubelik, because of his deep understanding of it. I consider that opening night my real Met debut, which is what I said when I was interviewed at the time. It marked a new and different relationship for me with the company, which I hadn't enjoyed under the Bing administration.

FOR MONTHS afterward, I was buoyed by the triumph of *Les Troyens*. A few nights after the opening I did a recital at Carnegie Hall. The sold-out house was tumultuous, even before I sang a note. You would have thought the audience was at the Met performance, because it was so frenzied. I smiled and bowed several times before starting the recital. I know it was a full five minutes before I began.

I returned to Paris to sing a second run of the *Il Trovatore* production at the beginning of 1974, and the audience there was also enthusiastic. I was received with new vigor in Europe, although I was already well known to many concertgoers there.

When I returned to the United States, I had a few orchestral dates. I sang "Dich teure Halle" (Hail great Hall) from *Tannhäuser* and Wagner's *Wesendonck Lieder*, with Tommy Schippers conducting the Cincinnati Symphony. We also took that concert to Carnegie Hall. Tommy was still recovering from a surgical procedure on his throat. His exquisite wife, Nonie, had died a year earlier and this devastated him. My heart went out to him, although we hadn't performed together for some time prior to that engagement.

After the Texaco Metropolitan Opera broadcast of *Les Troyens*, I had a spring recital tour and the glow from *Les Troyens* hadn't worn off. I was still so psyched for some of those dates, I had to do six and seven encores.

I came back to the Met to prepare for a role I was only moderately interested in, Judith in Bartok's *Bluebeard's Castle.* For some reason, it was a difficult role for me to learn. Maestro Kubelik talked me into doing it. I had to sit at the piano and analyze chords as I memorized the role. I felt at the time, and still do to a degree, that *Bluebeard's Castle* is an opera that works better in concert version than as a staged work. It has only two characters, which makes it relatively inexpensive to mount. That may have been one of the Met's considerations. I am always surprised when someone tells me how much they enjoyed my work in that opera. The company revived it a few years ago, with Jessye Norman singing Judith.

11

An Actor's Life

I ADORE the art of acting. I have a computer in my brain that constantly adjusts and calculates the emotional and intellectual meaning of each role. I usually asked directors to be very watchful of me,
because I was always trying something new. I was always thinking,
What if I did this? What if I did that? I really prepared for my roles.

I still read acting books. Some of my favorites were by Stanislavsky,
Uta Hagen, and Olivier. It was a Stanislavsky book that gave me the
idea of going inside of myself and asking, What if? I don't see acting as
coming onstage and transforming myself into a predetermined character. I cannot do that. When preparing for a role, I asked myself, What
if I were that person? What would I do? How would I walk? How
would I be dressed? Before this scene started, what could I have been
doing? And then the audience might believe that I was that person.

OUR CAST for the Met's *L'Assedio di Corinto* (The Siege of Corinth)
was announced to the public in the summer of 1973. Beverly was to
sing Pamira, making her Met debut. Justino Diaz would repeat his
Scala role as Maometto, and I would take on Neocle. Tommy Schippers

would, of course, conduct. The Italian tenor Franco Bonisolli, who sang Cleomene in the Scala production, was well known for being temperamental, so he wasn't considered for the Met production. The American tenor Harry Theyard was cast in the role for the Met production and also sang it for the Angel recording of the opera. The arrival of Rossini's most difficult opera at the Met had been some years in the making; preparations had begun in Italy at La Scala in the late 1960s.

Tommy Schippers had approached me then about singing Neocle for the La Scala production, but I declined. Marilyn Horne, an up-and-coming Rossini specialist, accepted when he asked her next. Ironically, after Renata Scotto (who was supposed to have sung Pamira in the La Scala production) withdrew, the management approached Beverly Sills to sing Pamira, which she agreed to do. The La Scala production of *L'Assedio di Corinto* turned out to be a big success for both Marilyn and Beverly, despite their conflicts with each other. Afterward, I regretted not having accepted the role. That opera is Rossini at his most challenging. To top it off, Schippers had come up with a big scene for Neocle, borrowed from Rossini's 1820 opera *Maometto II* (Mohammed II).

But as I have learned, we may get second chances. When discussions of mounting this opera began in the early 1970s, the Met asked Marilyn Horne to repeat the role of Neocle. Marilyn hesitated, because of the conflicts with Beverly in that La Scala production, and ultimately turned the Met down. The Met then came to me.

Siege was scheduled to open in April 1975. We recorded it for Angel Records in London during the summer of 1974. During breaks in the recording schedule, Beverly and I went antique shopping. Basil Horsfield, who was also Beverly's manager, gave a wonderful dinner party at his home in London for the entire cast and other guests. The build-up for Beverly's debut was already mounting.

I SANG Rossini in public every chance I got in preparation for performing Rossini's most difficult score. In January 1975, when Luciano

Pavarotti and I had a guest appearance with the Philadelphia Orchestra under the direction of Eugene Ormandy, I did "Una voce poco fa" (A voice said a little while ago) from *The Barber of Seville*. I also sang "O mio Fernando," and Luciano and I did the final duet from *La Favorita*.

The following month I did a complete concert version of *La Favorita* with the Opera Orchestra of New York at Carnegie Hall, with Eve Queler conducting. Alfredo Kraus sang Fernando; Pablo Elvira, Alfonso; James Morris, Baldassare; and Barbara Hendricks, Ines. Barbara, an African American, sang beautifully and has since become a star in this country and in Europe. I did some interpolations in the cabaletta "Scritto in Ciel" (It is written in Heaven) that took me up to a high C.

This was my first time working with Eve Queler and, to tell the truth, she was so comfortable on the podium, all I found myself thinking about was the music, which is as it should be. Her cues were always clear and she, too, believed in preparing the orchestra well. After that performance at Carnegie Hall, we repeated *La Favorita* in Hartford, Connecticut.

BY MARCH, the rehearsals for the opening of *Siege* were underway. Both the set designer Nicola Benois and the stage director Sandro Sequi had been involved with the 1969 La Scala performance and were making their respective Met debuts with this production. I had worked with Benois before in Italy, because he had designed the sets and costumes for my La Scala debut in *Samson et Dalila* and later for *Maria Stuarda* for the company. As it turned out, Tommy Schippers had further revised the score after the La Scala production, drawing on the tenor role in *Maometto II* and the 1826 French version of the opera, *Le Siege de Corinthe*. These revisions made Neocle more comfortable for me to sing, because the tessitura—the most used part of the vocal range—was higher.

On the cover of Angel's recording of *The Siege of Corinth,* I look very much like a woman, but that image is deceiving. In preparation for this "pants" role, I contacted the celebrated opera singer Risë Stevens (who had done several trousers roles at the Met), for a few coaching sessions on how to stand and walk like a man. She also cautioned me to avoid moving my hands in a particularly feminine way. I really enjoyed these sessions with Risë and admired her craft. The final touch to my Neocle look was the mustache, which was my idea.

Even at the dress rehearsal I knew something special was about to happen. I was singing half-voice and still was getting ample applause at the end of the scenes. After I finished the big aria, the applause continued for about two minutes, which is always a good forecast for opening night. Someone backstage began clocking the applause, and I knew then that I would be a big success.

Of course, the big event was Beverly Sills. When she uttered her first words onstage at that opening night performance, "Che mai sento!" (What do I hear!), the audience erupted in spontaneous applause. Her long-awaited debut was electrifying, and we all felt buoyed by it.

After my big scene in Act III in the catacombs, where Neocle vows to fight the Turkish invaders at all cost, the audience roared. The performance stopped, but I never broke character. Tears began to well up in my eyes, and part of me wanted to cry, but I held on. It was a glorious moment. Neocle demands a lightness and an agility that few audiences had heard from me before. The Met's management was also impressed.

I went on tour with the Met for the first time in *The Siege of Corinth* the following month. We stopped in Boston, Detroit, Cleveland, Atlanta, and Washington, D.C. I flew in and out of these cities instead of literally traveling with the company. At some point, Beverly received a threat from a woman who had stalked her in the past and had written her hate mail because she is Jewish. The stalker had apparently shown up at several of her performances. Beverly told me about these scary episodes.

The performances in Detroit were particularly memorable. As we took our bows on opening night, someone in the balcony threw a bouquet to the stage. I caught it. I then saluted like a soldier, standing at attention, and the audience really went wild! That tour gained a sizable following for me. Several cities wanted me to return in any role I wanted to sing.

Back in New York in October, we opened the 1975–1976 Met season with *Siege. Variety* magazine's review of the performance opened with "Sills Opens Met Season. . . . Shirley Verrett 'Stops The Show.'" Tommy Schippers made a few adjustments in the score, where he felt the opera dragged a little, but ended up withdrawing from several performances because of illness. Richard Woitach took over the rest of the fall performances and conducted the Texaco broadcast in January 1976. It was still an all-American cast, because Enrico Di Giuseppe alternated with Harry Theyard as Cleomene.

After the success of the 1969 La Scala *L'Assedio di Corinto,* I told Marilyn Horne I had been a fool to turn down the role of Neocle. After the opera's success at the Met, Marilyn told me *she* had been a fool to turn down the role when it was offered to her.

As great a personal triumph as the *Siege of Corinth* was, the best was still to come later that year at La Scala.

It is ironic that I should be so closely associated with Lady Macbeth. When Claudio Abbado first offered me the role, I felt it was too dark a drama for me. I was afraid of Lady Macbeth. She was power hungry. She drove herself insane lusting for power. She was so very, very dark. I didn't know if I wanted to go there. We first began musing about the part at a dinner party at Leyla Gencer's in Milan. Plácido Domingo was also a dinner guest that night.

Three years later, Claudio and I had done several performances together, and I trusted his musical instincts. Obviously, I appreciated his talent and loved working with him. Lou and I invited him to dinner at our home in Manhattan, and once again, Claudio spoke of my singing Lady Macbeth at La Scala. He felt the role was perfect for me. He liked the fire in my voice and thought this would be the definitive part for me. After resisting for two years, I told him I would look at the score and bought a full copy of it. As I began reviewing it, I could hear certain phrases in my mind and imagine how I would sing them with orchestra. It was a challenging part, but all of the notes were in my vocal cords. Even the high D-flat at the end of the sleepwalking scene was no problem.

When I looked at the score, I saw how brilliant it was. I saw what Verdi did with the Shakespeare and how he molded the music around certain aspects of the play. And it appealed to me as a great acting part. Oddly, in the stage version I was not as captivated by Lady Macbeth as I was when I saw the part written down in music.

At the outset, I asked myself, Who is this character? What do I want from this character? What does that character want from me? How do I fit into all this? What kind of person do I have to be to really portray this role correctly as an actress? I thought that Lady Macbeth was one of the great tragic characters. For some reason, this was the kind of role I think, by and large, I was born to play.

I had read Shakespeare's *Macbeth* while at Juilliard. I might have even seen the play onstage at that time, but I had never seen or heard the Verdi operatic adaptation. As it turned out, the Met was doing *Macbeth* that season, so Lou and I went to see it. He fell asleep during the first act. It wasn't a strong performance, but I could imagine myself doing the role onstage and how I would handle it differently. I imagined how I would use my hands for certain gestures and performed them even as Lady Macbeth sang the role onstage. I'm sure the people seated next to me in the theater wondered if I had lost touch with reality.

When I woke Lou up from his sound nap, he asked, "Why in God's name do you want to sing this boring opera?"

"What you heard on the stage is not what's in the score," I said. That's when I decided to call Claudio Abbado and tell him I was definitely interested in a La Scala production of the opera.

The opera was originally supposed to be staged in 1974, but it had to be put off a year. Instead, *Macbeth* would open the 1975–1976 La

Scala season on December 7, 1975. I coached the music with Warren Wilson.

Sarah Caldwell of the Boston Opera was also interested in staging the work. I told her we could talk over the opera before I did it at La Scala. I agreed to do it in Boston afterward. She and I met before I went to Italy. I sang the first-act aria, "Vieni! t'affretta!" (Come! Hie you hither!), to get her reaction.

Sarah always wanted to know, "What are you thinking about when you sing this aria? What are you about?" We talked a lot about the role. She was very helpful in my preparation. I respected her musicality and, what is more important, her sense and knowledge of the theater.

I was curious about her ideas, but, of course, I had my own. Some of them went against Verdi's. I remember reading in his letters that he thought Lady Macbeth should be sung with an "ugly" voice. I could not sing "Vieni t'affretta!" ugly or make my voice do it that way, because the line is too heroic. I hardly ever disagree with a great composer, but in this instance I did. I honestly believe that if Verdi had heard me sing it, he wouldn't have rejected my interpretation.

I recalled Igor Stravinsky's comment on *Oedipus Rex*. After I studied the music, my body was telling me something else about performing the role of Jocasta. Stravinsky told me, "All of those notations that I put in the score are for idiots! I love the way you sing the part. You're doing it with your soul, and because you are musical, you are not going to do anything that's not correct. Let your mind, body, and your senses tell you the way the music is supposed to go, regardless of what I have written there."

I approached Lady Macbeth with a similar conviction. She is physically stunning and that is part of her allure and mystery. An ugly woman would not have been able to do what she did. She is also a sensuous woman and knows how to use her sensuality in almost every instance. This was the background work I had done for the role, prior to my arrival in Italy.

I had been in communication with Claudio Abbado and Giorgio Strehler, the director, or *metteur-en-scene*. After finishing the fall run of *L'Assedio di Corinto* at the Met, I flew to Italy to begin preparing for *Macbeth*. I was there at least four weeks before the opening. Giorgio Strehler rehearsed me and Macbeth for hours! Some of the other singers slipped in and out for other engagements, but I was there the whole time. Strehler even sent for me on short notice when Macbeth was not available. We worked on the sleepwalking scene so much that I could nearly do it in my sleep! I practiced the final ascending and descending phrase of that scene so many times that Cessie, who frequently imitated my vocalizing, had it memorized.

The beauty of working with Strehler on *Macbeth* was that he used "mark actors" to give us a sense of how he wanted the scenes to appear onstage. For example, he used actors to demonstrate how he wanted Macbeth and Lady Macbeth to turn and look at each other, as they contemplated their next move. He wanted the long trains on their respective capes to overlap, encircle, and cross like the workings of the mind—a device, he said, that suggested the complex nature of the drama. This production of *Macbeth* was highly stylized and cerebral. All of this was to have a psychological impact on the lead characters, as far as Strehler was concerned. It was highly effective. He drove us hard in those rehearsals, but everyone knew he was working toward a great presentation of the opera.

The costumes also took some doing. We looked at several patterns or sketches, and I couldn't see myself singing the first-act aria in one costume or another. We eventually settled on a straight dark burgundy velvet sack dress for my first scene. The capes and the crowns really did most of the work. The first cape was a medium dark mauve. It was wonderful. The black hooded cape that followed concealed the dagger Macbeth used to commit the crime and then to wipe King Duncan's blood from the murder weapon.

My hair was styled in a very severe page boy. I didn't think I would look good in the wig, but it worked just fine. For the sleepwalking scene, Strehler wanted me in a gown with a long satin train that dragged on the stage floor as I walked across the stage. I sang the scene on a very elevated platform. The dragging train of the gown, with my hair hanging, gave me the appearance of added height.

The one complaint I had with the production was the lighting. I didn't think there was enough of it for my skin color. Strehler didn't want a lot of light, especially for this opera. Even the festive banquet scene where Macbeth is visited by Banquo's ghost was dark. He was after a silhouette effect. He wrote me a letter after the opening of the opera to tell me that he knew I wanted more light on myself, but he said, "Believe me, the picture is beautiful." When I asked Lou what he thought, he said, "Strehler was right, Shirl. You were wrong."

Another departure from tradition that Strehler wanted for this production was in the scene when Lady Macbeth first enters. In most productions of this opera, she reads the letter Macbeth has written, telling her of the witches' prophecy. In this production, we hear the letter being spoken in Macbeth's voice over a loudspeaker (as if in a fog) as Lady Macbeth enters the stage. She is reflecting on the letter's content before she begins singing. She walks downstage with her head upright, wearing a proud and confident smile. Her eyes are blazing with glee at the prospect of ultimate power. This effect was incredible.

Luciano Damiani designed the stage sets. This production of *Macbeth* was the latest La Scala collaboration among Abbado, Strehler, and Damiani. The cast was a singer's dream, with Piero Cappuccilli as Macbeth, Nicolai Ghiaurov as Banquo, and Veriano Luchetti as Macduff. It was different, being the only major female in the cast. My male colleagues were quite deferential to me, and, to be frank, I enjoyed the attention.

When the evening of December 7 arrived, I had the feeling that something special was about to take place. It was the same inner voice I heard when I was about to open in *Les Troyens* and *Siege of Corinth* at the Met. I went through my usual ritual of keeping quiet and vocalizing lightly. The performance was scheduled to be broadcast live throughout Europe over Italian television. From the moment I came onstage, I felt a surge of energy soar through my body that made me feel the role all the more deeply. I was so well-rehearsed, so well-prepared, so thoroughly involved, I felt I couldn't have made a mistake if I had tried. I have felt this way only a few times in my career, singing Neocle, Cassandra, Didon, Elizabeth I, and Norma.

After I concluded the cabaletta to my first aria, "Or tutti sorgete, Ministri infernali" (Arise, now, you Ministers from hell), when Lady Macbeth invites the evil spirits to rise up and "unsex me here," there was sustained applause. Basil, who was in the audience for the opening, told me afterward that it lasted three minutes on live television! I just stood there. I never broke character to acknowledge the applause, although people in the audience were waving at me. Others actually threw roses on the stage then! I never looked at one, not to mention touched one. That would have been Shirley Verrett reaching down to pick them up. This drama was just getting underway. I used only head gestures and my eyes to make clear that I was still very much the ambitious Lady Macbeth who was about to embark on the plot of her life.

After the applause died down, I swept aside some of the flowers with my huge cape. Under different circumstances it would have been an offense not to acknowledge the thrown flowers, but it was consistent with the single-mindedness of Lady Macbeth. If it made some members of the audience upset with "her," it was okay. I proceeded with my portrayal.

The following duet with Macbeth, after he murders the king, "Fatal mia donna! un murmure?" (My fatal lady, did you not hear a murmur?), was nothing short of theater at its height. It was almost as if we were engaging in some fiendish dance, because there was such unison of movement and anticipation of each other's gestures. Cappuccilli was compelling! The singing and acting he displayed in that performance were definitive. He helped to set a standard for Macbeth that other singers with whom I did the opera would have a hard time erasing. Ghiaurov and Luchetti were equally intense and persuasive. Even the minor characters were strong. This was the ultimate performance in a singer's career. I can't remember looking at Abbado in the conducting pit. I am sure I almost forgot he was there a few times. This is how well-rehearsed I was and how involved in the drama I had become.

When we arrived at Lady Macbeth's sleepwalking scene, I was in character well before I returned to the stage. As I said, the staging called for me to walk from stage right to left on a raised platform, about two feet wide and seven feet high. Two men, one on each side of the stage, had to hold it. It was intended to give me and the audience a greater sense of instability. I just sang and used my hands. In many productions, Lady Macbeth carries a night lantern to make clear to the audience she is sleepwalking. I had one at the beginning of the scene, but Strehler's directions called for me to drop it early, so I would be free to use my hands! The platform was also unsteady enough to look as if I were walking on some sort of high ledge. Just as I knew it would, that high D-flat at the end of the scene eased out of my mouth. It was so smooth, it could have been an octave lower, as far as I was concerned.

This was as unified a performance as I could ever recall. That December 7 was the night of my life! It was yet another career-defining experience. All I could say when the performance ended was, "Thank God! Thank God!" to praise Him for this success.

As exciting as the performance was, I was not prepared for what happened afterward. When Claudio Abbado came backstage, before we did our curtain calls, he kept saying to me, "I *told* you so! I *told* you so!" This was to say, I should have listened to him earlier. He knew I would score a major success in this role. The crowd was so ecstatic, people tossed flowers at me while I signed autographs. I signed them for about an hour and a half before I was ready to go back to the hotel. Two men picked me up on their shoulders and carried me through the streets to my limousine. A man shouted, "Noooo!" He wanted me to sign his program. A crowd began to surround us, throwing flowers at me and kissing my hands.

After the men put me in the limousine, the crowd around the car wouldn't let us move. The driver blew the horn, but no one budged. People began rocking the car then slowly pushed the limousine down the street, so that I could continue to sign autographs! The crowd pushed the limo all the way back to the hotel. The driver never had to do a thing except steer it. They were shouting, "Verrett! Verrett! Verrett!" The Italians are true opera lovers. When you have a good performance, trust me, they will let you know, as they did for me that December 7.

ONCE THE La Scala managers saw me in *Macbeth*, they were even more convinced of my future marketability. The managers came on-stage that evening with a blank five-year contract.

"Signora, just sign and we will give you whatever you want!"

I took the contract with me, because I knew I was in no position to think about business at the moment.

I wanted to accept La Scala's offer, but when I talked to Lou about it, he resisted. He said that he was an American artist and needed to remain in the United States at this point in his life. I felt that he could paint and be a university professor in Italy, just as easily as in the United States.

By then, Lou was a seasoned lecturer and teacher. He had already taught at the Pratt Institute, Parsons School of Design, Queens College, and Hunter College. To be fair to his position, he felt that although the Italians did offer to set him up at a university there, he had already had difficulties in finding basic things like the appropriate chalk and paint to do his work. I really think it boiled down to his not wanting to be too far away from the most vital art scene in the world—New York City. Finally, I gave in to the pressure, as subtle as it was. It was another career mistake. If I had it to do over again, I probably would have stayed in Italy for a time.

Lou regretted his decision for a period but was more than accommodating years later when other opportunities presented themselves. I reconciled the decision to decline the La Scala offer by reasoning that since the Metropolitan Opera Company had rolled out the red carpet for me, it would become my home house as Covent Garden in London had once been and I could return to Italy as opportunities came along. Ultimately, the entire episode was a brutal lesson; careers like mine don't always correspond to two people's agendas, particularly when the man and woman involved operate in different employment spheres.

THE ITALIAN reviews praised the *Macbeth* opening, and once again I was called "La Nera Callas" (The Black Callas). The reviews from around Europe all said the same thing. The broadcast had gone out from Italy and made my star status rise even higher. Had I accepted the La Scala offer, I would have been an even bigger star throughout the continent. Lady Macbeth became yet another signature role for me.

The *Macbeth* production was so well received around Europe that Deutsche Grammophon hastily struck up a deal with the company management to record the opera, based on the La Scala cast. There were a few cast changes—most notably, recasting Macduff for the recording. Veriano Luchetti had done a splendid job in the stage production and was subsequently followed by Franco Tagliavini in the run of the opera the following January, but Deutsche Grammophon wanted a more marketable name for the recording and was able to bring in Plácido Domingo to do the role. That recording still sells well, more than twenty-five years after it was made, and has won several awards. Veriano Luchetti did get the chance to do Macduff on disk when I recorded the opera a second time for the 1987 film.

I now began to get superstar treatment when I sang at La Scala and other theaters throughout Italy. By tradition in Florence, for example, the lead tenors were given the largest dressing rooms. Even in Callas's day, she had a small dressing room, because tenors were the "big cheese" in Italy. After the *Macbeth* triumph, I was given the large room when I sang there.

Piero Cappuccilli had been not only a great colleague in that production but a good friend as well. He came to my dressing room before the *Macbeth* opening at La Scala to wish me well, and Cessie took a liking to him. She saw him at the rehearsals and onstage. Macbeth's histrionics, throwing pillows and feathers, were great fun for her. She was all of three years old. Her sweet laughter was priceless.

HUMOR IS very important to me, even if I'm not exactly a cut-up. I'm not a kibbitzer like Martina Arroyo. She's a real card. But I love it when other people are funny. I will absolutely roll on the ground because I love to laugh. Although I've often been associated with dark, complex dramatic roles, I definitely have a flip side. When I do a funny song during a recital and want to make a point, I can focus on someone and solicit a response. I may be serious onstage, but I love to laugh in my private life. I can't tell jokes, but I love laughing at other people's. I love funny plays and movies. I love funny people. Laughter is so healthy. Whenever I have a really good laugh, even after something not so great has happened, it makes me feel better, healthier. I mean it. If I get angry at Lou, and I say, "I'm not going to smile today," it's hurtful.

AFTER THE *Macbeth* recording, I returned to New York to rest up for my next engagement at the Met. I was finally going to portray Adalgisa in Bellini's *Norma*. I had learned this role nearly ten years earlier, had recorded it, but had never sung it live on any stage. This was the only time in my career I sang the role live. The Met's production that February and March 1976 featured Montserrat Caballé in the title role, and although Franco Corelli was the announced Pollione, John Alexander sang the role. The performances went smoothly, and I was planning to go on the Met tour in the production the following May. I also reprised the role of Neocle in *L'Assedio di Corinto* with Beverly Sills. The January broadcast was our last performance together.

The January 17, 1976, issue of *Opera News,* which featured the broadcast of *L'Assedio di Corinto,* also featured an extensive interview with me, entitled "Diva." It was one of the most comprehensive interviews I had ever done. I spoke my mind, as I had in the past, but because of my recent celebrity, my words reached a larger audience. I was seen as "outspoken," because I was very frank in that interview about how African American men continued to suffer from prejudices in the opera world.

My specific comments on that issue were, "When we can see a black man standing next to a white woman, singing a love duet, without people cringing, then I think we will have made it into the human race." These were, and are, important issues to me. Over the course of my forty-year career, I saw many talented black men overlooked or somehow not chosen for things they were clearly capable of. I spoke earlier about Robert McFerrin in the mid-1950s, but it hasn't gotten appreciably better as we have now moved into a new century! The unspoken explanation is to avoid offending the audience—no African American men may appear on the opera stage in romantic roles opposite white women. Yet it is more than that. If that were the case, why are so few black men making orchestral and recital appearances—that is, nonoperatic roles—which supposedly would offend the public? As it is, Roland Hayes, Paul Robeson, and Robert McFerrin are among the few names that come to mind from the past. My colleagues George Shirley and Simon Estes gained celebrity in their turn, but few have reached those levels recently.

I was one of the few major opera singers who even had an African American accompanist. These are still very sensitive issues, but until we come to terms with how racial bias in this country ultimately holds all of us back, we won't succeed in a number of areas socially. It's like what Leontyne Price sang in that United Negro College Fund commercial, "We're not asking for a handout, just a hand." In other words, we want the opportunity to compete, to perform, to show what we can do.

In that interview I also caught people's attention when I said I would sing my first Norma in a La Scala production during the 1977–1978 season, with Montserrat Caballé singing Adalgisa. It was one of the roles I wanted the La Scala managers to stage me in, when they gave me the blank contract. This was the same piece, by the way, in which the interviewer made it seem that Maria Callas had given *me* advice about singing Norma, which she never did.

As I said, I knew from the late 1960s, when I prepared for Adalgisa, that I could also sing Norma. I had used "Casta Diva" as a vocalise as early as 1965.* All the notes were in my voice as I studied the score. As it turned out, my chance to sing the role arrived much sooner than I expected. *Norma* was scheduled to be performed on the Met's spring tour. Since I had announced my intentions to sing the druid priestess at La Scala, I was asked by the Met management if I would sing the role for its spring tour. I was pleased to say, "Yes." *Opera News* reported that I was the first singer since Giulia Grisi, who created the role of Adalgisa in 1831, to perform that role and that of the title character.

I INTRODUCED my druid priestess in Boston on April 19, 1976, to a sold-out house. When I emerged onstage, the audience applauded, I felt an instant surge of energy, and my mind briefly flashed back to the 1956 Callas performance at the Met as she came onstage in the role. When I sang my opening line, "Sediziose voci, voci di guerra" (Seditious voices, voices of war), I surveyed the other characters on the stage with a commanding presence and partly checked the audience for its reaction. I noticed that several people sat up in their seats when I began this recitative. As I sang "Casta Diva," a hush fell over the entire theater, which is what should happen when it is done well. The climax, of course, is the cabaletta when Norma expresses her anguished line "Ah! riedi ancora qual eri allora, quando, ah quando il cor ti diedi" (Ah! come back again as you were then, when I gave my heart to you then), over a chorus of druids clamoring for war. It continues to be one of the most poignant musical moments in opera for me. The audience's applause was thunderous.

It was even more thunderous when I decided to interpolate a D-natural above high C at the end of the Act I trio with chorus, "Vanne si, mi lascia indegno" (Go, leave me, base villain). I can't recall if I

---

* Vocalise is a musical genre in which the words may be left out to focus just on the notes.

warned John Alexander or Joy Davidson (the respective Pollione and Adalgisa) of my intention to sing the note, but neither of them batted an eyelash, which made clear to me that they were as caught up in the drama as I was. The audience didn't let the orchestra finish before people began cheering. This was another unforgettable operatic moment for me.

The rest of the tour went extremely well, and I received similar reactions for each of my performances. John Alexander was a strong Pollione. He had sung the opera live several times and recorded it. I'll come back to *Norma,* because even though it was one of my favorite roles, I have some feelings about how that opera has been given its exalted status and who should be singing it.

I WAS back in Boston the following month for Sarah Caldwell's long-awaited production of *Macbeth.* It was Sarah's turn to direct me in the opera. A short, stocky woman who appears not to pay much attention to things like makeup, wigs, and false eyelashes, she is a creature of the stage. Her sense of theater is awesome. People said she sometimes spent the night in the theater. I can't remember when we first met, but I believe that my PR director, Edgar Vincent, introduced us. We had talked about performing together for some time before we did. She had kept tabs on my success in the La Scala production of *Macbeth* and was clearly out to put her stamp on the opera. Her concept and execution of it were just as valid as Giorgio Strehler's.

Sarah went in the opposite direction from Strehler. His was a *Macbeth* of the mind, psychological and cerebral. Sarah wanted her version to be presented as if the audience had never seen or read the original Shakespeare play. She wanted to leave nothing to interpretation, and she dotted every "i" and crossed every "t." To give you an example of her theatricality, she had Lady Macbeth drop a sleeping potion from her ring into the drinks of the soldiers who were to guard Duncan while he slept. This made it easier for Macbeth to assassinate the king without being detected. She made several other scenarios more plausible with ideas such as this. When I did the sleepwalking scene, she had me mimicking everything I sang in the aria. Strehler's approach to this scene was very stylized.

The caliber of the supporting cast for the Boston performances was not at the same level as that in the La Scala production, but in fairness, it would have been hard for anyone to top that opening night in Milan. Ryan Edwards was a strong, intelligent singer in the title role. He seemed a little young at the time, but I clearly had Piero Cappuccilli as my reference. Giorgio Tozzi *was* an imposing Banquo. I hadn't sung with him since my RCA recording days in Italy. Joseph Evans was a local singer who did Macduff. He did an okay job, but we sang together after that with even better results.

When I finished *Macbeth* in Boston, I had one more performance of *Norma* to do on the Met tour, at Wolf Trap in Virginia. Nedda Casei sang Adalgisa and Robert Nagy sang Pollione. Robert Nagy and I had met at Tanglewood in the summer of 1956. There were high expectations for him in that program. He was the "flavor of the summer." Boris Goldovsky had him singing everything, because he had a lovely, huge voice. My ear, at the time, told me he was pushing it too hard. Unfortunately, when he went to the Met, it was in small walk-on roles like the messenger in *Aida.* Maybe with the right teacher things might have turned out differently. He wasn't really up to the role of Pollione, though.

Simon Estes also made an unscheduled debut as Oroveso in that Wolf Trap performance. He, on the other hand, was *superbo!* Our scene, where Norma begs her father to protect her children, was one of the best I had ever done of it. Overall, it turned out to be a wonderful performance.

I HAD the rest of the summer off, and the LoMonaco family went to our home in the Catskills. This was my annual rest period and the main reason we built this house. Lou had a studio over the garage and used the time to paint. I had the opportunity to be a full-time wife and mother. Francesca was a toddler, still running around and pulling things down. By this time, her speech skills had progressed considerably.

She knew that she was adopted early on, because we had heard horror stories about children not finding out until their adolescent or adult years and being traumatized by the news. The agency had warned us to tell her as soon as we thought she would understand.

We told her about the Asian part first. I remember her young voice saying, "No! No! I not 'dopted!" It took her about three days to adjust to the truth. Shortly after that, she and I were at a restaurant having lunch and several people came up to compliment her on her beautiful braids. One woman came up and told her how pretty she was. Cessie said proudly, "I'm 'dopted." The agency also said not to tell her we chose her, because she might reason that if we could choose her, we could also get rid of her. Instead, we were to tell her that we needed her in our family and in our lives, which is the way Lou and I did feel about our daughter. When she was older, I also told her that if she ever wanted to know her birth parents, I would help her reach them.

That summer Mother and Dad were visiting us from California, and Warren Wilson was also there, working on my recital program for the upcoming season. I had gone down to the playroom for a few minutes to rest, when Lou came downstairs in a hurry and said, "Shirley, I think your presence is needed upstairs." I looked at him with a quizzical expression, but he wouldn't tell me what was going on.

When I got upstairs, Warren, who is also Cessie's godfather, was upset. He and my parents had been playing with Cessie. She had been sitting in her seat at the breakfast table, talking to Warren, Mother, Dad, and Clarice, our housekeeper. Cessie said, pointing to Warren, Mother, and Dad in turn, "You are black, . . . but I'm not." Mother and Warren went up in smoke. Mother didn't know what to say and surely thought I was teaching her to be prejudiced. Cessie, in the meantime, didn't understand what she had done to upset everyone and started crying. That's when I explained to her the differences in skin color. I told her that although she wasn't as dark as Mommy,

Grandmother, Granddad, or Uncle Warren, she was also black and that's how she would appear to the world. I also told her, "It doesn't mean a thing. You are a beautiful and special little girl."

I never did find out where Cessie had gotten an idea like that, but it was probably from some of the children in her Montessori preschool. At three and a half, she was too young for me to question.

12

Somewhere In Between

I N 1976 La Scala Opera arrived in the United States for the first time in its history to commemorate the American bicentennial. I reprised Lady Macbeth in the La Scala production at the Kennedy Center in Washington, D.C., along with Piero Cappuccilli and Nicolai Ghiaurov.

There were a few drawbacks. Opening night, the curtain wasn't working properly, so we waited for close to an hour before we could begin. The Kennedy Center stage was smaller than La Scala's, and the effect of the trains on our capes, which was so crucial to the Scala production, was not as dramatic. But these drawbacks hardly mattered. Former vice president Nelson Rockefeller came backstage to greet me, the Kennedy Center gave a grand party for us after the performance, and *People* magazine covered it all. I was featured in the September 27, 1976, issue. Knowing that I may have been the only American in any of the La Scala bicentennial operas, *People* asked why the world-renowned Italian opera company used an American singer in the production instead of an Italian? I told the interviewer that there was one thing about Italians; if they liked you and appreciated your talent, as far as they were concerned, you could be from Mars.

In addition to the operas, Claudio Abbado led the La Scala orchestra and chorus in performances of Verdi's *Requiem* at Philadelphia's Robin Hood Dell and New York's Carnegie Hall. For the first time, I sang the soprano part in the *Requiem.*

Marilyn Horne sang the mezzo-soprano part in those performances. I came prepared to mend some fences with her because of something I had said off the record to a young interviewer. I had shared my personal views about who should be staged in what operas and used as an example a recent Met negotiation regarding the proposed production of *La Favorita,* where they wanted Marilyn and me to share the production. I told him Marilyn Horne was wonderful, an eminent Rossini specialist, but didn't look the part of Leonora di Gusman in *La Favorita.*

It was much more innocent than it sounds. But the writer misquoted these remarks in the news account and also in his book, and it hurt Marilyn. I could easily have imagined it would. The writer didn't print any of the positive things I said about her and her fabulous talent, only made it seem like I had said she was too "fat" for this part. Instead of picking up the phone and telling Marilyn what I had really said, I did nothing. It was a mistake I deeply regretted. It also caused some of her fans to be angry with me, which was understandable. I was foolish to think this writer wouldn't misquote me.

I apologized for my remarks. I told Marilyn I should have done it much sooner and I *had* been misquoted in the book. Marilyn was every bit as frank.

"Yes, Shirley, you should have called me. I would have understood."

I told her what I had actually said, but the way the writer put it was nasty and mean-spirited. In retrospect, I also see that it was wrong for me to even offer an opinion on who should be staged in what operas, because similar arguments have been used to justify not staging African Americans in certain operatic roles.

During the first Philadelphia performance of the *Requiem,* I noticed that she kept clearing her throat with a mild cough. I always kept a lozenge or two in my score. I quietly passed one over to her and she nodded her acknowledgment, without looking in my direction. The next day, she sent me a huge box of the lozenges. She was generous like that. I was glad we resolved that situation, because she remains a good colleague and a friend, and my carelessness had almost ruined it.

I love generous people. I think it is important to be generous, in both material and nonmaterial ways. It goes back to my religious upbringing. "Cast your bread upon the water." My church believed in giving something back to the world, in helping others, and in giving without expecting something back in return.

I give because I want to give. I give money, time, and support. I give to poor people on the street. I usually say to myself, "There but for the grace of God go I." I don't care if they're lying to me or not. I ask myself, Are they in true need? Maybe they'll go and buy wine or drugs, but that's not my business. I feel the need to give this way and so I give.

THAT OCTOBER, at the last minute before *Il Trovatore* opened the 1976–1977 Metropolitan Opera season, I was asked to sing Azucena. Luciano Pavarotti, Renata Scotto, and Matteo Manuguerra were singing the other lead roles in the production. Renata Scotto was coming on strong with production after production at the Met around that time. I had sung Azucena with Scotto in Paris a few years before, but this was her first time doing Leonora at the Met. She wanted us to do several things together, like switching between singing Norma and Adalgisa, as I had proposed to do with Montserrat Caballé. When I did the broadcast of *Il Trovatore* the following spring, I was asked, by the *Opera News* correspondent, why I was still singing Azucena when I was no longer a mezzo. I responded, "The composer 'wrote the role for a singer.'" From reading some of Verdi's letters, I knew he had planned to name the opera *La Zingara* (The

Gypsy), which is understandable, given the depth of Azucena's complex character. I am not sure if I had been to Verdi's home in Busetto by then, but in his wife's bedroom a plaque on a table in front of her bed reads, "Stride la vampa" (The flames are roaring), the opening line of Azucena's celebrated aria.

I played Azucena almost as a crazy woman. I changed my entire face, even down to the nose. I also wanted to look like someone who had been very beautiful but had degenerated as a result of that one horrible, life-transforming event. Some singers played her as a snaggle-toothed hag. I started out that way, but I matured in my thinking and in my approach to this role. I saw her as someone who had faded by living on the road as a nomad. I also portrayed her with a limp, as if she were arthritic, which she most probably was.

When you consider what this woman had to do, there is little wonder she was emotionally unstable. As she burns at the stake, Azucena's mother puts a terrible burden on her by demanding revenge. Azucena's feeble and confused effort (not to mention that she had to have been scared out of her wits) results in her throwing her own child into the flames instead of Count di Luna's child. She is then presented with the incredible task of raising the child of her mother's murderer as her own. The psychological impact of this played with her mind. It would be like raising a child you loved and hated simultaneously. Manrico should have been affected by all of this, psychologically, but Verdi gives us no indication of this. The only apparent manifestation of her deed is when, periodically, sometimes unconsciously, she calls out her mother's command, "Mi vendica" (Avenge me). I played around with the mother figure.

Some critics didn't like my ideas about the character, but my approach made me feel the part more deeply. I don't think the Italians liked this approach as much, because the role wasn't the big success there that it was everywhere else.

I grew to love playing Azucena. It was one of those roles I could do on a moment's notice. That is precisely what happened when I was called in to sing Azucena with the San Francisco Opera in an emergency in September 1975. That cast starred Luciano Pavarotti, Joan Sutherland, Ingvar Wixell, and Elena Obraztsova. Obraztsova began the run of the opera with laryngitis but after singing the opening performance was unable to continue. I received a call at home in New York and was asked if I could fly out to San Francisco to sing in her place. I had one rehearsal before the performance, which Richard Bonynge led.

I received a standing ovation at the end of the performance! Some people in the audience were actually waving both arms, as if they were in a football stadium. Part of this had to do with the crazed laugh I inserted at the end. It was incredible! The *San Francisco Examiner* reported the following day that I had stolen the show "right out from under Joan Sutherland, gaining a standing ovation along the way." When Azucena is strong, it strengthens the entire performance.

I also met Elena Obraztsova while I was in San Francisco. Perhaps it would be more accurate to say I was reunited with Obraztsova in San Francisco after more than a decade. She turned out to be the same young singer, Elena, whom I had met after a recital during my tour in the Soviet Union in 1963!

While she was becoming a big-name singer in this country, Elena related a story in a magazine article about how this "colored" singer had given her music to copy, with the notes and markings in it. Elena said that a Russian singer would never have done such a thing, but this woman had. As her name grew in the United States, I saw "Elena Obraztsova" in various trade magazines, but it never occurred to me that she was the same young singer I had met years before.

When she came backstage after the performance of *Il Trovatore,* she recognized me right away and everything fell into place. We hugged and cried. We remain friends today. She reminded me of when we first met and even remembered what I sang in the recital. I never realized that I was the "colored" singer in her story. She had come through her own personal trials under the old Soviet system, though. At one point she was required to denounce her mentor, soprano Galina Vishnevskaya, after Vishnevskaya and her husband, cellist and conductor Mstislav Rostropovich, defected to the West. Obviously, she did this to remain on good terms with the authorities at the time, because they had the power to squash her career like a bug. Had that happened, we would never have heard of her in the West, and that would have been our loss.

After the opening of *Il Trovatore* at the Met in 1976, I was scheduled to do a bittersweet engagement on October 31. My colleague, friend, and old RCA recording buddy Richard Tucker had died a year before. A voice competition had been established in his name to help up-and-coming singers. I was invited to participate in a memorial gala to fund the award. Many of the big names, including Martina Arroyo, Luciano Pavarotti, José Carreras, Anna Moffo, and Renata Scotto, were scheduled to sing that night. Unfortunately, I had to withdraw from the engagement on short notice because of illness. I later came to discover that I wasn't the only one unable to appear.

I HAD to be talked into my next opera production, Francis Poulenc's *The Dialogues of the Carmelites,* on the Met schedule for the following February. This was the first time the Met had staged it. The management wanted me to sing Mother Marie, the stern second-in-command sister. I was more interested in the character of the Second Prioress, Madame Lidoine, because of the discipline it imposed on me, so the management gave me that part. The Met never knew why I insisted on the Second Prioress. I needed this role to straitjacket myself onstage.

Lidoine was from a peasant background, definitely not an aristocrat like Blanche de la Force. Madame Lidoine takes her elevation to the top position of the religious order in very humble and spiritual terms.

Nothing in the dialogue or the music suggests that this woman is anything other than a resolute religious leader, who will look after the spiritual and emotional needs of the sisters and novices under her in the politically charged atmosphere of revolutionary France. Even as she approaches death and martyrdom, which was not her choice, Lidoine shows the other nuns how to mount the guillotine with bravery and certainty that the physical pain would be brief but the spiritual reward eternal. It was an emotionally taxing role, but I grew to love the character. I became far more involved in it than I had ever imagined. I always looked forward to the days I was singing the roles. The sets and costumes were beautiful.

In a rare coincidence, *The Dialogues of the Carmelites* was the February 5, 1977, Texaco broadcast *and* the premiere. The powerhouse of the production was Regine Crespin as the First Prioress, Madame de Croissy. She was nearing the end of her career by the late 1970s, but her performance was a real tour de force. In 1957, she had sung my role in the French premiere.

I really appreciated her work, especially in the scene where Madame de Croissy dies. Regine pulled out all the stops. I still remember her speaking the line "Mother Marie, in the name of God, I command you" with an almost delirious intensity. She was very dramatic and obviously a good actress. It was the only time we ever performed together.

The other big success in that production was Maria Ewing. She also did a fabulous job as the innocent Blanche de la Force. There was a situation that I am not too proud of now, but it did happen. I insisted on having the dressing room designated for the lead singer of the production. It should have gone to Maria Ewing, whose character in the opera was more prominent than mine. Madame Lidoine doesn't enter the opera until Act Two, but I wanted the "star" status. I was wrong to insist on it. We older singers came up in another era under different rules, which meant protecting one's turf or position, even when it came down to a dressing room. I learned about all of this in Europe. I suspect, though, that this practice hasn't completely vanished.

When the *Dialogues'* run finished, I had the spring 1977 run of *Il Trovatore* to do at the Met. Among the cast changes from the fall performances were Jimmy McCracken as Manrico and Louis Quilico as Count Di Luna. This cast did the Texaco broadcast in April.

*   *   *

THE 1976–1977 season was already a full one and it wasn't quite over. I had agreed to do Gluck's *Orfeo ed Euridice* for Sarah Caldwell and the Boston Opera, because I had done it at Covent Garden. She agreed to do the Paris version of the opera in Italian, which meant I was able to do the big aria, "Amour, viens rendre a mon ame" (Love, come to restore my soul), that I had recorded. Singing that aria made the opera worthwhile for me. Aside from that, I didn't like the production. Sarah was also staging Jacques Offenbach's *Orpheus in the Underworld* in the same season. She came up with the idea of using the same sets and costumes for both productions. Pink clouds floated across the stage. It was like something from the late Baroque era. I guess at one level it was very ingenious, but I didn't like the idea of appearing onstage in puffed sleeves, a pleated skirt, and tights, especially with my knock knees. This was the only production with Sarah that I disliked participating in.

As if *my* costume weren't silly enough, there was Benita Valente, who sang Euridice. She was put in a hoop skirt and some bizarre headgear. She sang the role well, I have to say. I felt that my performance was just okay, but it was also the last time I did this opera. It really was very low for my voice at this point. The straight-talking critic Robert Baxter, not a great admirer of mine at the time, said I gave an "uneven" performance. He was probably right. I think the criticism was aimed more at my doing this contralto role after having established myself as a soprano on the opera stage.

ILLNESS HAS always been the one great threat to my career. The body has to be in superb condition to sing well. The instrument *is* you. It's not something that is superimposed from the outside, like a violin or a piano. If something goes wrong, I can't change the strings. I have become very particular about not catching colds. I have worked hard to avoid anything that could cause a physical problem. Sometimes I have disappointed my body because I didn't have the patience to say I'm not going to eat that or do this.

To portray or sing a role correctly, the body must be involved. You must fill your lungs with air. If you can't, you can't get through the arias. The body is an important conveyer of meaning. Through it, the audience is sent these messages. Some opera singers don't know how to send messages through movement and gesture. They sing from the neck up. Obviously, they have good lung capacity, because anyone has to have good lungs to be a good singer. What makes the difference? The body and the brain must go beyond the limits of technical singing. I've seen a singer trying to portray a count while moving like a peasant. I will not move my body as Delilah in the same way that I do for Azucena or Eboli. Singing is holistic. The whole body has to be in good shape in order to sing and act brilliantly.

During the fall 1977 season, several health problems dragged on. I had a hard time getting rid of the flu. I would go to one town and sing beautifully, but as soon as I went to another town, I had breathing problems. Some of these symptoms weren't new, because I had had them before. For some reason, I was having more trouble than usual. Warren and I would do a recital and he'd tell me I sang okay, but I knew something was wrong. I always knew when I was good or just so-so.

In October I sang with Zubin Mehta and the New York Philharmonic in one of the "Live from Lincoln Center" televised concerts. I presented Mozart's motet *Exsultate Jubilate* and the "Liebestod" from Wagner's *Tristan und Isolde.* Zubin kept the orchestra down and didn't drown me out in the Wagner. He was among those who tried to get me to do more Wagner. Sarah Caldwell wanted me to do the role of Isolde. I had enough sense to decline both of those suggestions.

Right after that "Live from Lincoln Center" concert, I had a big recital coming up at Carnegie Hall at the beginning of November and later that month at the Kennedy Center. I also had a new production of Verdi's *Un Ballo in Maschera* at La Scala that December.

The program at Carnegie Hall was more soprano-oriented than some of my earlier recitals there:

I

HANDEL

Semele: O sleep why dost thou leave me
Joshua: O had I Jubal's lyre
Passion of Christ: Chi sprezzando

II

STRAUSS

Ruhe meine Seele
Zueignung
Wiegenlied
Fur fünfzehn Pfennige
Befreit

III

ROSSINI

Assedio di Corinto: Non temer

INTERMISSION

IV

SPIRITUALS ARRANGED
BY HALL JOHNSON

Honor, Honor
His Name So Sweet
A City Called Heaven

V

CHAUSSON

Dans le foret
Les Heures

Les Papillons
La caravane

VI

DEBUSSY

Enfant prodigue: L'Air de Lia

I sang at least four encores, including Guastavino's "La rosa y el sauce" (The rose and the willow), Joaquin Nin's "Pano Moruno" (Moorish Cloth), "Ma dall' arido stelo divulsa" (When at last from its stem I shall sever) from *Un Ballo in Maschera,* and "Pace, pace, mio Dio" (Peace, peace, my God) from *La Forza del Destino.* The recital was received well by the audience and the critics. As I recall, one reviewer complained about my stretching my voice to sing the Verdi encores. But I was pleased, overall, with how things went.

The Kennedy Center concert turned out to be an especially memorable event. I stuck pretty close to the Carnegie Hall program, although I substituted Mozart's *Exsultate Jubilate* in place of the Rossini *Siege of Corinth* scene. After the intermission, I sang Hall Johnson's arrangements of the spirituals. That's when I noticed there was something different about this audience. When I saw people put their hands up in the air as if they were in church, witnessing, it hit me that there was an unusually large number of African Americans, including people standing at the back of the theater. I grinned.

A few weeks before, I had done a telephone interview with an African American reporter who worked for one of the big Washington papers. I remember her being very thorough, which suggested to me that she had a musical background. The article came out before the Kennedy Center concert and, as I was told, a prominent African American Baptist minister read the article and persuaded most of his congregation to come to the recital.

There were hundreds of African Americans at that recital. The audience was so enthusiastic that it sparked me up. I could see the

gratitude and pride in many of their eyes. Many people came backstage after the concert to greet me. Some told me their pastor had
shown the congregation the story and then got up in the pulpit and
said, "We will all go and see *Miss* Shirley Verrett!" I had *never* been so
proud in all my life. It brought to mind Hall Johnson, who was long
dead by then. I wondered what he would have thought of me getting
this kind of reception from our people. He had to be smiling down
on me that day.

FROM THAT lovely experience, I went to Italy to do *Un Ballo in
Maschera* at La Scala. Claudio Abbado persuaded me to sing the
opera. This time, however, I was not doing Ulrica, but Amelia, the
guilt-stricken wife of the governor's counselor, Renato. The role never
appealed to me as such, and I can't say I identified with it, but Claudio was persuasive, and since he had been so accurate with his *Macbeth* prediction, I was more willing to trust him. Having said that, I
take full responsibility for having done the role, because neither
Claudio nor anyone else put a gun to my head. The problem was, I
arrived for rehearsals feeling under the weather, with what seemed
like an allergy combined with a cold. Some days I could breathe okay,
and on others I labored. None of this helped my singing, which, as
far as I was concerned, was substandard.

The cast for *Un Ballo* was a singer's dream. Elena Obraztsova was
Ulrica, Piero Cappuccilli was Renato, and Luciano Pavarotti sang
Riccardo. I always rented a short-term apartment when I would be in
Europe for more than two weeks. Luciano found an apartment for
me below the place where he was staying. He was such a dear colleague and friend. Luciano also taught me something about cancellations during that production. I would frequently hear him vocalize
above me. If his voice faltered just a little, I'd say to myself, "He's not
singing tonight," and indeed he would cancel. He *knew* the Italian
audiences and was well aware they would boo you off the stage. They
could be especially hard on tenors. He had been booed a couple of

times and wouldn't take certain chances. José Carreras stood in for him when he was indisposed.

During the dress rehearsal, I heard a few boos and hisses after I did one of the arias. This was not a good omen. It was the first time this had happened to me. The audience was partly justified, because I wasn't well. I went to my dressing room, feeling very dejected. Mirella Freni came back to comfort me.

She said, "Don't feel too bad, Shirley. It happens to all of us." I told her, "It hasn't happened to me before." I was on the verge of crying. In a sense I deserved it. I never should have done that role, feeling as I did about it. She told me when she had been booed and how it had hurt her. She added, in a lighter tone, "You haven't made it at La Scala until you've been booed." It brought a smile to my face. I may have chuckled, but my condition didn't get much better as the opera opened. I was also scheduled to sing a Verdi *Requiem* but withdrew from the performance. Agnes Baltsa or Elena Obraztsova replaced me. I was scheduled to sing thirteen performances of *Un Ballo in Maschera* but withdrew after seven.

I felt bad about withdrawing from the production and wanted to make it up to the Italian audience. I was asked to do a recital, because I did feel a bit better toward the middle of the run. I was a recital favorite in Italy, but this one was very impromptu. Since I hadn't brought a recital gown, the Italian designer Emilio Pucci sent over three for me to choose from. I selected a purple and white one, but he let me keep all three of them, which was very generous. Years before, I had been photographed in his atelier in Florence.

The recital went well. I did the Mozart *Exsultate Jubilate*, among several other things. It was a beautiful program and the audience really appreciated the recital. After I completed the printed program, I did several encores, including "Una voce poco fa" from *The Barber of Seville*. When I returned to the reprise of the aria, I began to interpolate certain ornamental passages. As I approached the conclusion of the aria, I heard a man's voice yell out from the balcony, "Lascia stare Rossini!" (Leave Rossini alone!). He apparently objected to the embellishments I had included in the aria. I immediately stopped singing and tried to compose myself but could feel myself becoming angry. As I stood there in silence, a few tears began rolling down my cheeks. I reached up with my finger to wipe away the tears so they wouldn't smear my eye makeup. In that split second, I walked to the edge of the stage and responded in the direction of my heckler in Italian, "Se lei non vuole essere qui, vada a casa!" (If you don't want to be here, go home!). The rest of the audience broke out into thunderous applause and started hissing the heckler. I surprised myself when I did that. It had to be a visceral reaction.

All of a sudden, I saw cameras flashing all over the theater. Paparazzi! It was as if they had come out of the woodwork! Several people from the audience, sitting in the front row, obviously saw the tears rolling down my cheeks and me wiping them away. A lady from the audience walked up to the edge of the stage and handed me a beautiful lace-trimmed handkerchief. If I had been sitting in the audience viewing all of this, I would have sworn it was staged! It was the kind of theater that Italian concertgoers thrive on. I treasure that memory because it was a beautiful gesture, and I had done a very good recital.

When I finished the recital, the usual crowd of well-wishers and fans came backstage to greet me. I changed out of my gown and went to sign autographs, after being delayed by reporters for an hour. The paparazzi were still clicking away. So many people had come back to see me, the management put me in a small booth at the entrance to the backstage area of the theater, where I could sign autographs without being mobbed. It became the standard practice for crowd control. People could stick their programs through the small window opening for me to sign.

My friend Marcella Bonsanti had come up from Florence to attend the recital. The Bonsantis had become like my family in Italy. Marcella was a petite Jewish-Italian woman from a very aristocratic Florentine family. During World War II, she had been hidden from the Germans to escape persecution. She smoked like a chimneystack but usually not in my presence. She sat in the booth with me as I continued to sign autographs. Suddenly, I got a feeling in the pit of my stomach as one particular "well-wisher" put his program through the window of the booth. I saw his face and a voice in my head told me, *This is your heckler!*

He put his face up to the window and said again in Italian, "I still say leave Rossini alone. You sing it very beautifully, but he didn't want . . ." Before he said another word, Marcella pulled her long cigarette holder from her mouth and said to the man in a very matter-of-fact manner, "Go fuck yourself." She put the cigarette holder back in her mouth as if she hadn't uttered a word and kept on puffing. My heckler didn't fare as well as before. Some of the fans in the area dragged him off and started shoving him around. I saw his head jerk back every now and then, which made it seem as if someone had punched him in the face. I don't know what happened to him after he was out of my sight. I stayed at the theater, signing autographs for another hour.

Even that wasn't the end of the story. The following day, I made the front page of several local papers. The headline in one paper read, "La Nera Callas piangeva" (The Black Callas cried), and showed a series of pictures of me being handed the lace handkerchief and wiping away the tears. Some of the papers reported that I broke down and cried. I did no such thing, but the entire incident certainly increased my standing among the Italian audiences.

The international wire services picked up the story from Italy. Lou and my parents called because they had seen the account in the papers. One paper in the United States said I was singing the opera *The Barber of Seville* (meaning the entire role) and broke into tears when the audience booed me after completing an aria. A few months later, I finally explained the story from my side when I did an interview for a newspaper in Cleveland, where I was to sing a recital.

In 1999 the Myto label released a recording of the live December 30,

1977, performance of *Un Ballo in Maschera* from La Scala. To my surprise, it didn't sound as bad as I recalled it. I still maintain that it wasn't some of my best singing, but I can be a little too hard on myself.

In any event, I did not have a good experience singing Amelia at La Scala. That was not a role for me. The Met had also asked me to do it. It was to have been a year and a half after La Scala, but I told the management that after the La Scala episode, I had decided to sing only the arias, not the entire opera. In fact, I had a friend and a PR person, Nini Castiglioni, pack my bags and put me on the flight to New York. I came home feeling very ill, emotionally and physically.

WHEN I arrived in New York from Italy in January 1978, I was in terrible shape. I was hyperventilating, so I immediately checked myself into a hospital. My physician ordered tests, but I just stayed overnight and checked myself back out. The best thing for me was rest. For the next two weeks, I did not leave my bedroom on the second floor of my home. The housekeeper brought me food and other small things I needed. I just rested. The rehearsals for the new Met production of *La Favorita* were about to start, and I felt that I had a lot at stake in this production that Basil and I had fought so hard for. The production also had a first-rate cast, with Luciano Pavarotti as Fernando, Sherrill Milnes as Alfonso, and Bonaldo Giaoitti as Baldassare. Jésus Lopez-Cobo, the Spanish conductor, was at the helm.

La Favorita is based loosely on the real-life fourteenth-century liaison between King Alfonso di Castile and his mistress Leonor de Guzman, who came from a noble background. Unlike the character in the opera, the historical Leonor de Guzman was far from a self-pitying weakling. She had several children with Alfonso (who was indeed married, as in the opera) and was his most powerful adviser. After the death of Alfonso, Leonor de Guzman died under mysterious circumstances, most probably murdered by her rivals in the court.

In the opera, Leonora is a sympathetic character who seems to have been led into a situation not of her own making. She left her father, expecting to marry Alfonso, only to discover he had a wife, and that she was to be his mistress. The twist in the libretto, which the Met production did not deal with, was that Alfonso's queen is Fernando's (the opera's hero) sister (who doesn't appear in the opera but is referenced several times). Baldassare, the severe prior of Compostela, where Fernando is taking religious orders, and the king's principal critic, is the father of both the queen and the novice. Fernando is, in fact, attempting to gain the love of a woman who is his brother-in-law's mistress!

Leonora's influence over the king has caused her to be reviled by the other advisers of his court. The only small joy in her sad life is her love for the young novice Fernando. She doubts, throughout much of the opera, that they can have any happiness because of her past, of which he is completely unaware. She sends her confidante Ines to tell Fernando about the nature of her relationship with the king, but the confidante is intercepted. Fernando instead receives the news in a public and humiliating manner from the king's ministers, after he has just married Leonora. He rejects her in horror and returns to the monastery. Leonora, disguised as a monk, finds him at the monastery to seek his forgiveness. He initially recoils, cursing and insulting her, but his love for Leonora is as strong as ever. He gives in and once more professes his true feelings. She arrives at the monastery to see Fernando one last time before dying (one of those inexplicable operatic ailments). It is a tragic opera, but I loved playing that role. Leonora wasn't heroic, as were the other heroines I played, but it was a challenge for me to play this woman who had almost no joy in her life.

This version of *La Favorita* included the fully staged ballets, which are usually cut. Jésus Lopez-Cobo was the conductor. The opera opened on February 21, and I sang all but one or two of the performances. I felt less than at my best. A few critics complained about the production, while others loved it. The audience was definitely in the latter category. Every time I finished "O mio Fernando," the show came to a halt. I had interpolated notes into the cabaletta "Scritto in Ciel" that I had never done before. Some of those performances were fueled by willpower alone. I was scheduled to go on the annual tour with *La*

Favorita, but I bowed out. I took another extended rest break. I may have even been feeling depressed, because I knew something was definitely wrong with my body, but I couldn't figure out what.

I just wanted to be alone after the run of the production. I didn't want to be around family or friends. I went to Florida for two weeks after *La Favorita* to try to sort things out. I told Lou I didn't intend to sing another note until I found out what was wrong with me, and I had some explanation for these periodic illnesses I was experiencing. I had been healthy once.

I ended up cutting my trip to Florida short because of a physician referral. I had spoken to someone at my daughter's school, another parent, who had similar allergy and breathing problems. She had gone to a physician in New York, who referred her to another physician practicing in Birmingham, Alabama. This Alabama doctor had done some groundbreaking work in the area. I made an appointment with this physician, Dr. Orion Truss. By this time, I had seen doctor after doctor in this country and Europe without success. I wasn't hopeful.

Dr. Truss's secretary knew of me and, when I arrived at the doctor's office, made me feel very welcome. When Dr. Truss and I met, we talked, it seems, for hours. His questions were very detailed and thorough. He asked questions dating back to my childhood. He described very specific scenarios like: When you woke up in the morning when you were young, did you feel . . . ? Amazingly, I could recall many things. After our discussion, he said, "I think I know your problem: candida albicans." He described it as a yeast infection that was usually vaginal but could be systemic. When I told him I could go to one place and feel fine and sing beautifully and just a few days later go to another and feel that something was wrong, he said these symptoms were consistent with the condition.

He gave me a small dose of medication in my arm. About a half hour later my nose started to open up. He said, "You may have other allergies, but this is the big one. Keep this one under control and you will be okay for a few more years." I felt a combination of relief, frustration, and joy. This probably doesn't adequately describe the mixed emotions I felt. I sat in the hotel in Birmingham and just cried. I mean, I cried! By the time of that diagnosis, I had been singing professionally for over twenty years! I had known as early as the 1960s that something wasn't right. I was given antibiotics for colds at the beginning of my Juilliard years, which was a mistake. I didn't know any better. I wondered what it would have been like if this had been detected much earlier. Would I have had an even bigger career? Would I have been able to accept more engagements? Would I always have to think of my vocal cords? Were they going to approximate correctly for singing? All of these questions surged through my mind. I couldn't sleep well that night. I tell you, I had a career as an opera singer in spite of my illnesses.

I began to wonder if other singers had experienced similar conditions that went undiagnosed and as a result gave up their careers. I don't expect many nonsingers to fully appreciate what I felt, but I liken it to people with moderate cases of dyslexia who don't have the condition properly diagnosed until adulthood. They may be able to function, but they know, as they grow up, that something is out of sync. Others around them may not understand what's troubling them because, depending on the severity, the dyslexic person appears to be functioning normally.

Dr. Truss gave me medication to take with me to help control this condition. I also gave myself injections. I still wanted time off to rest and recover after such a trying period. Now I keep myself functioning by using homeopathic treatments, and since I don't have to sing anymore, I occasionally eat things like bread, which has yeast in it, and some other things that make the yeast flare up.

In addition to Lou, I also informed Columbia Artists Management that I needed the rest break. My manager Ronald Wilford said I should take as long as I needed, and I did. I am not sure what performances I canceled, but there were several months' worth. Before the discovery of the allergic condition, I had questioned whether I wanted to continue my career. I reasoned that I had made a name as an opera singer, recitalist, and musician in general, so perhaps it was time for me to retire, even though I could still sing well. The treatments helped me enough that my confidence gradually came back.

I DID feel well enough to return to the stage to sing the San Francisco Opera's fall 1978 revival of Bellini's *Norma* in September. I reported for rehearsals in August. The conductor was Paolo Peloso, and others in the cast were Alexandrina Milcheva as Adalgisa, Nunzio Tedisco as Pollione, and Clifford Grant as Oroveso.

I felt that I overacted in the scene where Norma is about to stab Pollione in rage. A photographer caught me as I was running toward Pollione, robes flowing and all. I stopped in my tracks and dropped the knife. The scene was overdone, and that photograph with my right arm raised has become well-known. I looked like a wild woman. I sang "Casta Diva" (Chaste Goddess) and the cabaletta "Ah! bello a me ritorno" (Ah, return to me, beauty) very well. I always enjoyed doing it, because the tessitura was mostly above the staff, which has always been the strongest part of my voice.

The local reviewer of opera, who apparently didn't speak Italian, didn't like the performance because he felt that my diction was not precise enough—absurd! The European critic who reviewed the performances for *Opera Magazine* in London loved the production and the intensity of my portrayal of the druid priestess. It is all a matter of taste. It is ultimately a mistake for a singer to rely too heavily on a critique, whether the review is good *or* bad. These opinions can be wildly contradictory. Obviously, I tended to agree with the *Opera Magazine* correspondent, but even if he hadn't liked it, *I* had to be the final judge of how well I did. If you happen to a be a singer who doesn't hear yourself well, you need to have a few ears you trust and get a tape recorder to assist you. That should be the aim, anyway. That's what I teach my students today.

The local San Francisco reviewer who felt that I didn't do the Italian well must obviously preferred another legendary Norma in that production. That, of course, is his prerogative. I do have to wonder, however, what he would have said about *her* Italian diction! She had a phenomenal voice, but her vocal diction was perhaps one of her few weaknesses. "Bel canto" (beautiful singing) means paying attention to the beauty of the vocal line, but the drama and the text must also be communicated. Why did the composers write the operas, if all the singers merely stand up on stage and do nothing? If that were the case, you could go and hear a concert version of the opera, instead of a fully staged production.

I HAVE touched on my feelings about the role of Norma because, frankly, it is a role I have loved for a long time. It is, perhaps, one of my favorite roles, but I believe it has been blown out of proportion by historians, critics, conductors, and interpreters of the druid priestess. They, in turn, influence the public's thinking about it.

I have collected autobiographies of singers since my Juilliard days and have thoroughly enjoyed reading them. In Lilli Lehman's book, she cautioned students and other singers about singing Norma. She said she would rather have sung three of Wagner's Brünnhildes than one Norma. Somehow that statement became law and gospel. Even as a teacher, who am I to say that my students can't sing certain kinds of things because it was difficult for me? I don't have that right. I can guide and suggest. Only in rare instances have I found it necessary to insist. The student might find it easy to do the thing that was difficult for me.

From *my* perspective, I would rather sing three Normas than one Carmen. Carmen was a very physically demanding role, at least the way I did it. When you add the emotional intensity, it is even more challenging. When I sang it with an allergic condition, it was yet another challenge, because Carmen taxed that part of my voice where the water settled on my vocal cords. Other interpreters of the Bellini have expressed similar sentiments about the hype surrounding Norma and why that role has taken on mythic dimensions.

I approached the role from the standpoint of Norma as a mother. Although the maternal part of her life was surreptitious, she still had a tender relationship with her children. She was also a lover, even though she was supposed to remain chaste. She was a daughter and a friend as well. For me, above all, she was a woman. All of these aspects are made clear in the opera. Put them together, and it makes for a wonderfully developed character. Most interpreters, with the assistance of tradition, have made Norma so elegant and regal, as if she were a queen. From my standpoint this is a mistake. Nothing in the score or libretto requires Norma to be elegant, beautiful, or queenlike. From her outward appearance, at least, she has more in common with Madame Lidoine from Poulenc's *The Dialogues of the Carmelites*. Both are religious leaders, but Norma has a lot more power, prestige, and influence among her people.

When she sings "Casta Diva," she is the unquestioned leader of her followers, even though they have no idea she is covering up a secret life. She is praying to a goddess in that aria. Then comes the young, obviously inexperienced priestess Adalgisa, whom she comes to love dearly as a friend. Norma cries on the shoulder of her confidante Clotilde, and it isn't the "royal cry," but that of a woman who is afraid, feeling both betrayed by Pollione and a betrayer of her people's trust. Ultimately, her insecurity about her secret love relationship turns out to be justified.

Certain scenes in the opera touched my soul and tore me to pieces. From the point in the opera when Norma confronts Pollione with the power she holds over him and Adalgisa, "In mia mano alfin tu sei" (You are finally in my hands), to "Qual cor tradisti" (What a heart you've betrayed), Norma experiences rage and a thirst for vengeance. She then becomes a vulnerable and betrayed woman who evokes the audience's sympathy. This happens in about twelve minutes! I need to see those changes expressed dramatically. It is not just beautiful music. I sought to communicate this when I did the role. That was my approach. I'm glad I had the opportunity to do Norma in several different productions. I tried not to get too caught up in the role's psychology, but make no mistake, it was a difficult role and challenged me every time I performed it.

For me, Norma requires a spinto voice or at least a heavy lyric soprano. The difficult part to cast is Adalgisa. I know I have said otherwise in the past, but, to be truthful, my voice was not right for the role.
It should be a lighter mezzo-soprano or a lyric soprano with a little bite
in the voice, to suggest the innocence of the girl. Frequently, companies cast an Adalgisa with a booming voice like Fiorenza Cossotto's,
which is too robust a sound. Under such circumstances, she comes off
sounding matronly instead of like a *giovinetta* (a young girl). I had the
opportunity to sing Norma in several more productions than I actually
sang, but the various opera company administrations and I couldn't
agree on the choice of who would sing Adalgisa. This happened at
both La Scala and the Vienna Staatsoper.

ALTHOUGH MY very first *Tosca* took place at the Met in the fall
1978–1979 season, I had intended to debut the role in Boston earlier
that spring. I had to cancel the May engagement, and when Sarah
Caldwell attempted to reschedule, there was another conflict. Boston
rescheduled the performance for the fall, but Magda Olivero sang the
role in my place. I went to see her in it. She was already a mature
singer at that point but made up very well. She carried the performance off as a pro. For the Met *Tosca*, which I was to star in, the
company took the existing production and revised it with different costumes and sets. I was featured on the December 16th cover of
Opera News, wearing one of the several gorgeous costumes. The picture on the cover included a lovely dark veil. My favorite costume was
the one I wore when I entered in Act One, replete with a peacock-
feather headwrap. I wore a very low-cut deep-blue velvet dress with
lace trim in the second act. Tito Gobbi, the highly regarded Italian
baritone and celebrated Scarpia in the opera in his own time, directed.

James Conlon conducted, and he was excellent. I always appreciated it when a conductor discussed my approach to the character
with me. Some conductors considered singers to be dummies, only
interested in making beautiful sounds. I was fortunate not to sing
with many who had these "dark age" views. Even though Conlon was

young at the time, he discussed the character with me at length. His podium skills were also commanding.

Luciano Pavarotti sang Mario Cavaradossi in that production, and he was in splendid voice. I always enjoyed working with him, because he is such a good and caring colleague. He joked a lot in the rehearsals. Cornell MacNeil was a deviously superb Scarpia. This was the role I believe he was born to sing. At one point it seemed that he wasn't acting but living this character, right down to the way he looked at me.

Tosca wasn't an easy role, especially the second act. It wasn't a role I was madly in love with either. Lady Macbeth was also a difficult part, but I seem to have been able to relate to it better somehow. Lady Macbeth was one-dimensional. She symbolized drive and ambition, no matter what the cost, no matter who she had to take out to accomplish her goal. Tosca has a far greater emotional range, which isn't always easy to master. The physical demands of Tosca are also more challenging. The third act is a comparative "piece of cake." It is mostly wonderful singing, when compared to the second act, where the singer has to display humiliation, insecurity (which is a big part of Tosca's nature), murderous rage, and a few other feelings. The more I did the role, the better it became for me. Gobbi helped me with my initial interpretation, though. He paid me a compliment I will never forget, when he told me I caught on to the role faster than any other Tosca that he had ever worked with or observed. This came from the singer who had sung with practically every celebrated Tosca in the postwar era. I always kept that in mind.

When we taped for a national "Live from the Met" broadcast, I performed the role for the television cameras, which meant containing my movement, because television would have made my usual stage gestures look affected or exaggerated. My makeup was toned down for the television screen. The broadcast aired on December 19, 1978. A live Texaco Metropolitan Opera matinee was broadcast on January 6, 1979.

*   *   *

I WAS so pleased with my performances of *Norma* when I did it on the Met tour in 1976, I wanted to repeat it at the main house in New York. The management could not bring it back for the 1976–1977 or the 1977–1978 season, because those seasons had already been set. The earliest it could be revived was the 1978–1979 season. I was looking forward to doing it in New York, but the performances didn't turn out as well as I had hoped. I did not feel well during rehearsals for *Norma* and felt a flu coming on. I tried hard not to let it get into my chest, because that would have really complicated matters. The first week of March had arrived and things were getting worse. My inclination was to stop rehearsals and rest, but I didn't do that. Toward the end of the rehearsal period, I alerted the Met's management that I didn't feel I could sing opening night. It was a painful but, I felt, necessary decision. I went home and just wanted to block everything out.

This is when my star at the Met began to lose some of its luster. It started when I didn't take a call from the Met's then general manager Anthony Bliss. I thought he would try to persuade me not to cancel the opening night of *Norma,* and I didn't want to be talked into anything. I had played along in the past. I was not well. Even so, it was discourteous of me not to receive his call. Up to that point I think he really liked me, and I certainly liked him. I just told my housekeeper that I wouldn't take any calls. This is when I stopped being "beloved" by the Met's administration. That was my fault. The Met had to get Marisa Galvany to make an unscheduled debut as Norma, as a stand-in for me. I felt well enough to sing the next performance, which was the Met's live Texaco broadcast on March 17, 1979.

I heard a tape of myself in that performance singing "Casta Diva," and I sounded like I was singing on the edge of my voice, which is possible because I really was not well enough. I know that all of me wasn't there.

I continued to sing at the Met for another eleven years, but I didn't have the support I had once enjoyed. I had been on a roll. Bliss liked me a lot, and the management had plans to bring me to even greater prominence at the house. After that *Norma* incident, my relationship with the Met didn't go from great to poor, but it was certainly somewhere in-between.

On the whole, when compared to the previous years, the next fifteen years of my active career (that is, from the early 1980s through the mid-1990s) were not a lot of fun. I wanted to be out of it, even though I knew I could still sing well. I felt that I was at the mercy of what was happening to my body, that the surrounding climate was controlling me. Traveling had also become more tedious and tiring. Having said that, however, I still added another four or five opera roles to my repertoire, revived a few that I hadn't sung in years, and had several other major engagements.

13

Commandeur des Arts et des Lettres

S OMETIMES everything was on target and I sang beautifully. Yet
on occasion I felt that a performance was substandard, and I
wondered whether it was time to retire. I asked myself this question after another less-than-stellar experience with Bellini's *Norma,* at
a Covent Garden production in London. I was supposed to have
sung it there in 1976 but had asked if it could be rescheduled. Then,
when the opera opened the third week of November 1979, I was constantly at the doctor's office. To make matters worse, Josephine Veasey,
who sang Adalgisa, was also ill. Veasey made an announcement before
the opening performance. I should have done likewise but decided
not to do so.

I felt that my performances were adequate but not as strong as those
in San Francisco. The reviews were relatively generous, considering the
circumstances. The veteran Italian basso Cesare Siepi was the Oroveso
and was still singing well. I had first seen him perform the role in 1956
with Maria Callas. Lamberto Gardelli conducted and Pier Luigi Pizzi
updated the original sets and costumes designed by Sandro Sequi. He
had us costumed like nuns, but the effect was dramatic.

*   *   *

SOME PEOPLE were perturbed at my singing soprano roles. It seems to have gotten under their skin, as if I made a conscious effort to do so. I did not hold a news conference and announce that I was switching from one voice type to another. From the beginning of my career, I sang roles scored for soprano. The part had to feel right in my voice. If I felt that the role was right, I did it.

Just recently, an elderly woman who recognized me while I was shopping said, "You were the greatest mezzo-soprano in the world. Why did you switch to soprano?" I politely replied, "I began lessons in California as a soprano and sang what I felt was right for my voice, whether it was designated mezzo or soprano."

I didn't set out to put a tag on my voice. People are uncomfortable with that notion. They want to categorize you, put you in a box. I refused to be boxed in. To set the whole matter to rest, once I had my vocal cords examined. The laryngologist said my vocal cords indicated that I was a soprano more than a mezzo-soprano.

Among my new opera roles was the title character in Verdi's *Aida*. Leonard Bernstein had talked with me about doing a film version of the opera, to be shot on location in Egypt during the summer of 1979. He was to have conducted it and Franco Zeffirelli was to have directed it. Plácido Domingo was also scheduled to be in the film. Then Bernstein came back to tell me that he wanted me to do the "more dramatic" role of Amneris, and Clamma Dale would sing Aida. Clamma was a gorgeous young singer with a lovely voice who had once studied with Madame Freschl. I last heard her in the 1980s, when she did a wonderful Liu in *Turandot*. I withdrew from the *Aida* production, not because my younger colleague would be singing Aida, but because I had taken Amneris out of my repertoire. I don't believe the film was made, and if it was, I never saw or heard of it.

My first proper stage performance as Aida came in May 1980, in a production mounted by the Boston Opera, with Sarah Caldwell in the dual role of director and conductor. James McCracken sang Radames, Elizabeth Connell sang Amneris, and a wonderful young

African American bass-baritone, David Arnold, sang Amonasro. I enjoyed singing that opera. I knew the role from having sung Amneris earlier. Something in that opera affected me at a visceral level, because I always cried during the second act. It was a strange feeling of déjà vu, almost as if I had lived that scene in an earlier life. From the moment in the opera when the Egyptian king gives Amneris's hand to Radames in marriage, through the end of Act Three, I felt teary. I never had this feeling when I sang Amneris.

When I did those scenes with David Arnold in rehearsal, he said he couldn't look at me, because seeing tears streaming down my cheeks made him emotional. The line in Act Three when Aida sings, "O patria! O patria quanto mi costi!" (O my country, how much you cost me!), was particularly gripping. Aida's father has just castigated her and intends to force her to betray her beloved Radames for the sake of her country. I saw a tape of the performance, after the run of the opera, and was very pleased with that Nile scene. But I remember feeling torn up inside.

I had been wearing my hair in a short Afro hairstyle for a few years by that time but covered it with a wig on some occasions for certain operas. I thought the short Afro was an appropriate style for Aida, but a music critic who reviewed the production for *Opera News* called it a butch haircut. I found that remark particularly insulting. African women have been wearing their hair in this style for centuries. Sarah Caldwell liked this added touch to *Aida*. It was just new for the conservative opera stage. That remark didn't stop me from wearing it in subsequent opera performances or concert engagements. I then began wearing my hair in braids, a style that went over much better, for some reason—not that it really mattered to me. I was continually looking for an easy and uncomplicated hairstyle. For years I had worn wigs over my hair because it was the easiest way to look well-dressed. It also saved me many trips to the beauty shop, where it was often difficult to find a beautician who knew how to deal with my hair texture. Of course, it was easy to find African American beauty shops in many of the cities in which I performed. So, by making my life less complicated with the braided hair, I established a new tradition that other African American women in the concert world followed.

A FEW weeks before *Aida* opened in Boston, I sang a major benefit fundraising concert for the NAACP at Carnegie Hall to a capacity audience. I reduced my usual fee, because it was a benefit concert. It was nearly a repeat of the Kennedy Center recital with many African Americans in the audience, and, as with that performance, many African American well-wishers came backstage afterward to see me. Quite a few women (and men) were particularly complimentary of my Afro hairstyle. I was made a lifetime member of the NAACP on that occasion, and I keep the plaque in my studio at the University of Michigan.

I MADE an unscheduled debut with the New Orleans Opera Association in Bizet's *Carmen,* a role I hadn't sung for some years. The originally scheduled singer had to withdraw because of illness, and the Opera Association director pleaded with me to step in. I wanted to know who else was in the cast. I accepted when I learned Harry Theyard was cast as Don José and Justino Diaz would sing Escamillo. I had performed with both of them before. It was like a reunion. I don't believe I had sung with either of them since the *Siege of Corinth* at the Met. Once I agreed to sing the role, the New Orleans Opera Association made a big pitch in the media that I would be singing Carmen. The spin they put on my appearance was the local girl who made good and came back home to save the show. Of course, I hadn't lived in New Orleans for the better part of forty years. The two performances were sold out. I arrived with a slight cold and asked the opera management to make a pre-curtain announcement to that effect. I did all right, given that it was a spur-of-the-moment decision. I still had the role in my voice. It was also good to be in New Orleans to see relatives and friends.

*   *   *

THE NEXT big production in 1980 was again at Covent Garden a few weeks after the New Orleans *Carmen,* in a reprise of Puccini's *Tosca.* The production opened in November and was a resounding success! It was better than when I first sang it nearly two years earlier at the Met. Gianfranco Cecchele was a surprisingly strong Cavaradossi. He was very intense during that all-important second act. The Scarpia was Kari Nurmela, a Finnish baritone I recall having sung with only on this occasion. In his makeup, he resembled Cornell MacNeil, who was in the Met production.

I added another Verdi role, Desdemona in *Otello,* to my repertoire in 1981. I premiered it with the Boston Opera on May 21. Unlike *Aida,* however, those performances of Desdemona in Boston were a first and a last for me. I continued to sing the aria from the fourth act because I truly enjoyed singing this very touching and beautifully composed music, but the character of Desdemona didn't quite suit me. As I prepared for the role, I kept thinking that by marrying a black man (a Moor), Desdemona was a young lady trying to defy her father. I believe, however, that she truly loved Otello. I don't know how I came to that conclusion, but Sarah didn't disagree with my interpretation.

The Boston production paired Jimmy McCracken and me in the lead roles. He had been one of the reigning Otellos for years and unquestionably earned his richly deserved celebrity for the part in that production. He was dramatic in his entrance. I even paid attention to it over the speakers in the dressing room. He was such a fine and supportive colleague. I am sorry we didn't get to sing together more often before his death.

There were strong reviews for my portrayal of Desdemona. Perhaps I shouldn't have given up on the role, but, overall, I didn't find it satisfying. I had an interview before the opening performance and, as I expected, the question of a black woman playing a white character in an opera in which race is a central issue came up. I answered the question with a question, "Did you pose that question to James McCracken?"

I don't recall a response, because the question was rhetorical. I *did* lighten my complexion slightly, because I was portraying a character in which race was a dynamic, but it was nothing like the way I was made up to play Elizabeth I in *Maria Stuarda.* Instead of blond hair, I wore a brown wig with highlights to complement my makeup color.

I WAS invited to sing for the inauguration of Ronald Reagan in Washington, D.C., but had an engagement in Pittsburgh that I was unable to cancel, but I did sing at the White House for the Reagans later that year at a state dinner for the Japanese prime minister. I learned a Japanese song about the cherry blossom to surprise him. He and his wife kept smiling and nodding their appreciation at the gesture.

I sang for President Reagan, despite my disagreement with his politics. Although I would vote for a Republican candidate if I believed in his or her politics, I have yet to vote for a Republican for president. In the summer of 1976, the Democratic Party's National Convention Committee invited me to sing the "Star-Spangled Banner" at its convention in New York City. I'm not sure if my performance was televised, but the main attraction of the convention was, of course, Jimmy Carter. After he won the presidency, I was invited to sing at a concert honoring the seventy-fifth birthday of Marian Anderson at Carnegie Hall, which included Leontyne Price and Clamma Dale. I sang "Songs My Mother Taught Me," and James Levine accompanied me at the piano. First Lady Rosalynn Carter was in attendance and was delighted with my performance. I believe that she facilitated my later being invited to sing a recital at the White House for a state dinner honoring the Italian premier, Giulio Andreotti. Somehow, Mrs. Carter became aware that I collected antique furniture and had me appointed to the White House Commission for the acquisition of antique furniture and artifacts, so I had several opportunities to return to the White House for meetings.

IN THE early summer of 1981, I went on a European tour with the La Scala chorus and orchestra, performing Verdi's *Requiem* under the baton of Claudio Abbado. We began the tour in Milan at a large cathedral. Mirella Freni and I alternated singing the soprano part, after I sang the first performance in Milan; Elena Obraztsova and Lucia Terrani-Valentini sang the mezzo part; José Carreras sang the tenor part in Milan but didn't go on the tour. Nicolai Ghiaurov and Paul Plishka alternated singing the bass part. I ended up singing a majority of the performances, because Mirella did not feel well for at least three that she was scheduled to sing. We sang in Athens, Dresden, Prague, and Sofia. The amphitheater, which was some miles outside of Athens, had incredible acoustics. From the top level of the amphitheater, you could drop a coin and hear it hit the stage below.

This was the first time I had gone out on tour and remained for two weeks. The soloists and Maestro Abbado traveled together; we ate our meals together and generally enjoyed each other's company. There was not even a hint of negativity throughout the entire time. That was a rare occurrence, with so many stars assembled.

Elena Obraztsova and I kept each other company on the flights. We were sitting one day, laughing like two little girls about something that had happened the day before, when Nicolai Ghiaurov came up to us and said, "It's nice to see the world's two great powers getting along so well," joking about her being Russian and me, American.

That July, after the La Scala tour, I sang the mezzo part in a performance of Verdi's *Requiem* at Tanglewood, where I hadn't sung in years. To my surprise, Mirella Freni and Nicolai Ghiaurov were the soprano and bass soloist in the quartet. When Mirella saw me at rehearsal, she ran up to hug me and said, "Shirley, I didn't know we would be singing together." We had been together just a few weeks earlier, touring in the same work. Ermano Mauro sang the tenor part at Tanglewood and did a very fine performance. His voice had grown richer since we last performed together. Seiji Ozawa conducted this star-studded performance.

I had two major productions of Saint-Saens's *Samson et Dalila* coming up in the fall of 1981. Both productions were filmed for television and released commercially. The first was at Covent Garden with Jon Vickers in September and October, under the direction of Sir Colin Davis. Jon sang well but was not pleased with the lighting overall. He complained to the lighting designer, Nick Chelton, about not getting enough light and actually yelled up at him during dress rehearsal, pointing his finger in the direction of the lighting booth, "I know what you're doing up there!"

"It's not your scene," someone yelled back.

"I don't care! I want some light, too!" Jon replied.

Elijah Moshinsky, director/producer, attended to every detail. For costumes, the silk material came from China. The colors were hot and passionate tones and patterns never before seen in *Samson et Dalila*. Imagine a chorus of maidens, singing about love and the beauty of the day, silhouetted against a dark red backdrop. Samson is also onstage, wearing a white robe; then Dalila appears, seemingly out of nowhere. While soft notes are ascending in the string section, she gazes at Samson, who is clearly transfixed by her beauty. In this scene I wore a beautiful red sleeveless top with a contrasting dusty-pink leaf-patterned skirt.

In the all-important love scene, when I bewitched Samson with the celebrated "Mon coeur . . . ," I wore a stunning pink-silk robe with a red oval-shape pattern. Inside the oval shape was a gold contrast. This was the most impressive costume of the four I wore. Everything was stunning, including my hair, which I wore naturally. I can't remember if the choice of style was mine or not, but my short Afro was perfect.

THE SAN Francisco Opera production of *Samson* followed soon afterward. It featured Plácido Domingo, with Julius Rudel in the orchestra pit. In certain respects, this production was stronger than London's because of the subtle psychological nuances stressed by the director, Nicolas Joel. For example, when I entered, Joel had me walk on as seductively as possible, swaying hips and all, and immediately begin working on Samson. So I moved in Samson's vicinity like a shark circling its prey. I lightly touched his shoulder, and with each motion I lured him into my sphere of influence. I followed with a suggestive dance, fully aware that Samson noticed my every move.

The critics were ecstatic. The reviewer from the *San Francisco Examiner* said, among other things, that it boasted "three excellent principals, an extraordinarily handsome scenic and costume design, crisp, effective stage direction," and the article was equally complimentary of Rudel's conducting.

FROM THIS point onward it became increasingly difficult for me to perform. By the end of the 1970s, I began to experience certain physical changes. I had no idea these were the beginning stages of menopause, which didn't hit me properly until I was in my fifties. Menopause caused more water to build up in my body. I think the same thing happened to Christa Ludwig nearly ten years earlier, when I sang the opening performance of *Les Troyens* at the Met. Blood vessels and capillaries in the throat often burst. Other physical manifestations occurred. It was rough. Yet sometimes I could sing a recital, and everything would be just fine. I had no trouble floating notes or doing whatever I wanted with my voice. On other occasions, my ears stopped up and threw off my pitch, and I wouldn't be fully aware of it. I knew several singers who didn't realize that they were sensitive to certain things, assumed they were losing their voices, and finally gave up.

I was still trying to be a supermom, a superwife, and a superstar. Believe me, it was a challenge. I must be honest about what was happening with my family. I was just irritable. If Lou said, "Black," I would say, "White." It seemed as if I criticized everything. This was a stressful period. Then, the hot flashes started. I began taking estrogen, but that caused me to gain weight and my blood pressure to rise. I eventually stopped, to switch to more natural treatments, but my discontinuing estrogen meant that I could sleep only a few hours a night and I was left with a weight problem.

* * *

A FALL 1981 issue of *Opera News* had a lengthy article about Grace Bumbry, featuring her on its cover. The interviewer apparently raised the inevitable question of our rivalry. Grace was quite outspoken about it. She is reported to have said that the problem of our "rivalry" was more mine than hers, because I had to follow in *her* footsteps. She also said she had nothing against me, personally, but thought that my switching voices (i.e., from soprano to mezzo roles) was very strange. Well, I suppose I had become accustomed to hearing people say such things after I took command of Norma. She may have had a point about my following in her footsteps, early on. I did, after all, emerge as a big-name artist after her success at Bayreuth. I debuted at the Met after her, but someone had to be first. She was. Circumstances, or fate, placed her in certain situations before me. What cannot be disputed, however, was that by the mid-1970s and throughout the 1980s, I was not following in her footsteps. I was a bigger-name (and bigger-fee) artist than she was, especially in this country. I have more commercial and noncommercial recordings, had more television appearances, and, for that matter, appeared in bigger productions with other big-name artists.

In that *Opera News* article Grace also mentioned that we might possibly do a joint concert but was vague about the details. This is when much of the concert world became aware of a planned joint engagement featuring Grace and me. Grace's manager, Herbert Breslin, who had also been a PR person for me, dreamed up the idea of our doing the joint concert. Someone else decided that the engagement should be timed to celebrate Marian Anderson's eightieth birthday. The concert promoters played up the idea of the great singer having inspired both of our careers. I must say, I was a little hesitant, but in the spirit of celebrating Miss Anderson, I went along.

Grace and I decided on a program, or at least I thought we had. As the performance date neared, I wanted to make a slight change. After an orchestral overture, the program was to proceed with the dramatic soprano/mezzo-soprano duet from Ponchielli's *La Gioconda,* "L'amo come il fulgor creato" (I love him as the thunder of creation). I was to immediately return onstage and sing the letter scene from Verdi's *Macbeth*. In viewing the arrangement, I felt that it was too much singing following the first duet. When I suggested an alternative, Grace said no, because we had already agreed to the format. She, of course, was correct. A week or so later, however, she came to a meeting in one of the rehearsal rooms at the Met with her accompanist and wanted to make a change in the arrangement. I held her to the same agreement that she had held me to a little earlier. I told her, "No, it cannot be. When I tried to change something some time ago, I was told I couldn't do it, so we have to stick to the program as it is." As if I hadn't said a single word, she continued with the changes she wanted. When I attempted to object again, she talked right over me. At that moment I stood up, slammed my score on the table, and said, "*Basta!* Do the bloody concert yourself!" I got up and walked out. She yelled after me as I left, "You didn't want to do it in the first place!" I responded, "*You* can sing the whole program. I don't care!"

Herbert Breslin's associate Hans Boone was present during this entire exchange. He followed me out of the rehearsal room and immediately began pleading, "Shirley, it won't look good on anybody's account if you don't do this concert." It took close to an hour before I agreed to return to the meeting. There had clearly been a breach in the relationship with Grace, which had been coming along okay up to that point. Incidentally, there were *no* changes to the program we had agreed on.

After we met with Eve Queler and the orchestra, it seemed that Grace went out of her way to antagonize me. If she thought I had made a mistake, she would gesture, roll her eyes, or do something else to call attention to it. For example, I did something in a cadenza and she said, "What was *that* you sang?" I said dryly, "Whatever it was, it was correct." *She,* in fact, was making mistakes.

This entire dynamic really bothered me. I talked to Lou and Warren about it. They both said I should forget it. It is always easy for people to give this kind of counsel about situations they are not involved with. A girlfriend referred me to a therapist. I wasn't interested in reclining on a sofa and digging up past events for the next year; I just wanted to talk to someone about the negative experience I was having with Grace. When I explained the recent incident to the therapist, she wanted to know more about my previous encounters with Grace and how we ended up in the current dynamic. I told her everything about our past dealings—from my perspective, of course. I was a little embarrassed, initially, but spoke frankly nonetheless. The therapist suggested that my problems with Grace went back to my childhood. They were rooted in my relationship with my sister and the competition between us for our father's love. My sister, Elvira, was completely in the dark about any of this.

But the moment the therapist said it, I had a catharsis. I broke down and sobbed. I saw myself doing things as a little kid, when I was five or six years old. The competitiveness I felt toward my sister was a big clue in understanding my personality. It helped explain my drive, my will to do things perfectly and better than anyone else. The therapist said that in order to counteract this negative energy, I should send out love. She taught me a mantra to use to surround the person and the negative situation with love and light.

THE CONCERT to celebrate Marian Anderson's eightieth birthday was scheduled on January 31, 1982. Actually, Miss Anderson had taken a few years off her age, which several singers did. She was born in February 1897, so it was really her eighty-fifth birthday we would celebrate. The concert was being heavily promoted as two celebrated rivals, two black women, pitted against each other in a cutting contest. The idea seemed to work. Someone told me that a man went up to buy tickets for the concert and asked for tickets to the "feud." The public had no idea how close to cancellation that concert had come.

Harold C. Schonberg, the *New York Times* magazine music critic, wrote a story for the January 17, 1982, edition, entitled, "A Bravo for Opera's Black Voices." Grace and I were in costume for the cover of that issue. I wore my favorite costume from the recently revived Met *Tosca* production, complete with headwrap and peacock feathers.

Grace wore a costume from *La Gioconda,* I believe. The photo session was shot by the celebrated photographer Annie Leibowitz.

Grace and I appeared on the late-night *Dick Cavett Show.* We both dressed in purple and sang the letter duet from Mozart's *Marriage of Figaro.* Dick Cavett made the point that our first joint public performance was *not* on the stage of Carnegie Hall but on his show. The Carnegie Hall concert itself was sold out. We both sang well, and Eve Queler and the American Opera Orchestra were in great form.

Grace's arms were the first to hug me at the end when we finished Bellini's "Mira o Norma." There were tears in her eyes. God is good. He works in mysterious ways. This was a real turning point for me in our relationship.

Miss Anderson, frail but radiant with her beautiful white hair, was at the concert. Her presence made the strained relationship between Grace and me seem a little trivial. Neither of us might have achieved our celebrity had it not been for her and her trials. Although Grace and I still had a tug of war, we did that program several times after the initial Carnegie Hall engagement.

WITHIN A few weeks, I returned to Boston to do a reprise of *Aida* with the Boston Opera. This run of the opera went better than the first time. I was still emotionally moved by singing the role. At the same time, I was also learning another new role to introduce at the Met, Leonora in Beethoven's *Fidelio.* I had coached it with Warren Wilson before the Met's rehearsals but felt under the weather, physically.

Leonora was not a role I was particularly interested in, but Joan Ingpen of the Met management persuaded me to do it. I was hesitant but talked it over with a few associates and acquiesced to do the opera. My performances weren't strong, and I was panned in the reviews. I should have been. I was again having allergy attacks and withdrew from the production, to be replaced by Joanna Meier. I went to the countryside to rest. Then Joanna Meier became ill, and the Met management called me to ask me to come back and sing in *her* place. I agreed to do it but really didn't have the stamina. I just stood and sang, but the big arias weren't strong. I was foolish, because those people had paid to see Shirley Verrett do the role properly and I also disappointed them. I also disappointed myself.

The audience comes to hear at least a good performance. If some illness comes on, and you feel that you can make it through without damaging your vocal cords, you should make an announcement before beginning the performance. I believe the audience will take that into consideration. When you go out knowing that you shouldn't have gone out, and you don't make an announcement, be prepared for the results. I always took that responsibility on myself. If I sang badly, it was my mistake. I never put the blame on anyone else.

Part of my reason for writing this book is to explain what was going on in my life during those times. I had edema as a result of the menopause. It is typical for women to get edema, which means you get water under the vocal cords or in other places in the body. I talked about my symptoms a lot at that time, in hopes I would get some guidance. I looked healthy, so people just couldn't understand my situation. I was going through hell. I was still doing recitals, but during those years, I had to cancel several of those as well. The allergies also reemerged during this part of my career. I could sometimes feel a hot flash coming on during the middle of a phrase, as I sang onstage. It began as a gradual heating up of my chest, followed by a rush of heat to my face and body. I started to combat it by returning to the diet I had when I was a Seventh-Day Adventist. I had always eaten fruits and vegetables. I continued to drink herbal teas, especially those that were supposed to relieve allergies and menopausal conditions. I also read everything I could find on the topic.

Menopause complicated my life in a variety of ways. My bronchial tubes became full. When I started the estrogen treatment, I gained weight and had to take a diuretic to release the water, but that didn't take it from around my vocal cords. I wasn't sleeping very well either. I eventually saw a physician in Louisiana, Dr. Bellina, who suggested that I get estrogen and progesterone injections to help me sleep. I was in New Orleans to do *Tosca* and met him through a friend, who happened to be in the city while writing a book with the doctor. I began to sleep all right, but there were side effects.

I gained even more weight. My breasts enlarged and grew almost two cup sizes. The treatment also exacerbated a fibroid condition I had had for years, but that had caused no problems before the estrogen treatment. After treatment began, the fibroids grew and I had to have a partial hysterectomy. They had become the size of a grapefruit over my uterus, which was otherwise in very good shape. I saw the fibroids on an X-ray. The gynecologist couldn't peel the fibroids off, so he had to take out the uterus, but he left the ovaries. The effect of that procedure caused a weakening of my body. I'll come back to the severity of what I experienced, because it continued to manifest itself in my career.

THE *Fidelio* incident further eroded my relationship with the Met. After Schuyler Chapin left the Met management, I was with Columbia Artist Management, and that firm wasn't handling my career the way I thought it should be handled. A conflict might come up with Jimmy Levine or someone else at the Met, and my management just suggested that we let things "happen naturally," instead of setting up a meeting to talk things out, as Basil Horsfield would have done. It was an unhappy situation and I take 50 percent of the blame. I recall refusing offers to do eight operas at the Met.

I was not invited to sing at the Met's centennial celebration in 1983. This was an apparent fall from grace. I was, however, invited as a guest and went backstage to stand with former Met artists and current colleagues. Levine had asked me to do Mozart's *La Clemenza di Tito* and made it clear that I could do whatever role I wanted. I said no. I also declined another Met tour, which was also a mistake, because touring is how you continued to cement a following for recitals, to fill a concert hall, particularly in the midwestern markets.

Filling halls was getting harder for everyone. It got to a point where even Joan Sutherland couldn't do it. This is when Massimo Bogianckino's call came.

*   *   *

I FIRST met Massimo Bogianckino in Italy in the early 1970s, when he had been the sovrintendente with the Rome Opera and later director of the Florence Opera Company. He had wanted me to sing for him for a long time, but the right opportunity had not presented itself. There were just so many opera houses and concert halls that one could sing in during a six-month period, which was the limit to my being away from home. He was leaving Italy to become general manager of the Paris Opera and wanted me to go there with him as one of his featured artists.

Bogianckino and I met again in 1972 in San Francisco, when I performed *L'Africaine* there. At the time, I explained my scheduling situation to him and my commitment to my husband to be away from home no more than six months of the year. He thanked me for my frankness. He also admitted that he had heard about my family arrangement but was glad I had explained it to him directly. He asked if I would sing with him if the opportunity arose. I told him I would be delighted. It took eleven years for that to happen, but we worked it out. Basil helped to put things in place in Paris. This seemed to be the opportune time, given the difficulties I was having at the Met. I discussed it with Lou and he agreed to the plan, because France would be a different place for us. We stayed in Paris for three years, from 1983 to 1986.

I wasn't scheduled to leave for Paris until the summer of 1983, and I had several engagements to finish in the United States before going. I had another *Norma* scheduled for Boston in April. This was a new production that Sarah Caldwell mounted especially for me. It was a wonderful production, and I *loved* the costumes Ray Diffen designed. He was wonderful; I had worked with him before in the revived *Tosca* at the Met.

For some reason, there was a big hoopla over this production, with pre- and post-production parties and interviews about singing that role. *Norma* still maintains that sacrosanct position in the operatic repertory, much more so than Lady Macbeth, which is, frankly, a more challenging role. It is strange!

The Boston production featured Rose Marie Freni as Adalgisa, Joseph Evans as Pollione, and Donald Gramm as Oroveso. I believe it was the last thing Gramm sang in Boston before his untimely death. In this production, Cessie, now ten, and Rose Marie's daughter, made up to look like boys, played Norma's children. It was Sarah's idea.

Musically, Sarah pulled out all the stops. This woman conducted like no one I had ever seen before. She inserted the sections that were traditionally cut, like the interim chorus of the "Casta Diva" cabaletta, "Sei lento, si sei lento, o giorno di vendetta" (You come slow, oh day of vengeance). The aria takes on a more extreme tone when that section is put back in, because Norma again quells the angry druids before reprising the cabaletta.

The dramatic trio with chorus that ends Act One was so exciting, because Sarah put back in Norma's repeats, which emphasized the intensity of her threat of vengeance against Pollione and Adalgisa. The applause was so thunderous when it ended. I was ready to repeat the trio with chorus, if Sarah had signaled us to do so. Her conducting gestures were so forceful, I thought she might strain a muscle. To see this short, stout woman in the pit, pulling that kind of sound out of the orchestra and singers, was astounding.

Norma has been one of my favorite roles of all time, but this was as close to a definitive performance as I can recall being in. I finally felt vindicated in this role, after the experiences at the Met and at Covent Garden in 1979. I not only sang well, I didn't overact in the confrontation scenes with Pollione and Adalgisa. I now felt that I *owned* the role. I would have been comfortable recording the Bellini, had the opportunity presented itself at that point. Even the music reviewer Robert Baxter, who had criticized me in the past, praised my performances. This is one production of this opera I can look back on with a great deal of appreciation, because everything seemed to come together. Rose Marie Freni was a superb Adalgisa and reminded me just how much I loved *that* role. We blended especially well in the duets.

One woman came backstage after the performance, still weeping at hearing the "Qual cor tradisti" ensemble at the end of the opera. Her expression brought tears to my eyes because it is such a touching moment in the drama.

The management in Boston had always been wonderful to me. It was an old theater, which meant lots of mold, so they covered my entire dressing room with heavy wrapping paper to keep the mold in check. They had people scrubbing like mad to keep the bathrooms clean. I loved Boston. I always did. Sarah and I had a wonderful working relationship. She could always put an entirely different spin on various opera roles and productions. She is a gifted individual and a fabulous musician. This was the reason I happily returned to Boston each time I was invited.

A few weeks before *Norma* opened in Boston, I sang a recital in London, in which Geoffrey Parsons accompanied me. The recital was wonderful. I sang Schubert's "Gretchen am Spinnrade" and "Ganymed," as well as Strauss's "Befreit," "Fünfzehn Pfennige," "Wiegenlied," and "Zueignung." I also did a Brahms set, and that recital went well. Everything was lined up and in place for the big sojourn to Gay Paree.

PARIS AND New York are so different. In New York, you can shop anytime you want to, even on Sunday. In Paris, there is a great sense of relaxation. You have more time to meditate. You're not in a business mode, 24-7. In Paris, they take real time off for lunch. The smaller businesses close up shop for the summer or at least for a month and a half. Life's slower. It's also easier.

When it comes to ideas and culture, though, I don't believe those clichés about the French being smarter or more culturally sophisticated than New Yorkers. The French are not necessarily more intellectual or more opera- or theater-oriented. I can find the same culturally sophisticated people in the United States and especially in New York and other big cities.

The move to Paris, the City of Light, was less traumatic for Lou and me than it was for Cessie. She was in the early stages of adolescence, where friends and peer pressure become paramount. She, of course, hated the idea of leaving New York and her friends for a foreign country. As a compromise/bribe, Lou and I told her she could have a dog when we arrived in France, provided we could find suitable housing that allowed pets. She had wanted a dog before, but I had vetoed that idea because of possible allergies and I didn't want to raise a dog in New York City. We bought a beautiful black poodle outside Paris but didn't give it a name right away.

Warren came for a visit shortly after our arrival. We were driving through southern France, and Warren asked Cessie what she would name her dog. She said, "I don't know." Just then we drove through a town named "Uchaux." Cessie and Warren began laughing at the name of the town, which she first pronounced as "O shucks," making fun of the town's name. Afterward, the name of the poodle stuck, "Uchaux" after the town in France.

When she arrived, Francesca was thrown neck-deep into the French language. We encouraged her at home by speaking French periodically there. She is still fluent in it today.

For the first three months, we rented an apartment from some friends, Christianne and Antonin Besse. We wanted a permanent place before the opera rehearsals started and, eventually, with the help of our new banker and friend Bernard Soubrane, found a beautiful apartment. He had an apartment in the same building. Ours was huge and shaped like a horseshoe. We had four bedrooms, each with a bathroom; a large dining room; a living room; and a music studio. From the front balcony we could see the Invalides, where Napoleon is buried. The back balcony overlooked a beautiful garden. It was wonderful. I had always wanted to live in Paris and enjoyed my time there. It was a delight to walk the streets, seeing the lights, and crossing the Alexandre III Bridge to go home from rehearsals and performances. Paris is such a romantic city.

Lou was also ready for a change. Through his ingenuity, he created

a studio space in our apartment building. Each apartment had a cage
area in the basement known as a "cave." Lou set up appropriate lighting in the area and blocked off a wall, and it became his studio. He
also worked on a book and did a lot of his research at the Biblio-
theque Nationale in Paris. The work, *La Gravure en Taille douce*
(Etching and Engraving), was published in 1992. It outlines the history of most printmaking procedures over a period of five hundred
years. While there, he met a friend, Baronne Petra de Montigny, who
helped him get his book published by Flammarion.

My first production during the fall 1983 season was a staging of
Rossini's *Mosé*. In 1968 I had sung Sinaide in a concert version in Italian. The 1983 Paris production was in French. Although the role was
still in my voice after fifteen years, if the truth be told, the coloratura
wasn't as fast as before. The costumes weren't that flattering. Samuel
Ramey did a magnificent job in the title role. It was also the only time
I performed with Cecilia Gasdia, who sang Anaide. She was an
emerging name in the opera world, but I don't hear much of her today. She was a big Callas fan. She even had a poodle that "sang" like
Callas's dog. A recording of that performance was recently released.
When I heard it, once again I sounded much better in the role than I
had imagined I would at the time.

That December, Grace and I did a reprise of our joint recital at
Covent Garden in London. The performance was videotaped for
broadcast in Europe and the United States. The conductor was
Michelangelo Veltri, leading the Royal Opera House Orchestra. They
cut out the most important duet, which was from Donizetti's *Anna
Bolena:* "Dio, che mi vedi in core" (God, who sees into my heart).
This is the dramatic meeting between Anne Boleyn and Jane Sey-
mour. As far as I was concerned, it was the best singing we did jointly.
We were told that the duet was too long. This was upsetting, because
it was a nice showpiece.

It seemed to come out of the clear blue sky, but when I received
this official-looking package from the French government, I hesitated
briefly before opening it. To my complete shock, I had received the

government's Commandeur des Arts et des Lettres (Commander of Arts and Letters), which is given to those whom the government believes have significantly contributed to cultural and world development through the performing or literary arts. I had no idea I was even being considered. I had received the Chevalier des Arts et Lettres in 1970 and made a big deal about it. These awards are not given out lightly. The Commandeur is much more prestigious. I did not quite know how to respond. There was no ceremony, no one to thank. When I inquired, I never found out if anyone even nominated me. I do pride myself on its receipt and wear the pin for any public event I attend.

IN THE summer of 1984, I debuted at the Verona Arena as Tosca. The performances were spectacular. The sets and everything were wonderful. Every time I sang the big aria "Vissi d'arte" (I lived for art), I had to repeat it, because the audience wouldn't let me continue the opera. The rain stopped one performance for about a half hour. Montserrat Caballé had told me some years earlier that they had a policy at the arena of not refunding the money to the audience, so if it rained, the singers just sat around until it stopped. She said she had known of performances to last until 2:30 A.M.! In fact, during the same summer, several of my colleagues had to wait well into the morning when the weather interrupted the performance.

The performance space was so huge, I had to begin walking from backstage toward the stage nearly a minute before singing, "Mario, Mario!" I had attended performances there as an audience member years before but had no idea how large the stage actually was from the other side. Even the orchestra pit seemed twice the size of one in a regular theater. Acoustically, the space was fine. As I recall, I was the first of three singers to sing Floria Tosca in the run of the opera that summer. Even more singers did Cavaradossi and Scarpia. Giacomo Aragall was one of the tenors with whom I sang, though. The management of the Verona Arena wanted me to come back to do *Aida* and several other roles over the years, but I decided not to, because singing outdoors wasn't that good for my health. I hardly ever did it, and this was especially true in my later years.

ON NOVEMBER 26, 1984, my Juilliard teacher and friend Madame Marion Freschl died in New York. I flew in from Paris for the memorial service. I was supposed to sing for it but felt I wouldn't hold up well enough to make it through such a performance. Instead, organizers played a recording I had made of Brahms's *Four Serious Songs* when I studied with her. Then I spoke some words in her memory.

I had seen Madame Freschl before I left the United States for France. She and I became estranged during the late 1960s, because of a misunderstanding stemming from her comments about a recital I had done in New York, but we got back on good terms by the late 1970s. By the time of her death, her health and memory had declined significantly. It was necessary to repeat things to her several times before she remembered them. It was difficult to see her in that state, because she had been such a vital and caring human being.

In 1984, Basil decided to do an hour-length documentary of my life. It was a British production, although I was living in Paris, which is where it was filmed. The film crew followed me around to several rehearsals and performances. The documentary included footage from the La Scala production of *Carmen* in 1984, as well as from several Paris Opera productions I starred in, including a new production of Gluck's *Iphigenie en Tauride*.

During the filming, I took Francesca and our neighbor's daughter on a skiing trip to Switzerland. I was on skis the first day after going through the training instructions. I became a little ambitious and was skiing down a hill at about fifty miles an hour, which was too fast. I could not turn as I had been instructed and could not stop myself either. Finally, I told myself, Fall, Shirley! which we had been told to do if we got into trouble. As I did so, I stuck out my left arm at the last possible moment and sprained my wrist. I instantly saw stars. The pain was excruciating! Two days later, though, I was back on the ski slopes.

For some reason, the production crew didn't show me skiing in the documentary, but, unless I am not mistaken, they caught my spill on camera. They did, however, film me trying on clothes in the Missoni Paris boutique and singing on the balcony of my apartment, on boats, outside of castles, and, of course, in opera houses during performances. The documentary ended up being a contemporary portrayal of me. I sang several popular songs, such as, "With a Song in My Heart," "I Love Paris," and "Hello, Young Lovers," and even did the Hall Johnson arrangement of "Witness." The *Shirley Verrett: Film Biography* was shown in the United States on the Bravo channel. The pianist who accompanied me in the documentary was Chris Walker. Aside from Geoffrey Parsons, while I was in Europe, I worked with one other pianist, Christian Ivaldi. Christian is a superb accompanist and musician, and we performed together many times throughout Europe. He was a joy to work with, because he wasn't excitable, was always very helpful, and threw no tantrums.

The production of Gluck's *Iphigenie en Tauride* was quite elaborate. The metteuse-en-scene, or director, was Liliana Cavani. She is very well known in Europe, mostly as a movie director. Liliana was an effective director but wanted me to sing in some contorted positions. She really loved Gluck's operas, many of which are not well known, apart from *Orfeo*. This was only my second role by him, but I soon added the title character of *Alceste* to my repertoire.

Alceste opened at the Paris Opera in May 1985. It was my first time singing the role, and Pier Luigi Pizzi directed the performances. He also designed the sets and costumes. One of the dresses was a gorgeous deep-blue satin gown. *Alceste* was another tour de force, and again I was in wonderful shape for the performances. Barry McCauley sang Ademete in the run of the opera. It was a promising young voice, and he was a natural actor, right down to the eye gestures.

GRACE BUMBRY and I did the joint concert again in Los Angeles and San Francisco in the summer of 1985. On our way to a rehearsal in the limousine, Grace looked at me and said, "Shirley, you've changed." Tears were streaming down her face. Little did she know that I had prayed mega-prayers for this change. I had taken the therapist's advice, to surround our recent relationship with love and light. Since then, we have been friends.

Mother, Dad, Elvira, David, Milton, Leon Jr., and Ronnie all attended our Los Angeles concert. I have to say, I really sang well, both there and at the San Francisco performance.

You can imagine how surprised I was when the *Los Angeles Times* music critic tore both of us apart! My sister read the review and said that she must not have been at the same concert as him. For the first time in my life, I called a music critic to challenge him on what he wrote. I asked him how he could say I didn't sing well? As it turned out, he had a grudge against Grace from years before.

That encounter was one more reason for me to take what music critics say with a grain of salt, especially after I already had an established career. Sometimes they are just carrying out personal vendettas. Grace and I were supposed to have sung the same concert at Wolf Trap, in Vienna, Virginia, but I had to cancel because my allergies flared up big time at my parents' home. I literally couldn't speak. I know it had something to do with the air-conditioning system.

MUCH OF the summer of 1985, I rested. In fact, I was required to rest a mandatory six weeks, the minimum time after having the surgical procedure I had just undergone. I decided to come back from Paris to have a hysterectomy at Dr. Bellina's clinic in Metairie, Louisiana. I recuperated at the summer home that Lou and I had in the Catskills. I vocalized a little to keep things in place but did no heavy singing, which would have involved strenuous use of my abdomen.

Psychologically, the 1983–1985 seasons in Paris had been good ones for me. I had several wonderful engagements, and it seemed that my momentum and joy of performing were back. I was still dealing with the effects of menopause but was able to go onstage and deliver a solid performance. That was more important to my well-being as an artist.

Although Jean-Louis Martinoty replaced Massimo Bogianckino as director of the Paris Opera (under circumstances I did not fully understand or inquire about) before my three-year contract ended in 1986, I still had another major opera to do, Luigi Cherubini's *Médée*. Liliana Cavani also directed this production. She had a real flair for these dramatic operatic female characters. This was the second opera she directed me in, and, as was the case with Iphigenie, her interpretation of Medea was no less compelling.

Medea fluctuates between being the woman scorned and an evil sorceress–like creature. The latter wins the contest. She murders her children and stands outside the temple in glee, to watch the people run in fear of her evil. Liliana directed me to look as wild as possible, wide eyes included. It was almost as if Medea had gone insane. I discussed my preparation for this role at length with the Greek designer George Stavropoulos. He stressed the severity of a Greek woman murdering her husband's sons, as Medea does, as being tantamount to murdering her husband (i.e., his bloodline).

Liliana relied on a lot of symbolism, not unlike Giorgio Strehler in the La Scala *Macbeth*. For example, she had my costume fitted with a long red sash, which I gradually pulled out of the cloak and formed into a circle. It was a symbolic trail of blood left by Medea.

Pinchas Steinberg graciously held the orchestra back in certain sections, because a good deal of the role lay in the middle of my range, which has always been the weakest part of my voice. He, too, had opinions about the music, which made this a striking and exciting production.

THE PARIS Opera performances of *Médée* were in February and March of 1986, but in April I had to come back to New York to sing Eboli in *Don Carlo* at the Met. Aprile Millo sang Elisabeth in those performances and her career began in a big way. I, too, enjoyed huge success in that production. Every time I finished "O don fatale," the audience applauded for several minutes after I left the stage. I thought once or twice that I would have to come back on again. Although I was not on the best of terms with the Met managers at the time, they knew I could still sing rings around most people when they needed a big name for *Don Carlo* or *Il Trovatore.*

Just a few years earlier, after that disastrous *Fidelio,* critics claimed I had lost my voice and announced that my career was over. Nonsense. It is irresponsible of some writers to say such things, because the voice isn't a mechanical device. The vocal cords are muscles, subject to stress (emotional, physical, and psychological) just like every other muscle in the body. Luciano Pavarotti cracked on one note in a performance of *Don Carlo,* and it was heard around the world. We heard that he was through. I guess that sells papers. They predicted that Plácido Domingo would lose his voice if he sang *Otello.* He was *still* singing it years after having first performed the role.

I never have come to terms with that kind of criticism, but I have learned to live with it. It is like being in a Roman arena. If you don't perform well, be prepared to be torn to shreds. It made me somewhat reclusive, because I always had to think about protecting my voice and my health. I felt obliged to stay alone on many occasions. In this business, you are only as good as how well you sang the day before. Of course, I had loyal fans, but some people just move on to the next "flavor of the month." This is, however, the career I chose, or perhaps it chose me. You have to take what comes.

RIGHT AFTER the Met *Don Carlo* run, I had to go back to Europe for several recitals in Italy. I was supposed to sing Cherubini's *Medea* (in Italian) with Sarah Caldwell and the Boston Opera in June, but we had a conflict. Sarah wanted me there for four weeks of rehearsal, but since I already knew the opera, I felt I could give no more than three. She had an elaborate, but potentially effective, change for the production that involved doing the recitatives in Greek and English. The process got a little complicated, and I didn't feel I could spare the time. It created some tensions between Sarah and me, because I had looked forward to singing Medea again. As it turned out, the sets Sarah planned to use in the production were being shipped from overseas. There was a complication in the arrival. Since the sets and costumes for *Tosca* were available, we agreed to substitute the Puccini for the Cherubini. The performances were in early June. The *Medea* tickets had already been printed, so although I did *Tosca,* the tickets had *Medea* printed on them.

I did, however, go back to Europe to do the soundtrack for the film version of *Macbeth,* scheduled to be on location the following summer. After the recording was complete, Lou, Francesca, Uchaux (the dog), and I packed up to come back to the United States. The transition to New York wasn't that bad. I think it was harder on my family than on me, since I was so accustomed to traveling during my career.

WHEN I left Paris in 1986, I symbolically left behind a dear friend of more than twenty years, Basil Horsfield. The year before, I had informed him that I would be leaving his management. Given the closeness of our relationship, readers deserve an explanation of how we separated after such a long and fruitful association.

In the early 1980s, Basil went through a traumatic experience when he and his business and personal partner, John Davern, split up after eighteen years. It was a friendly separation, but Basil began to lose focus and drink heavily. He sustained a serious injury when he fell down a flight of stairs and had to be hospitalized. He healed quickly enough, but he wasn't the same old Basil. He forgot appointments, certain schedulings, and generally was not working at the level I was accustomed to from him.

I, too, was at a crossroads, because I knew I wouldn't be singing much longer, so it seemed like the right time to move on where management was concerned. I invited Basil to lunch in Paris to tell him about my decision. He was startled, but persistent about continuing. I tried to soften the situation by saying that I didn't expect to be performing much longer, but he maintained that we could work together another ten to fifteen years! I gently but firmly told him that although this was the end of our professional relationship, our personal friendship would always remain intact. I kept my word to him. Unlike the departures from Siegfried Hearst or Herbert Barrett, I remained friendly with Basil. I had no choice. There was too strong a bond. I loved him very much. He had been the architect of my career for two decades, a trusted friend, a confidant, and an adviser.

I HAD several major engagements coming up that fall of 1986 but had to withdraw from a performance of *Tosca* with the Connecticut Opera. There was a new production of *Macbeth* with the San Francisco Opera in November, led by Terry McEwen. Pier Luigi Pizzi designed the sets and costumes for the production. I didn't sing the high D-flat at the end of the sleepwalking scene, because I had difficulty singing that passage with the pianissimo, as I had when I first began singing the role. Terry gave me an alternate passage. Deborah Voigt, the singer playing Lady Macbeth's lady-in-waiting, caught my eye. She was paying very close attention to what I was doing onstage and was very complimentary. Deborah is now a beautiful and successful singer and has become a celebrated interpreter of Lady Macbeth in her own right. That is a significant talent, which I fully expect to see flourish even more in the future.

In December 1986, I did a Christmas concert with the Mormon Tabernacle Choir in Salt Lake City, Utah. The program, carried on PBS channels around the country, was called *Christmas with the Mormon Tabernacle Choir and Shirley Verrett*. I sang standard Christmas carols, including several with chorus, but I recall the music director, Jerold Ottley, being particularly well-prepared. I would have felt comfortable with him conducting me in an opera. He paid close attention to detail, and his gestures were extremely clear and precise. The people in Salt Lake City were also very gracious and made my appearance a grand affair. Because PBS was broadcasting it for fundraising purposes, I was asked to make a fundraising pitch. I believe this is when the idea of doing voice-overs first occurred to me. That program was shown for several years during the Christmas season. I wore a beautiful Stavropoulos-designed silver gown and was just gleaming. I also wore my hair in braids then. I frequently wore wigs when I performed, but the braids were stylish and I sported them proudly, just as I had the Afro.

M Y   N E X T   outing with *Macbeth* was not so fair as the San Francisco performances. To be honest, I could very easily have avoided discussing this production of the opera, because recalling it is quite painful. Since it was a part of my career, I should relate the incident. I was scheduled to sing Lady Macbeth with the Rome Opera House in February and March 1987, with plans to return to this country to sing *Aida* in Miami. The performance was a disaster and I take full responsibility for the outcome. I became ill, because they were doing renovations in the Hotel Quirinale, which is where I was staying. It was a block away from the opera house. I stayed in the Verdi suite, as usual. Elena Obraztsova was in Rome to appear in a production of *Carmen,* but she, too, became ill and had to withdraw from a few performances.

It was a wonderful production of the opera, with Giorgio Pressburger directing, Renato Bruson singing Macbeth, and Giuseppe Patane conducting. During the dress rehearsals, I showed off by singing "O patria mia" (O my country) from *Aida,* because I planned to sing the role after returning to the United States. Some large pots on the stage were producing smoke for the witches' scene. I walked by one at the dress rehearsal and whatever was in it burned my throat so badly that when I got back to the hotel, I could hardly speak, much less sing. I saw a physician, who gave me medicines, but I still couldn't manage a full octave. All I could do was speak.

On opening night I was begged by the opera company to go on and finally I decided to *speak* the role instead of singing it. It was the worst moment of my entire career! I made a fool of myself. When the audience realized what I was doing, some of them became agitated. Predictably, I got catcalls and hisses, but others wanted to hear me speak it. My friend Alessandra Bonsanti, who was in the audience, asked me, "What were you thinking?" I thought I was helping to save a performance, but it was still a *dumb* thing to do.

To make matters worse, this was my debut at the Rome Opera. I had sung several recitals in the hall before but never an opera. I didn't make it through the first act. I just walked off the stage and went back to the hotel, where I should have stayed in the first place. The management canceled the rest of that evening's performance. The company had goofed as well, because it had not provided an understudy. Ghena Dimitrova was called, to take over at least one or two of the performances. I stayed around Rome for two weeks, hoping for a recovery, but nothing changed. Whatever it was, was deep down in my trachea.

The report of the performance went out over Associated Press, United Press International, Reuters, and several other news organizations. "Verrett has lost her voice!" I read in one of them. If anyone had bothered to ask, I would have explained that I did it knowing I couldn't sing that performance but wanted to help the management of the Rome Opera. I have referred to certain things I did before as mistakes, but going onstage under those circumstances was *stupid.* I strongly advise against it, because the audience ultimately does *not* appreciate such a stupid sacrifice, nor should they!

Our egos can sometimes get the better of us. I have certainly been guilty of this. The only thing I could possibly salvage from that experience was my determination to continue. I absolutely would *not* leave the stage under these circumstances. I felt that my very reputation and legacy were at stake at this point. After my recovery from that Rome *Macbeth* fiasco, I probably would have sung free recitals, just to demonstrate to the public that I still had a voice. Fortunately, that wasn't necessary. I was able to give other first-rate performances for several more years. Most important, my fans, who still believed in me, forgave me. A final irony is that my friend Richard LeSueur told me of a pirated copy of that Rome *Macbeth* performance. When I am ninety-five, I may bring myself to listen to it. Maybe my hearing will be gone by then.

PART FOUR

14

My Greatest Fan

I T   T O O K close to three months for me to recover from that Rome *Macbeth* debacle, and I obviously had to cancel the *Aida* perform- ances in Miami, as well as a few other engagements. I was well enough to return to Europe that summer of 1987 to participate in the film version of *Macbeth*. I had recorded the soundtrack the summer before, with Leo Nucci singing the title role and Riccardo Chailly con- ducting. The soundtrack was also released as a commercial recording of the opera.

Claude d'Anna directed the film version of the opera. It was a big production with a large crew. D'Anna wanted a primitive look. Our costumes were large, dark gray with fur, and very heavy. There were helmeted guards in practically every scene, all suggesting medieval Eu- rope. We were on location in the Ardennes in a Belgian castle that had once belonged to the celebrated Crusades warrior Godefroy de Bouil- lon. The production lasted several weeks, and we lip-synced the music.

Filming at four in the morning was so cold, you could see your breath as you spoke or mimicked the singing. Sometimes we sat around for retakes, which could take hours in those heavy costumes

and makeup. I loved *every* moment of it, though. There was such ca-
maraderie among the cast and crew, I hated to finish filming. We had
wonderful dinners and occasional tours around the very beautiful
Belgian countryside. There is a custom in the film world for the principal actors to host a dinner for the entire crew during filming, which
I was more than happy to do.

Much of the production was shot outside. For example, the
witches in the opening scene emerged from caves at dusk. They were
actresses with long black wigs, wearing only loincloths and with dirt
smudged all over their bodies. They looked more like prehistoric
cavewomen crawling around than like modern human beings. Plenty
of corpses were strewn all over the filming site. Some were impaled,
some hanging from ropes around their necks; all were fake, of course.

Lady Macbeth's first big scene was filmed in the dungeon of the
castle. As I sang the first aria, I walked through various portals, descending to deeper levels of the cavernous dungeon. I ended the cabaletta by burning Macbeth's letter and dropping it into a bottomless
pit. The whole scene was very dark and ominous. While rehearsing
the scene where the Macbeths meet after the murder of Duncan,
Macbeth refused to release the blood-stained dagger. I got caught up
in the scene and spontaneously reached down to bite his hand to
force him to drop it. I don't know where the gesture came from, but
D'Anna liked it and decided to keep it in. Playing that role could
bring out primal emotions and gestures from you.

Samuel Ramey sang the role of Banquo for the recording, but a professional actor portrayed the role in the film. Veriano Luchetti finally
got his opportunity to record Macduff, but that part, too, was portrayed by a professional actor in the film. I loved watching professional
actors work and asked many questions about their interpretations,
to compare them with mine. I was curious about the differences in
how singers (many of whom are not known for their acting skills) got
such roles under their belt, in contrast to methods used by professional actors.

I worked hard on the sleepwalking scene, which was creatively filmed. For example, in the musical prelude leading up to it, the witches emerged while scavenging from a banquet table, where they competed for leftovers with live rats! This was an eerie setting for the scene. I moved within a contained part of the castle, and as the scene ended with the high D-flat, I descended into a pit. It was a wonderful effect on the big screen.

I had to take certain tempos a little more slowly because my muscles weren't responding as they had before. I made some fond relationships as a result of the *Macbeth* project, and I am proud of the results of that production.

According to theater world folklore, to utter the word *Macbeth* is believed to bring bad luck, and many can tell stories of mishaps surrounding productions of the Shakespeare play. Yet with the obvious exception of that Rome experience, it has been a good luck role for me. I thought the film would be my last formal involvement with the Verdi opera, but I was talked into singing in a production in Japan in 1988. Justino Diaz sang Macbeth, and the rest of the cast was Japanese. It was a befitting conclusion to my thirteen-year association with this wicked grande dame.

IN JULY 1987, Lou, Francesca, Shody (my nickname for Uchaux), and I moved to California. I was tired of living in New York and wanted to go home. I also wanted my daughter to get to know her relatives on the West Coast. After returning from France and entering high school, Francesca became a proper black nationalist. She wanted to wear her hair in an Afro and talk about the white man's injustices to black people. I think some of the rhetoric may have hurt her father's feelings, but I knew it was a phase teenagers go through. Earlier, I had advised her to identify with her African American heritage, because her life would be a little easier than if she tried to straddle the fence. I had seen enough of passant blanc when I was young in New Orleans.

Lou wasn't too thrilled with the idea of moving to California but went along because he wanted to please me. We bought a beautiful huge home in the East Bay area, complete with an indoor swimming pool and a lovely tennis court. The person who sold it to us was a fan of mine and wanted me to have the house. We lived there for only four months, though, because I found that one cannot go back home. One good thing did come from being on the West Coast: for those four months, I got a chance to spend some quality time with Dad, who had been diagnosed with prostate cancer and was in poor health by then. We did a lot of talking, though.

I told him, among other things, that if I had to choose my parents, even with the strictness of the Seventh-Day Adventist Church they had imposed on me, I would have chosen him and Mother all over again.

I felt profoundly aware of how Leon Verrett Sr. had affected my life in ways he had never known and I had barely understood before. Sitting in the presence of this now frail old man, who had defined the essence of responsible manhood in my life, earlier experiences and feelings came back to me as if pouring through a floodgate.

In the early 1970s he and I were a bit estranged because of a business deal that went bad. I remember talking to him calmly on the telephone one night, and the next thing I knew, I was yelling at the top of my voice about things that had irked me as child. It is amazing what you can drag up and use against your parents, regardless of how privileged a life you have had. I had never done such a thing before. I was immediately sorry and cried out of shame for my behavior. After that incident I felt so guilty, I can't recall even raising my voice to him again.

Through all of this I never lost my love for Dad. I could identify better with his view of raising a child now that I had one of my own. I certainly had more than a few episodes with Francesca, and she was an only child who lived an even more privileged life than I had. Dad had raised six children to responsible adulthood.

He taught us to keep on trying, to never give up. The word *can't* was not acceptable. He never gave up. I am sure it was because of him that I was determined to continue my career, even with some of my maladies.

*   *   *

I MADE my debut as Azucena in *Il Trovatore* with the Chicago Lyric Opera during the 1987 fall season. I was trying hard to fight a cold and doing all kinds of holistic treatments to avoid it. I soaked my feet in cold water and then in hot water. I drank a lot of wheatgrass juice. I wanted to keep the cold in my head, because once it moved to my chest, I could not have sung.

Luciano Pavarotti was the announced Manrico, but illness caused him to withdraw from the production one week before it opened. He received a lot of bad press about it, and the Lyric Opera managers said they would never invite him to sing with the company again. Fortunately, I made it through just fine.

It was hard for me to deliver a bad performance of Azucena. I had been singing the role for nearly twenty years and had not become bored with the character even once. Anna Tomowa-Sintow sang Leonora, and Leo Nucci and Piero Cappuccilli alternated as Count Di Luna. It was the first time I had sung with Cappuccilli in a long while. I believe this was the last time we performed together onstage. Cappuccilli was scheduled to sing all of the performances but felt under the weather, so Leo Nucci flew in from the West Coast and sang a few performances until Cappuccilli could re-assume the role. Giuliano Cianella, the tenor who stood in for Pavarotti to sing Manrico, was scheduled to take over later in the engagement, but he ended up singing all of the performances.

That was the only time I sang with the Chicago Lyric Opera. The company had asked before, but the management at Columbia had vetoed a few things without consulting me. Herbert Breslin told me that a few opera companies, including San Francisco, felt that I had slighted them, because my management hadn't handled negotiations properly. Breslin had me call and personally speak with the management there, and some of the misunderstandings were laid to rest.

After the *Trovatore* performances, Lou, Francesca, Shody, and I left California and moved back to New York City. We later built a home in Warwick, New York.

I had a scheduled performance of *Norma* in Paris, but it didn't take place. I can't remember why I didn't sing it, because I had another performance scheduled in Monte Carlo at the beginning of 1988. The Monte Carlo run of *Norma* turned out to be my last performances of the opera.

It was a memorable *Norma* for several reasons. It was the first and only time I sang with this opera company. I enjoyed it because the theater was so quaint and tiny. It was a nineteenth-century–sized theater, which meant it was excellent for the voice.

This was a first-rate production of *Norma*. Pinchas Steinberg did a superb job with the orchestra and the chorus because they were exceptionally strong. He was also a precise conductor, and singers felt comfortable with him. I sang with a fine mezzo, Susanne Mentzer, who was a strong Adalgisa. Of the Adalgisas whom I sang with (close to ten different singers by then), she was memorable because of her musicianship and, more important, how well we blended in the duets. Hers was not a pushed or heavy sound. Her coloratura was also quite clean in the Norma/Adalgisa duets. Bonaldo Giaiotti was ever imposing as Oroveso. He was such a talented artist, whom I can never recall being late or canceling a performance. The Pollione was, perhaps, the weakest link in the production.

Then the call from Lou came. Dad had died. Because I was singing my last performance of *Norma* in Monaco, the family decided to hold the body until I arrived in California a few days later.

The final performance of the opera that I sang before returning to the United States was, as you might imagine, emotionally taxing. I was okay until the final act, where Norma pleads with her father to protect her out-of-wedlock children, "Deh! non voleri vittime" (Ah! do not let them be the victims). I suddenly got a rush of reality thinking of my father's death. The emotions started to come out in my singing. Tears began streaming down my face and I nearly stopped to cry. I paused for a few phrases in the aria to compose myself while the orchestra continued. Maestro Steinberg just glanced at me and kept things moving. Bonaldo Giaiotti sensed that something was wrong and physically held on to me. He obviously thought I had become too involved with the drama. I'm not sure if I told him afterward that my father had just died. After the performance, I said my good-byes and immediately left.

All I could think about on the flight back to the United States was the happy four months we had spent together. I felt some sense of peace about that. As he was dying, I spoke with him about my attitude about organized religion. Both he and Mother thought I should come back to the church.

My answer to both my parents was that I could not be what they wanted me to be as a Christian. I can only live my own Christianity. And my Christianity is within my soul and within my total belief in the goodness of man. Even though we live in a world of chaos, still I believe there is goodness in the world and that it is inside of me. I never had a religious conversion, as my parents did. I was born into the church, but my belief to this day is that I could not join another denomination.

Yet each person must decide for himself what is right. Despite his strict Adventist faith, my father was happy for me. What mattered most to him was that I was in music, doing what he had predicted for me all those years ago. Many years later, when he saw me in *Carmen* for the first time, he said, "Oh, boy, you're happy now, aren't you? You can do all the things you wanted to do and couldn't do as a child!"

But Dad had not died in peace. He was in a lot of pain, what would have been called in his mother's time a "hard death." The cancer had spread to his bones. Mother said that at the end, she prayed, "Please God, take him," because he was in so much pain. It was a terrible thing for him to go through.

Lou and I arrived from New York the day before the funeral, a painful experience for all my brothers, my sister, and me. I had never touched a dead person before, but during the visitation I kissed Dad's forehead. I immediately broke down and sobbed uncontrollably, letting out pent-up feelings. It was the last time I would see my daddy.

Mother couldn't go to the funeral. She had had a mild stroke and was in the hospital. It was probably a good thing, after all. After

Dad's death, Mother stopped sleeping in the master bedroom of their home, because she felt his presence there too strongly. He is buried in a crypt in a memorial park in Sacramento.

Leon Verrett Sr. was a good husband, father, and Christian man. I am very much like him, very opinionated. I often called him up and we got into very lively discussions. I look at his picture even today and say, "I wish you were still here to advise me." I know he is an ancestor now and is still providing his assistance in a spiritual way. I loved my father very much and he loved me. I became "Shirley Verrett" largely because he saw my possibilities. He was my greatest fan.

15

An End and a Beginning

DAD'S DEATH devastated me. I wanted to run away and hide, yet I knew he would never have approved. I did take some time off, though, just to deal with my feelings. Regardless of the relationship with your parents, you will miss them terribly after they die.

Lou sensed the pain I felt and took over many day-to-day things, just to give me a chance to recover. This was only one of the many ways in which he enriched my life, protected me, and supported my career. When it was time for me to return to the stage, he kept asking, "Are you ready?"

MY NEXT big opera production took me back to San Francisco. It was a revival of *L'Africaine*, which hadn't been in the repertoire of the company since I first performed in it sixteen years earlier, in 1972. Plácido Domingo returned with me, but everyone else was new. Ruth Ann Swenson sang Ines, and Justino Diaz sang Nelusko. It was one of those engagements where one performance would be strong and the next mediocre. I had obviously gained weight from the menopause changes since performing Selika in 1972. I asked for less-revealing costumes than before. I was especially sensitive about the size of my arms and insisted they be covered with sleeves or something. The stage was raked and, because of my weight gain, my breathing was more labored at times.

Some reviewers wrote that I was stronger in the role in 1988 than in 1972. One said I was experiencing a "vocal renaissance." In truth, I felt ill in one performance and didn't trust what my support was doing to keep my pitch in place. As I sang the lullaby to Vasco (Plácido), I asked him to give me a signal if he heard the pitch sagging. A thumbs-up sign meant for me to raise the pitch. Thank God, he had to signal me only once. He was wonderful, as always, both as a colleague and as a singer. The opera, overall, was very beautiful and I enjoyed it. I had forgotten what an impressive production it was. I sang Selika's death scene much better in the 1988 performances than I had done it earlier.

The others in the cast were just as strong. Justino Diaz and Ruth Ann Swenson were superb. Ruth Ann was just beginning as a young prima donna, and Justino, of course, was an old pro. He is still singing well, after more than thirty years on the stage. The conducting was certainly much stronger. Maurizio Arena was clearly in control. He had every phrase worked out in the score and had complete command of the orchestra, unlike the conductor of the 1972 performances. As it turned out, he knew quite a bit about the voice. He had coached singers and was interested in the blend of singers with the orchestra. Obviously, his direction put me at ease. Kurt Herbert Adler was still general manager at the time. I am glad the performance was filmed for commercial release. It gives me a chronicle of how I sang toward the late part of my operatic career.

SOON AFTERWARD I sang Berlioz's *La Mort de Cleopatre,* a work I had learned specifically for a concert at the newly renovated Carnegie Hall. John Eliot Gardiner led St. Luke's Chamber Orchestra in the work. I had begun to study the score a year earlier but put it away for a while. I had to coach it again with Warren as the performance date neared. I didn't enjoy singing the work very much, and I am not sure why. The music is actually quite beautiful. I think it had more to do with my experience in the hall.

The acoustics in the hall were not as good as they had been before the renovation. To tell you the truth, it was horrible to sing in. You had to stand facing straight out while singing. If you turned your head to the left or to the right, the sound was lessened. If your voice hit a certain spot, it sounded metallic. It was unfortunate, because I had sung so many wonderful performances in that hall. They were trying to minimize the sound of the subway or something, but it didn't work well. I believe that parts of the hall had to be redone after the initial renovation.

I LEFT for Europe right after the Berlioz performance, to star, along with Luciano Pavarotti, in another production of Donizetti's *La Favorita* in Venice. Pavarotti, however, did not sing Fernando but made his debut as a stage director. He asked me to be in the production because of our other collaborations; he had always liked the way I portrayed Leonora. The production was supposed to run from the middle of December through the end of the month, but it started later than scheduled and ran through the middle of January 1989.

Luciano did a good job as director. Pietro Ballo, one of Luciano's young protégés, sang Fernando. He had a very strong, lovely voice. He just needed to learn to be subtler in his singing. This production of *La Favorita* was a big break for him at the time. The singers who did Baldassare and Alfonso were also quite young but surprisingly strong.

When I finished the big aria, "O mio Fernando," the opera stopped. The applause seemed neverending. It reminded me of *The Siege of Corinth* at the Met. Minutes passed before we could start again.

Gabriele Ferro was the conductor, and I remember his *tempi* being a little slow. I had worked with him before, when he conducted me in an album of French arias for the Fonit Cetra label, which was a very good recording. It is hard to find in the United States, but I own several copies of it. Ferro was adequate as a conductor, but he was much loved in Venice. When he mounted the podium, the audience went wild.

I was in Italy for Christmas, one of the few times I was away from home during the holidays. Lou and Francesca joined me, and we had a beautiful Christmas in Venice. It was lovely at that time of year, because there were fewer tourists and one could really see and enjoy the magnificence of that great city. My family and I did a lot of shopping and sight-seeing. We visited Randy Mikelson and Pier Luigi Pizzi, who had magnificent homes in this divine city.

When I came back home in January, Luciano presented another one of his *Pavarotti Plus* programs. The telecast featured me, along with June Anderson, Ruggiero Raimondi, Sherrill Milnes, and several others. I think I sang a duet from *La Favorita* with Pietro Ballo, with whom I had sung the opera in Venice. I also sang the Macbeth/Lady Macbeth duet with Sherrill Milnes. Of course, we ended the program with the "Brindisi" from *La Traviata,* as had been the custom of the *Pavarotti Plus* series.

Before going on, I was backstage doing a yoga stretch, touching the floor, and then slowly rising up. It helps to circulate the blood and relaxes you. Luciano came over and asked what I was doing, so I told him. He started the stretch and, before I knew it, several of the other singers in the program were also doing it. It was quite a sight to see all of us bent over, dressed in evening wear.

A few weeks after this concert, I sang Aida for the third and final time in Boston. It was my first appearance with the company since the *Tosca* performances in 1986. My Aida was even stronger this time around. These were bittersweet performances, because my colleague and friend James McCracken had died a few years earlier. Jimmy was a seasoned Verdian tenor. It is unfortunate that he didn't record more, but at least our earlier performances of *Aida* were recorded, although not commercially available. I would really love to have a copy of that performance. The tenor, Franco Bonanome, who sang Radames, wasn't in Jimmy's league. David Arnold, on the other hand, was a stronger Amonasro than when we first sang the opera together. David is a real solid musician and also a talented pianist.

I HAD a relatively busy recital schedule in this country, but I also had a new project to complete in Europe. The film *Maggio Musicale* marked my big-screen debut in a speaking role. The movie also starred the tenor Chris Merritt and Malcolm McDowell as a frustrated opera producer, who runs into trouble when he attempts to direct a *very* temperamental opera singer (my character, can you imagine?) in a European production of Puccini's *La Boheme.* The project came about through Simonetta Lippi. The movie's director, Ugo Gregoretti, wanted me to be obnoxious as the American prima donna. In the death scene, where Mimi is supposed to be dying of tuberculosis or another of those "opera diseases," I appeared the antithesis of a tubercular woman as we rehearsed Mimi's death scene. Of course, Mimi is a role I never would have sung onstage.

The movie was not shown in the United States. It was supposed to have opened at a theater in New York City, but didn't, for some reason or another. I hope it does eventually, because I was quite pleased with the nonsinging part.

While I was in production of *Maggio Musicale,* I received a request from Luciano. He was recording *Rigoletto* again, this time with June Anderson as Gilda and Leo Nucci as the morally corrupt jester Rigoletto. Luciano asked as a personal favor that I participate in the recording to sing the relatively small role of Maddalena, who appears only in Act Four. Whomever was scheduled to do it had to back out. I agreed, after much coaxing, but requested a note be included with the recording that I was singing this role as a personal favor to Luciano. It wasn't a particularly suitable role for me to record, because it was so low. I didn't memorize the part but mostly worked from the score. Although I have always loved the music, the celebrated quartet "Bella figlia dell'amore" (Lovely daughter of love) forced me to use chest voice a little more than I wanted. The results were okay.

Maggio Musicale was my movie acting debut, but it wasn't my first opportunity to appear in a speaking role in a feature film. Although the 1984 movie *Diva* was based on an incident that happened to Jessye Norman, I was asked to appear in the film as the American opera singer. The writer had asked Basil Horsfield to speak about it to me. I was sent the script and I looked it over. For some reason they kept having production delays, so I didn't think it was very serious and withdrew from the project. It turned out to be a mistake, because that film became a cult classic. Wilhemina Hernandez did a superb job in it. When I eventually saw the finished film, I was a little surprised because the script I had seen had a more substantial role for the singer. The aria from Catalani's *La Wally,* which was featured in that film, was not the one I would have sung, had I done the movie. I don't think we even discussed what I would sing before I withdrew from the production. Given the film's great popularity, it would have had significant implications for my acting career.

JULY 14, 1989, was the bicentennial of France's Bastille Day, a celebration that was observed worldwide. To mark the occasion, the Opera Bastille was inaugurated with a star-studded gala featuring world-class opera stars, including Plácido Domingo, Alfredo Kraus, June Anderson, Barbara Hendricks, Ruggiero Raimondi, Teresa Berganza, and me. The evening was called "La nuit avant le jour" (The night before the day) and featured French opera arias, ensembles, and choruses. The women were given specially commissioned gowns by Yves Saint-Laurent, Christian Dior, Givenchy, and Christian Lacroix, among others. Mine, a Saint-Laurent original that I still own, is a beautiful gown of black and gunmetal gray silk taffeta with velvet trim. The men were as elegantly dressed in designer suits and tuxedos.

The French president, François Mitterand, was there, along with other world leaders, including Britain's Margaret Thatcher.

Georges Prêtre conducted the orchestra, and Robert Wilson directed the arias and ensembles. Prêtre and I were backstage, reminiscing about our thirty-plus years' association. He was just as feisty in the late 1980s as he had been in the 1960s. He is still one of my favorite conductors.

I was in good voice when I sang the celebrated aria from Gluck's *Alceste,* "Divinites du Styx" (Gods of the Styx).

FOR ABOUT a year the Met and I discussed my singing in a production of *Samson et Dalila.* It took me a long time to decide, for several reasons. It had been close to ten years since I had last sung the role. Also, it was too low for a voice like mine; I needed the correct conductor to make it work. But I finally decided to go ahead with it and went into rehearsal, to sing Dalila in February 1990 with my perennial Samson, Plácido Domingo. Under the circumstances, I couldn't have imagined a better colleague. John Macurdy was cast as the old Hebrew.

I knew from experience that if you had the wrong conductor for that opera, it could be *disastrous.* The Met management promised me a good conductor. Charles Dutoit was not that person. I spent a total of one half-hour with him in the studio to run through the entire score. Dalila was a role I hadn't sung in years, but that was not the biggest problem. I had been accustomed to ensemble rehearsals to achieve a greater vocal blend. There were no ensemble rehearsals with the other cast members. We went right to the stage. I think Dutoit was practicing on us, because he was about to record the opera, or so I was told. Because the duets were in a part of my voice that was weaker at that point, Plácido held back.

I was frustrated and angry at how the rehearsals were going. Then James Levine came onstage after one of the rehearsals and told me how *well* things were going! In my sometimes brutal honesty, I retorted, "I will never sing this role again!" I'm not sure whether I shocked him or not, but I once again proved myself to be too outspoken.

James Levine will always deserve respect. After all, he brought to the Met several African American singers, including Kathleen Battle,

Jessye Norman, and Florence Quivar. He really brought Florence in properly, because before that, they had her understudying roles. Her voice is far too striking an instrument for an understudy. Levine also brought several African American men into the ranks of the Met, including Vincent Cole, Gordon Hawkins, Arthur Thompson, Terry Cook, and the late Ben Holt.

But the performances of *Samson et Dalila* were so-so, from a vocal standpoint. I liked the drama of it all, but I wasn't altogether pleased with the singing. I had certainly done the role better. Nevertheless, after one of the performances, a group headed by the then president gathered in the green room and presented me with the twenty-fifth-year watch. It was a moving ceremony. It was significant because I had been with the company for only a little over twenty-two years. Florence Guarino had been instrumental in bringing the honor about. She strongly argued that I deserved recognition for many excellent performances with the company.

THE BASTILLE Opera performance of *Les Troyens* opened in March 1990. I sang Didon and Grace Bumbry sang Cassandra. Based on that opening performance, some reviewers claimed that I was finished, but I proved them wrong again, as I had in the past. The American critics must have come to my stronger later performances, because those were more favorably reviewed.

Because of a choral strike at the Bastille Opera, one show was suspended and had to be rescheduled. The rescheduled performance conflicted with a recital I was booked to do at La Scala Opera House. I had made the Bastille Opera management aware of this La Scala engagement when my contract for *Les Troyens* was signed. Therefore, they knew I would not be available for the rescheduled *Troyens* performance. But they announced that because I was "indisposed," Grace Bumbry would sing Cassandra and Didon in the same performance. They did not reveal my previously booked engagement. I put the blame for this mix-up on my French management's shoulders. But at least Grace got her opportunity to do what I had done seventeen years earlier at the Met.

MY LAST formal appearance at the Metropolitan Opera House took place in April 1990. I was called in to replace the scheduled Azucena in *Il Trovatore* at the end of April. Sharon Sweet was making her company debut as Leonora, and Franco Bonisolli sang Manrico. Hers was a good voice. Bonisolli was more interested in outsinging everyone than in totally involving himself with the drama, but I got along with him very well. When I look back on it, there couldn't have been a more fitting farewell opera for me at the Met.

I probably understood Azucena as well as any other role I had performed. The following June, I finally recorded it. Zubin Mehta conducted the orchestra and chorus of the Maggio Musicale Fiorentino, in a performance featuring Luciano Pavarotti as the Troubadour and Leo Nucci as Count Di Luna. Luciano Pavarotti and Leo Nucci had been wonderful friends and colleagues throughout my career. Antonella Banaudi, who sang Leonora, wasn't ready for a recording with a cast of this caliber. She told me she was a protégée of Carlo Bergonzi and had won a contest a few years before. She wasn't bad but needed a little more maturing. That may have been one of the reasons London Records (the label we recorded the opera for) didn't release this *Il Trovatore* until 1995, although we recorded it in 1990. I later learned that Antonella Banaudi was a replacement for Susan Dunn, a more established name, who was scheduled to be in the stage production and the recording. Luciano and Banaudi were in the stage performances of *Trovatore* at the Maggio, while Leo Nucci and I came in specifically for the recording.

I sensed this would be my last time doing the opera, almost certainly my only opportunity to record it commercially, so I went all out, with my usual high C at the end of Act III when Count Di Luna captures Azucena. I had fun.

*   *   *

THAT *Il Trovatore* was my final commercial opera recording but not my last opera performance. In 1989, on location with the film *Maggio Musicale* in Pistoria, Italy, I ran into my old friend Dr. Luciano Alberti, who had featured me in Donizetti's *Maria Stuarda* at the Maggio Musicale in Florence in 1967. He had become the sovrintendente of the opera company in Siena and asked me to come and sing Santuzza with his company the following summer. He said they were doing a new production of Pietro Mascagni's *Cavalleria Rusticana*. I couldn't say no. It was 1990. Nearly sixty years old, I was adding a new opera role to my repertoire! *Cavalleria* was double-billed with some music that Mascagni had composed for a film score. The orchestra played Mascagni's film score in the first part of the program, and *Cavalleria Rusticana* was done in the second half. The staging of *Cavalleria* marked the centennial of the opera.

The conductor, Baldo Podic, took time to communicate his ideas and solicit mine. Most important, he understood that I was performing the role for the first time and gave me the care and attention I needed.

Santuzza is very different from the other operatic grande dames I had performed, like Norma, Lady Macbeth, Tosca, Leonora, or even Azucena. Santuzza is a small-town woman who sacrificed her reputation by taking up with a younger man, Turiddu. This love interest ultimately betrays her. She then has to live as a disgraced woman, rejected by the small-town mentality that even forbids her to worship in church. She humiliates herself further by going to her lover's mother, begging the mother to intercede on her behalf. It wasn't an easy role for me to identify with.

The obvious solution for someone in Santuzza's position would be to leave the town and start fresh elsewhere. Instead, against the reality staring her in the face, she opts to cling to the hope of Turiddu returning. The sad thing is that she was probably no more than a fling for the suicidal Turiddu, who had always been interested in another woman, Lola. The sound of Lola's voice was enough to turn Turiddu's head. Santuzza plays the dejected, jealous, vengeful, and self-pitying woman all the way. For example, in her pleas to Turiddu, she says, "Battimi insulttami, t'amo e perdono" (Beat me, insult me, I still love and forgive you). Within a few minutes, she puts a curse of all curses on him, "May a Bloody Easter fall on you!" Of course, that's exactly what happens to him.

Perhaps, given my own personality, those were some of the areas of the character I found difficulty identifying with. Santuzza's weakness and, frankly, stupidity didn't appeal to me. At some level, though, many women make poor decisions when it comes to relationships. I was certainly not immune. This was how I ultimately made the role believable in my mind and portrayal.

Kristian Johannsson sang Turiddu, and he was very strong. He had a full voice, too large for the small theater we sang in. He was a good actor and has deservedly become a big-name artist.

Even then, I had made no firm decision to stop singing onstage. Other engagements were to come.

Before I left Italy, I did an all-Gershwin program in Positano. I was trying out my new program for future use. Simonetta Lippi was responsible for my performing the Gershwin. After some years of not seeing each other, we reunited in the Hotel Villa Medici in Florence and, after talking a long time, renewed our friendship.

Among the 250 people in that receptive and enthusiastic audience, one caught my attention almost immediately—Basil Horsfield. I hadn't seen him for some time, although we had maintained contact by telephone and an occasional letter.

The intervening years since we had last seen each other had not been kind to him. To put it bluntly, he was in a bad way. Basil had gained a lot of weight. He apologized for not getting to see me in the *Cavalleria* run but had followed the reviews of the production. Our conversation was warm and friendly, but there were awkward moments when I spoke about where I was performing. In the past he would have known my whereabouts. I tried to tone things down by saying how demanding it was, physically, to be onstage, and it was surely time for me to put this career behind. We parted with a warm embrace and promised to do better about staying in contact. I don't believe that six months passed before I received a call from his secretary, saying that he had died.

I GRADUALLY reached the decision to scale down my management and just stopped accepting opera roles. Allergies made my delivering consistent performances problematic. I also struggled with my weight. At one point it appeared as if I had a double chin when I opened my mouth to sing a high note. I could feel weight under my neck. My arms and hips were too heavy. I disliked my body at this time.

Yet this wound up being a busy period, anyway. In 1991 I had several engagements in Boston. I did a recital in April, my first there in more than a decade. The following month I returned to appear with the Boston Pops Orchestra, with John Williams conducting. The program highlighted music from the American Civil War era and was taped for broadcast on PBS in mid-May. That program also featured the legendary folk singer Odetta, my lifelong friend Roscoe Lee Browne, and the Harlem Boys' Choir. I was on the board of the Boys' Choir at the time.

An even bigger reward was the chance to return to Russia. By the late 1980s, Sarah Caldwell had made cultural strides in the former Soviet Union. She had recruited several singers there to appear with the Boston Opera and eventually began taking various U.S. artists with her to perform in Russia. She had invited me before, but in 1991 I was available and went. It had been nearly thirty years since I was last in Russia.

I did a recital in Moscow and sang, among other things, Schumann's song cycle, *Frauenlieben und Leben,* a group of Strauss songs, and a group of spirituals. They went over as well in 1991 as they had when I sang them in 1963.

My final concert in the Great Hall of the Moscow Conservatory closed a festival of musical activities. My program was in two parts. In the first half, I sang arias from Verdi operas, including *Macbeth, Otello,*

Aida, and *Don Carlo.* My friend Richard Dyer, who is the music critic for the *Boston Globe,* was also in Russia to report on these events. He said I sang "*Aida's* aria 'Ritorno Vincitor!' (Return Victorious!) better at sixty than I did at forty-nine." All I know is that I had fun singing it. The Russian conductor Alexander Mikhailov led the Moscow Radio Symphony Orchestra. He did, I must say, a superb job.

The second half of the concert was an all-popular-music section. The orchestra was reduced, and Warren Wilson conducted me and the orchestra in songs like "The Man I Love," "Our Love Is Here to Stay," and "Lover Man." I hammed it up by moving around on the stage, occasionally singing to someone in the audience. People were just as ecstatic as in 1963. Irina Archipova, the great Russian mezzo-soprano, was there, too. It was a delight to see her after nearly twenty years. She had retired and was teaching at the Moscow Conservatory. She had become quite a celebrity there, as you can imagine.

The changes I saw in 1991, compared to 1963, were astounding. It was like the difference between night and day. People spoke freely. In the 1960s, people hesitated to speak to Americans, yet when I borrowed magazines like *Time* and *Newsweek* from the U.S. embassy, they looked over my shoulder on the flights, trying to see the pictures. This time around, our interpreter joked about the KGB and Mikhail Gorbachev. In 1963, the people stood in queues to buy bread—in 1991, for hamburgers at the new McDonald's.

FINALLY, IN May 1992, as part of World Expo 92, I sang Leonora with Alfredo Kraus in *La Favorita* for the last time at the Teatro de la Maestranza in Seville. The performance was repeated in Madrid. Alfredo Kraus spun his high notes as usual in "Spirto Gentil." I was proud to say I had not lost my touch with "O mio Fernando," even after thirty-five years. I became determined to lose the weight.

This *La Favorita* turned out to be my final series of opera appearances.

*   *   *

I CONTINUED to sing recitals in the United States and, of course, in Europe, but suddenly that changed. In the early 1990s, Europe experienced an economic recession. France and Italy are still recovering from it. The year 1992 was the worst of my career, because three months of recitals in Europe were canceled. When you are not singing at the Met and La Scala or appearing on broadcasts and European radio and television, you lose your center and part of your audience. After one or two years, people begin to forget you. They want the flavor of the month. It all comes down to selling tickets. The opera companies and concert promoters are in business. I understand that side of it very clearly. Joan Sutherland, at one point, couldn't fill a house. Companies couldn't keep paying high fees when seats were going unfilled. I was getting a high fee, but when my career slowed down, I didn't draw the audiences I once had. I was not Miss Prima Donna at the top of the heap.

I became sad and depressed. I had planned to put twenty-five years into a singing career and then to turn to the legitimate theater. By 1992, I had been at it for over thirty-five years. People would talk me into another production or another tour; I loved what I was doing. When my career slowed down, it was a big shock. At sixty-one years old, I finally concluded that God was trying to tell me something.

Even in my seventies, I can do some things with my voice that I couldn't do when I was young. Likewise, I can't do things now that I could do just ten years ago. I cannot, for example, sing Lady Macbeth in its entirety, because that high D-flat is no longer in my voice. Or, at least, it comes and goes. It is not as reliable as it once was. With lessening elasticity, the vocal cords don't work as they once did. This is brought on by age and, in my case, allergies. I used to sing the "Alleluia" from Mozart's motet *Exsultate* as fast as any coloratura soprano could sing it. Now I must sing it more slowly and it is frustrating. That facility is no longer in my voice. I still vocalize faithfully every morning, though, except when I am on vacation.

On the other hand, some things I'll be able to sing until I am eighty or ninety, but it won't be Lady Macbeth or Norma. I believe

God was trying to move me on to something else. I had postponed my retirement from singing long enough.

I confess that even now I awake on some mornings feeling very well and say to myself, "How nice it would be to sing one last performance of *Norma, Macbeth,* or *Aida.*" When I come to the reality of that, I say, "Are you kidding? Be happy it is finished for you. You hated being on the road those last years." Packing and moving to different hotels became a chore, and although I tried not to show my distress to Lou or Cessie as I left home time after time, I certainly felt it. I was living like a nomad.

I sang beyond 1992, mostly recitals and almost exclusively in the United States. In 1993 I participated in a program called "The First Ladies of Song." It was a musical tribute/fundraising effort to have a statue of Eleanor Roosevelt erected in New York at Seventy-Second Street and Riverside Drive. I sang a Hall Johnson arrangement of "Fix Me, Jesus," and Aaron Copland's "Zion's Wall." Several other singers, including Marilyn Horne, Rosemary Clooney, Lena Horne, Julie Wilson, and Teresa Stratas, also participated.

Now I sang when I wanted to, but I declined most offers. One recital I did feel obliged to do, however, was August 1, 1993, for the National Association of Negro Musicians in Oakland, California, at the convention center. This is an organization like the NAACP, which has helped many African American musicians who might never have had the opportunity to achieve. I couldn't say no to them. It was *some* recital. We had a few organizational and logistical problems—for example, the stage platform wasn't available, so I had to sing on the same level as the audience. My friend Willis Patterson was impressed that I did not make a federal case of this inconvenience.

The audience's reaction brought me to tears. It was like a church homecoming. I can still remember seeing all the bright smiles. Old ladies who had been musicians in their time praised me. It was as if *I* had fulfilled some of their musical career aspirations. Several were of my generation or maybe slightly older.

It was a memorable occasion, made more special because my

mother was in the audience. August 1 also happened to be her eighty-seventh birthday, and I sang "Happy Birthday" to her. Everyone complimented her on how grand she looked.

I BELIEVED that it was time to say good-bye and move on. And then, Rodgers and Hammerstein's *Carousel* came along.

I was in my country home when I received a call from Roz Starr, a highly respected New York musical figure, asking me if I were interested in doing voice-overs for films. She put me in contact with an agent, Bob Waters. Ron Ross, an agent in his office, knew me as an opera singer. Two weeks later I received a call, asking me if I would be interested in the role of Nettie Fowler in a Broadway revival of *Carousel,* to be staged by the young British director Nicholas Hytner. Thinking my name would draw in people who had known me as an opera singer, the producers wanted me to audition for the role.

All kinds of thoughts swirled through my mind. Was this the right move? Maybe I needed more time to think about it, to prepare myself. What would my opera-world colleagues and associates think? Would I be perceived as a once-great opera singer trying to hold on to a career by pandering to a Broadway audience? Then I told myself that Ezio Pinza, Claramae Turner, Robert Merrill, and Frank Guerrera, among others, had made successful transitions from opera to musical theater.

So I said I would consider the role, but even with all of this, I vacillated about my decision. By November 1993, news leaks that Shirley Verrett would be in the production began to circulate, even though I hadn't firmed up anything. I was annoyed by the presumption. Frankly, I was also a little put out by being asked to audition, as if I were an inexperienced singer.

I called Ron Ross and told him I was no longer interested. He was disappointed and said that he thought it was a mistake for me to refuse the part. I then called my longtime friend Maurice Berger, the cultural critic and writer, to ask for his input. Maurice was familiar with Nicholas Hytner's reputation and also thought it was a mistake not to do the role. He urged me to reconsider and began calling every other day, attempting to persuade me to change my mind.

After the *Carousel* casting process moved to England, the Gemini in me came out—we can change our minds at the drop of a hat—and my spirit of adventure and curiosity took over. So I relented and told the producers that if they didn't find someone there to do Nettie, I would audition after all. Two weeks later, they arranged a special audition to hear me do an excerpt of the musical.

I really hammed it up at the audition. That's when I first met Nicholas Hytner. Before the audition, I could have cared less whether I got the part, but after meeting Nicholas I really wanted it.

Interestingly enough, I was called back. The casting personnel wanted me to read through the scene where Nettie is standing over the dead body of Billy Bigelow. Afterward, Nicholas came up to me and said, "I have been an admirer of yours since I was a young boy."

I drew my head back in surprise and said, "Really?"

He said, "I saw you at Covent Garden and I want you to know you were the greatest Tosca I have ever seen in my life."

He told me Nettie was the hardest role to cast, because she was the pivotal character in the drama, the one who brings love and reprimand to the group. He wanted a seasoned professional playing that role, and he did not want anyone else but me.

The production opened in the spring of 1994 and the rehearsal schedule was grueling, but I enjoyed every minute of it. I was at rehearsals even when I was not being staged but wanted to blend in with the other cast members and absorb everything. It was wonderful working with a group of young actors and singers. Others in the cast were Michael Hayden as Billy Bigelow, Sally Murphy as Julie Jordan, and Audra MacDonald as Julie's friend Carrie Pipperidge.

The children in the cast really impressed me, because they were so adorable and talented. Some even said, "Hi, Grandma," when greeting me. It didn't bother me. Nearing my sixty-fourth birthday, I was perhaps the senior member of the ensemble. The other cast members began calling me "Madame Verrett," but I told them just to call me "Shirley."

I had wanted to be a truthful Nettie. What if I were Nettie? I had thought. What if I were in this situation, what would I do?

Nettie is the ray of light in this dark, tragic story about a mixed-up human being. *Carousel* is about death. It's about a young girl's life squandered. Nettie encourages Julie at the height of her despair. Nettie personifies health and life. She is the person everybody runs to, the mother-confessor. She's a fixer-upper. She likes people to get along.

On opening night, several of the cast members were obviously nervous. Some commented on how poised I appeared. Little did they know what was going on inside. I felt the tension rising. I was doing something that few renowned opera singers would have ever imagined. My God, some must have thought, what was the world coming to? Shirley Verrett, who has sung dream roles like Aida, Lady Macbeth, Tosca, Norma, Medea, and Delilah, is now singing "June Is Bustin' Out All Over!" Opera purists would look down on my decision, not caring at all that I saw it as an opportunity to reach a new and wider audience.

I questioned myself again about how the theater world would receive me. Are they going to have unrealistic expectations of me? Will my vocal chords respond well? What if my allergies flare up? I wondered. Then I told myself, as I had on so many other occasions, It has to work. Whatever will be, will be. I made one last adjustment to my wig and went onstage.

The clambake scene and "June Is Bustin' Out All Over" went well, but the big scene for Nettie comes when she sings "You'll Never Walk Alone." An unexplainable feeling of serenity came over me as I sang that night:

When you walk through a storm,
Hold your head up high,
And don't be afraid of the dark.

At the end of the storm
Is a golden sky
And the sweet, silver song of a lark.
Walk on, walk on with hope in your heart,
And you'll never walk alone!

"You'll never walk alone." I held my head very erect in a frozen position, as I had done for years at the end of countless arias, waiting for the audience to express itself with applause. But the theater was silent. My mind was really racing fast with possible explanations. I then heard people sniffling, and I saw a few in the audience wiping tears from their eyes. I decided this was a good omen for a Broadway actress.

I grew into the role in subsequent performances, and I feel that I really came into my stride by the middle of the run. I did eight performances a week and maintained a heavier theater schedule than I had in the prime of my opera career. The result was that I was nominated for an Outer Critics Circle Award for Best Supporting Actress in a musical in 1994, and I was one of the honorees of the Drama League. All in all, I was glad I had felt compelled to take a chance and break with tradition.

It was exhilarating to kick up my legs as Nettie Fowler on one night and go back on the recital stage as Shirley Verrett on another. I was still singing Schumann's *Frauenlieben und Leben,* and, as a mature woman who had gone through several life-changing events, I had a more sympathetic approach to this work.

During the run of *Carousel,* I was also invited to sing at a benefit honoring Bishop Desmond Tutu; the event was tied to the recently held elections in South Africa, in which Nelson Mandela was voted president. I sang "You'll Never Walk Alone."

I had been approached twice before, first in the early 1970s, about singing in Johannesburg and said no. The concert organizers offered a substantial fee, but as far as I was concerned, no fee was worth singing in front of a segregated audience again. South Africa was waging its propaganda war around the world, saying apartheid wasn't as bad as reported. I suspected that if the perpetuators of that system could bring a prominent African American opera singer there to perform, they would claim that the racial situation couldn't be as bad as the West had heard. All of this was before the artist/athlete boycott was in place against South Africa. I had had enough experience with segregation in this country, which was a form of apartheid in itself.

DURING THE run of *Carousel,* I received a call from my longtime friend and colleague George Shirley, following up on a vocal competition that I had judged recently in New York City. One of his students had competed. George wanted my take on things, and I told him what I felt. We were also catching up, because it had been many years since we had seen each other. He mentioned the possibility of my teaching at the University of Michigan, and I assumed that he meant teaching some master classes. He also wanted me to become involved with the National Opera Association. He kept asking me about my interest in a possible teaching appointment. I resisted, thinking it would tie me down.

George said to Lou and me, "You would really like it at the University of Michigan. The school of music is nationally renowned. I think you should consider it." I said, "That might be a possibility, but I am not leaving my husband behind after all these years." George said he didn't think it would be a problem.

It took some negotiation, but it worked out. Lou joined the art faculty and his students love him. We began our respective teaching appointments in the fall semester of 1996. I had been approached by universities years earlier and said no, but this was the right place at the right time.

ANN ARBOR is where I am supposed to be. I have a strong commitment to developing younger talent at this point in my life, which is why I took the position. But it was my name, frankly, that opened the door for me. I had to prove my worth after I got there. The institution knew me as an opera singer, but few knew that for a major part of my career, I was my own voice teacher. I had to go around all kinds of little turns to get up on stage sometimes and perform. That turned out to be a wonderful road to learning about my own voice and what the technical voice is all about.

And because of that, I feel that I am a very good teacher. When I tell students something, it's not something I've guessed. It works. Teaching voice truly is a one-on-one endeavor. I feel that vocal cords are like thumbprints. I try to teach each student according to what God put into his or her throat.

My approach to teaching voice and singing are similar. Most teachers say they try to teach in the most natural way, but many do not. Natural production, as I call it, is singing as you speak. English diction was required of all singers at Juilliard, because everyone needed to learn better enunciation, regardless of whether they were from Kentucky or Maine. This process involves learning how to connect the words.

I also spend a lot of time speaking about the correct form and position of the mouth, to create space for the sound to resonate—the soft palate. Often we see singers position the mouth as a horseshoe, which, as I see it, is more appropriate when singing a buffa opera but not the ideal position for the most efficient sound. I didn't always practice this throughout my singing career, but, as I experimented, it gradually came to me, and when everything was in alignment, it was almost as if I were speaking on pitch.

The breathing process is also very important in singing. I have always had a small ribcage for a singer, which meant that I had to do exercises to breathe correctly. I also have a sway back, so I had to be on guard to not let this interfere with my correct breathing. The position of the tongue is another important factor. Some teachers suggest that the tongue stay in one position, but it does not do so when we speak; it has to be free to move quickly. It should be the same process when one sings. All of these processes encourage correct vocal cord adduction and the beauty of the sound. There are many approaches, to be sure, but this has worked for me.

Teaching basic technique is a given, but I'm interested in the whole person. How you present yourself is crucial. If you want to make a strong impression, don't walk onstage in a dress with a crooked hem, a dress that's too tight, or shoes the wrong color.

I have a rule. When my students sing in the master class, they may not come into class with jeans or clunky shoes. I had arguments about this when I first came to Michigan. The students told me that they didn't have lockers. I encourage them to find a way. Step in front of the audience in unbecoming clothes, and you will create a barrier between you and your audience, even before you open your mouth. I tell my male students the same thing. Walking onstage with your shirt coming out of your pants, without a jacket, or with unshined shoes is *verboten*.

I teach my students that their bodies are important—their entire bodies. A teacher of one of my students told her to sing "Una voce poco fa"—a wonderfully coquettish aria—with a stiff body and head. She didn't want the student to move a muscle. I set this young woman straight.

"Live the part that you're singing. Let them see in your eyes or the elegant, gentle flip of an arm that you know what you're singing about."

In her student recital, she did it the way I taught her. She got rave reviews from the students. How could her very experienced teacher have had a career? I say, go with the mind and the heart. Get up on the stage and don't bore me. Don't make me think you're singing the telephone book.

I also teach my students to respect and be courteous to their colleagues. Your piano accompanist is not your lackey. Without your accompanist, you can't do your recital, unless you're singing a cappella. I want my students to understand from the beginning that they are in a partnership with their colleagues. Ultimately, I teach my students how not to be a prima donna or a primo uomo. It's wonderful to be a prima donna in the true sense of the word but not the fake kind, the temperamental diva who goes around snapping at everybody.

Ultimately, I know that all of my teaching and my students' hard work will not necessarily lead to a major career. No matter how beautiful the voice, most of my students may not have great careers. But many of them will continue to sing and do other things. Many of my students walk into my classroom and think they're going to have a career handed to them. I tell them the truth: "I can help you with your voice. You have a wonderful voice. I cannot predict whether you're going to have a career. That is up to you and the gods. I have no jurisdiction over it."

Nobody will "make" you. *You* make you. You have the greatest responsibility for your life. I tell students to find teachers with whom they feel they have synergy, but to remember that the passion has to come from within. This is why it is so important to study only when you are ready. When I was young, my Dad started paying for my voice lessons. I stopped him. I asked him not to waste his money on me. I knew myself well. I knew that I wasn't ready to sing yet. I also knew that my dad hated to waste money. He appreciated my honesty. I wasn't ready to work then. I was singing at the Rotary Club and at school, and that was fine for me. When I was finally ready, I found a teacher in the yellow pages. I'm afraid most of my students will have a more difficult route.

AMID THIS atmosphere of change and renewal, my grandson, Tamarquis, was born on April 5, 1997. It was a difficult pregnancy for Cessie. She had to spend about three months in the hospital, and the baby was born prematurely. He looked so shriveled, because he hadn't even grown into his skin. When I saw this little bundle with a cap on his head and goggles on his eyes to protect them, and I held him in my arms, I melted like butter. I couldn't hold back my tears and just cried. It was truly love at first sight for me. All I could think was, "This child really wanted to live. He really wanted to come here."

*   *   *

IN JUNE 1999, I returned to New York City to go onstage once more in the revival of the 1903 musical comedy *In Dahomey*.

Some of the greatest African American literary and musical talents of the turn of the century, including Paul Laurence Dunbar and James Weldon Johnson, wrote the lyrics. The celebrated musician and performer Will Marion Cook composed the music, which featured many catchy ragtime-like melodies, along with a well-known dance, the "Cake Walk." The work was historically significant as the first all-black musical to be booked at a mainstream Broadway playhouse, the New York Theatre. Among the talent for the premiere were the great vaudevillians Bert Williams and George Walker. After its successful Broadway run, the musical toured Europe for some time and, for all practical purposes, went into obscurity.

The 1999 production, rewritten and directed by Shauneille Perry, was an auspicious event of a different kind. It resulted from a ten-year effort by its producer, Woodie King Jr., the director of the New Federal Theatre, an off-Broadway playhouse in the historic Henry Street Settlement on Manhattan's Lower East Side, and at the last minute it was still coming together. While studying the dual roles of Cecelia Lightfoot in Act One and Queen Ayat in Act Two, I had to learn new music one week before the opening. In the opera world, that could have sent some prima donnas packing. I had a ball.

MY LEGACY, as far as I'm concerned, may be that I've always been more versatile than many other singers. Not many went in and out of different styles and languages with as much ease. My career would have been a lot easier if I had followed only *this* path or *that* path, but I couldn't. I did it my way. I sought the arduous parts and tried to capture their essence. Added to that, it's never been enough for me just to be good; I always had to be very good. I don't mean I had to be better than anyone else, but I really had to be the best of what I could be. You can't be perfect. You do what you can do, and then you let it rest.

So, like a song, this life of mine goes on, always beginning again even as some things end. Lou and I remain soulmates. Our cherubic granddaughter, Anastasia, born May 18, 2001, had a routine delivery. On December 20, 2001, Elvira Augustine Harris Verrett departed peacefully in her sleep at age ninety-five. In tribute to Mother, I re-fashioned the opening chapter of this book and read it at her funeral. I think she would have been pleased.

Opera Synopses

Listed in the order that Shirley Verrett first performed them, here are summaries of the operas featured in this book. Characters and plot twists not central to the storylines have been minimized or eliminated for ease of reading. For a complete, scene-by-scene account of these operas, please consult *The New Kobbé's Opera Book,* edited by Anthony Peattie or *The New Grove Book of Operas,* edited by Stanley Sadie.

Lost in the Stars
WEILL/ANDERSON
based on Alan Paton's novel, *Cry the Beloved Country*

Verrett performed the roles of Linda, a brash singer, and Irina, a sympathetic young woman, in separate productions. Set in the early years of apartheid South Africa, the opera concerns the dilemmas of a pious rural minister, Stephen Kumalo, and his son, Absalom, caught in a vise of racial prejudice. Absalom has impregnated Irina and joined a street gang. Linda tries to seduce him. Irina reaffirms her love for him. But trouble stalks Absalom, who is condemned to death by hanging when his gang kills the son of a wealthy white farmer. As the hour of execution arrives, however, Kumalo learns that brotherhood can rise above racial prejudice when the father of the murdered man befriends him.

Der Tod des Grigori Rasputin
(The Death of Grigori Rasputin)
NICOLAS NABOKOV

Verrett portrayed a gypsy temptress in this opera, which centers on the 1916 assasination attempts on Rasputin, the spiritual advisor to the doomed family of the last

Prepared by Christopher Brooks

Russian tsar. While satisfying an insatiable sexual appetite, Rasputin meets the seductive gypsy and subsequently, his death.

The Rape of Lucretia
BENJAMIN BRITTEN

Verrett performed the role of Lucretia, the faithful wife of a Roman officer, Collantinus, in this opera set in Rome around 500 B.C.E. Prince Tarquinius Superbus rules. To tweak Collantinus, a fellow officer, Junius encourages Tarquinius to woo Lucretia. Tarquinius rapes her. Full of remorse and shame, the grief-stricken Lucretia stabs herself and dies in her husband's arms.

Oedipus Rex
IGOR STRAVINSKY
based on Sophocles

Verrett performed the role of Jocasta, the queen of ancient Thebes, who was widow of the murdered king Laius and wife of the new king, Oedipus. With the city suffering from plague, Jocasta's brother, Creon, reports the oracle of Delphi's prophecy: while Laius' killer remains in Thebes, the plague will continue. When a blind soothsayer declares Laius' murderer is himself a king, Oedipus accuses the blind man and Creon of complicity to overthrow him. Jocasta attempts to settle the tension between the king and her brother. But the truth unravels relentlessly. Oedipus turns out to be her long-lost son by Laius, and his father's unwitting killer. Jocasta hangs herself; Oedipus, in despair and shame, blinds himself.

Carmen
GEORGE BIZET

Verrett performed the role of Carmen, a gypsy factory worker in nineteenth-century Seville. Suitors surround her, but she expresses the fickle nature of love. That Corporal Don José is indifferent intrigues her. José has a childhood sweetheart, Micaela, a village girl, and he vows to marry her according to his ailing mother's wishes. But Carmen ensnares him. Ordered by Captain Zuniga to guard her after she cuts another factory girl, José gives in to her plea to loosen her bonds and her promises to meet him afterwards. José is arrested for allowing her to escape.

José deserts the army after a fight with his sergeant but maintains a jealous devotion to Carmen. She grows bored with him. Months later, outside the bull ring in Seville, Carmen enters with her new love, the famous toreador Escamillo. Warned by her friends that José is lurking nearby, she finds the once proud officer, broken and disheveled. José pleads with her to return, but she will not have it. When Carmen attempts to leave, José stabs her and falls sobbing over her body.

Athaliah
HUGO WEISGALL

Verrett performed the role of the Old Testament queen Athaliah. Daughter of the infamous Queen Jezebel, Athaliah has assumed the throne by having her son, King Ahaziah of Judah, and his children murdered. Unknown to her, however, one child, Yehoash, was spared and raised in the temple by the Jewish high priest Yehoyada and his wife, Yehosheba, under the name Eliakim. After some years, Queen Athaliah learns the truth in a dream. She wants to raise the boy as a son in the palace, but he refuses. Athaliah and her troops surround the temple where Yehoash is sheltered. But when Yehoash appears dressed as the lawful King of Judah, her soldiers abandon her to swear loyalty to him. Athaliah is executed.

Luisa Miller
GIUSEPPE VERDI

Verrett recorded the cameo role of Frederica, the wealthy duchess who wants to marry Rudolfo, who is in love with Luisa Miller, the heroine.

La Forza del Destino
(The Force of Destiny)
GIUSEPPE VERDI

Verrett recorded the role of Preziosilla, the fortune-telling gypsy who encourages the men of Spain to fight against the Austrians. She praises the joys of war.

Orfeo ed Euridice
CHRISTOPH WILLIBALD GLUCK

Verrett performed the trouser role of Orfeo, a hero in Greek antiquity. Orfeo laments the death of his beloved wife, Euridice, until the god, Amor, says Orfeo can rescue her from the underworld if he does not look at her on the way back (in some versions he may not touch her). Orfeo arrives at the gates of Hades. His singing is so touching the evil spirits allow him to proceed.

Orfeo calls out to Euridice to follow him to the land of the living. He remembers not to look at her, but Euridice mistakes this for indifference. Believing Orfeo no longer loves her, she decides to stay among the dead. Orfeo relents, looks at her and embraces her, and she dies once again. As a despairing Orfeo draws a dagger to kill himself, Amor appears again. She tells him he has passed the test of undying devotion and brings Euridice back to life.

Un Ballo in Maschera
(A Masked Ball)
GIUSEPPE VERDI

Verrett performed the roles of the soothsayer, Ulrica, and the wife, Amelia, in separate productions. The opera is set in colonial Boston (in some productions, Sweden). The plot centers on a conspiracy against the governor, Riccardo, and his infatuation with Amelia, the wife of his trusted aide, Renato. Amelia, also attracted to Riccardo, turns to the old soothsayer to break the spell. In her den, Ulrica calls out fierce incantations. She advises Amelia to gather a certain herb at midnight in the feared hanging grounds. Hiding behind a curtain, Riccardo overhears everything.

After Amelia leaves, Riccardo invites the soothsayer to read his hand. She forecasts that the next person who shakes it will be his assassin. Rushing to the den to check on the governor's safety, Renato shows up and shakes Riccardo's hand.

At midnight at the hanging grounds, a frightened, veiled Amelia appears. Riccardo has secretly followed her. He declares his love and she unwillingly admits hers. Renato arrives and urges his friend to flee from the approaching conspirators. Riccardo leaves only after Renato promises not to seek the identity of the "veiled" woman. But when Amelia's veil falls, Renato recognizes his wife and joins the conspiracy to kill Riccardo.

On the night of a masked ball, Amelia warns Riccardo that his life is in danger. He bids her farewell and is stabbed by Renato. Dying, Riccardo asserts Amelia's innocence and gives Renato safe passage out of the town.

Lucrezia Borgia
GAETANO DONIZETTI

Verrett recorded the trouser role of Count Orsini, friend and companion of the young Genaro, unknown son of Lucrezia Borgia. Orsini has had a brother poisoned by the villanous Borgia and is himself poisoned in the opera.

Maria Stuarda
(Mary Stuart)
GAETANO DONIZETTI

Verrett performed the role of Queen Elizabeth I of England. The plot concerns her rivalry with her cousin Mary Stuart, previously Queen of Scotland, now imprisoned by Elizabeth on suspicion of sedition. Courtiers Talbot and Leicester plead on Mary's behalf. Elizabeth harbors secret feelings for Leicester, who prevails on Elizabeth to see Mary. Frightened, Mary begs her cousin for clemency. Instead of compassion, Elizabeth becomes more haughty and insulting, causing Mary to denounce Elizabeth.

Urged to sign Mary's death warrant, she wavers until Leicester begs for Mary's life. At that point, Elizabeth, feeling betrayed, signs the warrant, and orders Leicester to be present at the beheading. Talbot, revealed as a Catholic priest, grants Mary absolution before she is led to the executioner's block.

Aida
GIUSEPPE VERDI

Verrett performed the roles of Amneris and Aida in separate productions. Set in ancient Memphis, the opera concerns the Egyptian warrior Radames and his love for the enslaved Ethiopian princess, Aida. Both Aida and her mistress, the Egyptian princess Amneris, are in love with Radames. Aida recoils as she realizes he is going to battle against her people, but she asks God's pity. Amneris tricks her into revealing her true feelings for Radames.

In battle, the Egyptians take Ethiopian prisoners, among them Aida's father, King Amonasro. He compels her to trick Radames into revealing where the Egyptian forces will be next. Radames confesses his love for her and agrees to desert. Amneris comes on the scene and calls Radames a traitor. Aida and Amonasro escape and Radames is arrested. Initially angry, Amneris is moved to pity for Radames, but he refuses to defend himself and is condemned to be buried alive. Once placed in the tomb, he discovers Aida has secretly hidden herself there. The two die peacefully together.

Mosé
GIOACCHINO ROSSINI

Verrett performed the role of Pharaoh's wife, Queen Sinaide. In the last days of the biblical era of the Israelites' captivity in Egypt, the brothers Moses and Aaron have a niece, Anaide, beloved by Queen Sinaide's son Amenophis. He contrives to make her abandon her people. When she resists, he plots against Moses and the Israelites. Sinaide attempts to comfort her son and urges Pharaoh to liberate the Jews, as he promised. But Pharaoh goes in pursuit. Moses parts the Red Sea for the Israelites to pass through; when the Egyptians attempt to follow, they are engulfed.

Don Carlo
GIUSEPPE VERDI

Verrett performed the role of Princess Eboli against the backdrop of a Flemish revolt in midsixteenth-century Spain. Eboli loves Prince Don Carlo, but he loves the new queen, Elisabeth. At court, Don Carlo's father, King Philip, is suspicious of his wife. Carlo waits outside the queen's garden in response to a letter he receives arranging a meeting. A masked Eboli meets him instead. When Eboli realizes he expects the queen, she becomes enraged and threatens his downfall. Carlo's friend Rodrigo intervenes.

The feared Grand Inquisitor wants both Carlo and Rodrigo put to death for their support of the Flemish revolt. Carlo is imprisoned, and Philip has found his picture among Elisabeth's jewels. Eboli confesses to the queen that she gave the jewel case to Philip. Given the choice of exile or the convent, Eboli curses her beauty but vows to save Carlo's life. The king arrives to release Carlo as a mob led by Eboli also arrives to free him. Carlo escapes. Elisabeth waits at the tomb of Charles V to bid Carlo farewell. Surprised by Philip and the Inquisitor, Carlo is saved when a friar posing as Charles V's ghost emerges from the tomb and drags Carlo in.

Les Troyens
(The Trojans)
HECTOR BERLIOZ

Verrett performed the roles of Didon and Cassandra in separate productions and both roles in one production. **Part One**, *La Prise de Troie* (The Capture of Troy), begins with the Trojans wondering in amazement at a huge wooden horse. The prophetess, Cassandra, predicts danger ahead, but her betrothed Corebus as well as others question her stability. The Trojans bring the horse inside the gates of the city over her protests. Greeks pour out of the horse and capture Troy. The ghost of king Hector appears to the sleeping hero Aeneas to tell him of Troy's capture and orders him to lead his remaining troops away and discover a new kingdom, Italy. Cassandra and other priestesses hide in the temple of Vesta. She determines that before becoming slaves of the Greeks, they should commit suicide. After chasing off the few who refuse, Cassandra and the others kill themselves.

Part Two, *Les Troyens a Carthage* (The Trojans at Carthage), opens in the kingdom of Carthage. Queen Dido (Didon) is hailed by her people for maintaining years of peace and prosperity. She extends hospitality to a fleet of Trojan sailors. With news of an enemy army advancing on Carthage, Aeneas steps forward and offers to fight the enemy on Didon's behalf. Aeneas and Didon fall in love.

The ghosts of Corebus, Hector, and Cassandra appear to Aeneas and command him to sail immediately on his own mission. As he prepares to embark, Didon arrives and pleads with him to stay, but he is resolved. Humiliated, Didon bids farewell to her people and stabs herself with Aeneas' sword as she makes two prophecies. The first is of a great Carthaginian warrior, Hannibal, the last of an emergent Rome.

Samson et Dalila
CAMILLE SAINT-SAENS

Verrett portrayed the biblical temptress, Dalila (Delilah). Set in Gaza, where the Hebrews pray for liberation from the Philistines, the opera takes off when the Hebrew hero Samson kills an attacking Philistine commander. Samson's Philistine lover, Dalila, calls on the gods to help her to subdue Samson. She seduces him into revealing that his superhuman strength is tied to his long hair. While he sleeps, Philistine soldiers shave Samson's hair and blind him. Samson prays to God to have mercy on his people despite his weakness and for the return of his strength. He pulls down the pillars, crushing everyone, including Dalila.

Il Trovatore

(The Troubadour)

GIUSEPPE VERDI

Verrett portrayed the tormented gypsy Azucena. In fifteenth-century Aragon, the story is told of how a gypsy was burned at the stake for bewitching the Count Di Luna's younger brother, and her daughter threw the boy into the same flame. The gypsy Azucena tells the troubadour Manrico the same story. In truth, she is the avenging daughter, but she says she threw her own child into the flames instead. Manrico has reason to be interested in Di Luna. He reveals that he and the count recently dueled. About to strike the deathblow, something tells him not to. Manrico also loves Lady Leonora, Count Di Luna's love. Lady Leonora is about to enter a convent. Over Azucena's protests, Manrico goes to stop her. Manrico and Di Luna's men fight, and Leonora and Manrico escape but are caught later.

Azucena is questioned in the affair. When Captain Ferrando recognizes her as the murderer of Di Luna's brother, she calls out for her son Manrico. In prison, he comforts Azucena. Meanwhile, Leonora convinces di Luna to free them by promising to marry him. To escape the consequences, she takes a slow poison. But Di Luna is not fooled. As Leonora dies, Di Luna orders Manrico's execution and forces Azucena to watch. Half-crazed, she screams that he has killed his own brother, and her mother is at last avenged.

Dido and Aeneas

HENRY PURCELL

Verrett portrayed the sympathetic Queen Dido. In the royal palace of Carthage, Belinda, the sister of Dido, persuades the queen to receive a foreign visitor, Prince Aeneas, and find love again. Meanwhile, a jealous sorceress reaffirms her hatred for Dido and conjures up a way to prevent it. As Dido and Aeneas enjoy a hunt, the sorceress sends a rainstorm and later sends her elf disguised as Mercury, who orders Aeneas to continue his mission. Aeneas is ready to resist the god's order, but Dido sends him away, and with a broken heart, resolves to die. She asks her people to remember her without blaming Aeneas.

La Favorita

GAETANO DONIZETTI

Verrett performed Leonora, King Alphonso's mistress. In fourteenth-century Spain, Fernando, a novice, discusses with Father Superior, Baldassare, his attraction for a young woman he met in church. As it turns out, the woman, Leonora di Guzman, is equally interested. A powerful mistress of the King Alfonso, hated by his court, she arranges Fernando's commission to the military.

Alfonso praises Fernando's military heroics and grants him whatever he wishes. Fernando asks for Leonora's hand, not knowing she's the king's mistress. Alfonso keeps his word to Fernando. Leonora, filled with doubts, writes a letter confessing to Fernando, but it is intercepted before delivery. Leonora sees Fernando before the wedding and assumes that he has forgiven her. They marry. Fernando learns the truth and returns, devastated, to the monastery. Leonora arrives, ailing and disguised as a novice. She only seeks his forgiveness and dies in his arms after receiving it.

Anna Bolena

GAETANO DONIZETTI

Verrett recorded the role of Jane Seymour, the reluctant rival of Queen Anna Bolena (Anne Boleyn). Although Jane loves the British monarch, Henry VIII, she agonizes because it costs Anna her life.

L'Africaine

GIACOMO MEYERBEER

Verrett performed the role of the exotic Queen Selika. In early sixteenth-century Portugal, the explorer Vasco da Gama, presumed lost, returns from the far east with Selika (not known to Vasco to be a queen) and her attendant Nelusko. In Lisbon, Vasco learns that his beloved Inez, believing him dead, is promised to Don Pedro. Don Pedro orders Vasco's imprisonment. While he sleeps, Selika expresses her love for him and warns of Nelusko's jealousy.

Inez agrees to marry Don Pedro, so Vasco is freed. This sets in motion a series of events as Don Pedro sets out for Selika's land with Inez, followed by Vasco. Nelusko intends to destroy them all, with the exception of his queen. Nelusko's followers attack. Many die. Vasco is saved when Selika announces that he is her husband. But recognizing Vasco's rekindled love for Inez, Selika orders a ship to return the couple to Portugal. As the ship sails away, she breathes the aroma of the deadly mancanilla tree and dies. Nelusko does the same.

Norma

VINCENZO BELLINI

Verrett sang young priestess Adalgisa once, but thereafter portrayed the high priest-ess, Norma, in several productions. In ancient Gaul during the Roman occupation, Oroveso and other druids acknowledge Norma. They do not know that her secret lover, Pollione, the Roman proconsul, has two children by her. He now loves one of her priestesses, Adalgisa. Pollione woos Adalgisa into leaving for Rome with him, and the girl seeks release of her vows from Norma. When Norma realizes this be-trayal, she contemplates killing the children. But she drops the dagger and sends for Adalgisa. She tells the younger woman to go to Rome with Pollione and take the children with her. Adalgisa refuses. She offers to ask Pollione to return to Norma, in-stead. The two women swear eternal friendship. But Pollione is obsessed. He takes Adalgisa by force and profanes the druids' holy place. Norma calls for war against the Romans. Pollione is captured but refuses to give up Adalgisa. Norma accepts her culpability. The druids are shocked, but Norma asks her father to protect her chil-dren and mounts a pyre to die. Pollione joins her.

Bluebeard's Castle

BELA BARTOK

Verrett portrayed Judith, the headstrong eighth wife of the infamous Duke Blue-beard. Resisting all advice, Judith becomes his bride. To change his gloomy castle into a bright place of happiness, Judith insists that she must have access to all locked doors. The first conceals a torture chamber, the second a room full of weapons, the third a room full of jewelry and increasing amounts of blood. She becomes more in-trigued. The fourth door opens into a beautiful garden, but with more blood. The next door reveals the Duke's kingdom. The sixth door shows a river of tears. As Ju-dith opens the seventh door, apparitions of Bluebeard's previous wives appear and she realizes she must now join them in death.

L'Assedio di Corinto

(The Siege of Corinth)

GIOACCHINO ROSSINI

Verrett performed the Corinthian warrior, Neocle. Set in midfifteenth-century Corinth, the popular young Neocle has been promised the hand of Pamira, the daughter of the governor, Cleomene. She, however, has fallen in love with a man whom she only knows as "Almanzor" until Maometto, leader of the Turkish forces, captures Corinth. Pamira recognizes the feared Turk as Almanzor. Maometto offers to make peace in order to marry her. Cleomene refuses and, at first, Pamira defies him. But she is torn between her love and her patriotic duty to Corinth. Maometto attempts to comfort her. Neocle tries to halt the wedding but is spared only because Pamira says he is her brother. Finally, Pamira renounces Maometto who allows her to leave but vows to destroy Corinth the following day.

Neocle reconciles Cleomene and the repentant Pamira. The Greeks rally temporarily, but Maometto returns to claim Pamira. She stabs herself rather than submit.

Macbeth
GIUSEPPE VERDI

One of Verrett's crowning roles is the wicked Lady Macbeth. In eleventh-century Scotland, her husband Macbeth and his fellow military commander, Banquo, happen onto a group of witches who prophesy Macbeth's rise to Thane of Cawdor and eventually king. Lady Macbeth clearly sees her role in facilitating his rise to the Scottish throne and seeks the aid of demons. She tells Macbeth he must assassinate Duncan, the king, which he reluctantly does that night. The following morning Macduff, another Scottish noble, and Banquo discover the dead body.

Macbeth and Lady Macbeth see Banquo as their next threat. Assassins kill Banquo; his son escapes. Macbeth sees the bloodstained ghost at a banquet and decides to consult the witches again. In a cave, Macbeth and Lady Macbeth determine to slaughter Macduff's family. This time, it is Lady Macbeth who is guilt-ridden; she sleepwalks, confesses, and is driven to her death. When Macduff takes his revenge and kills Macbeth, all hail the death of the tyrant.

The Dialogues of the Carmelites
FRANCIS POULENC

Verrett portrayed the second Prioress, Madame Lidoine. Set in eighteenth-century revolutionary France in a Carmelite convent, a young noblewoman, Blanche, announces her intention to become a nun. Her father, the Marquis, and brother, the Chevalier, reluctantly agree. The ailing Mother Superior Madame de Croissy reminds her that the convent is a place of prayer, not heroics. Blanche takes the name Sister Blanche of the Agony of Christ. Later, Mme. de Croissy dies with Blanche weeping by her side.

The new Mother Superior, Madame Lidoine, addresses the sisters. She, too, reminds them that their duty is to prayer and not heroics. The new republic has forbidden the nuns to practice their religion. A commissioner announces the convent must be vacated immediately and the nuns must stop wearing their religious dress. In Mme. Lidoine's absence in Paris, the nuns vote for martyrdom. Blanche runs off, terrified.

Madame Lidoine returns to discover what has happened and instructs Mother Marie to find Blanche, who has taken refuge as a servant in her former home. Blanche tells Mother Marie her father was guillotined the week before. In a prison cell the Carmelites wait with Mme. Lidoine. The sisters took the vow in her absence, but she now embraces it with them. At the Place de Revolution, the crowd awaits the Carmelites' execution. Mme. Lidoine leads the way, singing the *Salve Regina* with the others. As the guillotine silences the last voice, Constance, Blanche steps forward with poise and fearlessness to die next.

Tosca
GIACOMO PUCCINI

Verrett portrayed the fiery opera singer, Floria Tosca. Set in Rome in the early nineteenth century, a political prisoner, Cesare Angelotti, is hidden in a chapel by his sympathizer, Mario Cavaradossi, an artist. When Mario's beloved Floria Tosca, the celebrated singer, arrives at the chapel, she is suspicious of the locked door and thinks he is concealing another woman. Mario sneaks out of the chapel with Angelotti just before the feared head of the secret police, Baron Scarpia, arrives. He, too, is enamored with Tosca. Scarpia sees his opportunity. He shows Tosca a woman's fan "suggesting" Cavaradossi's infidelity. Tosca vows revenge and agrees to meet Scarpia later.

Cavaradossi is apprehended by Scarpia's men and interrogated near Scarpia's meeting place. Tosca arrives, hears Cavaradossi's screams of torture, and impetuously reveals Angelotti's hiding place in order to save her love. Mario curses Tosca, but Angelotti kills himself before being captured. Mario is taken to prison. Scarpia offers Tosca a deal; in exchange for her fidelity, he will stage a "mock" execution and offer safe conduct papers to Cavaradossi. After feigning acceptance, Tosca stabs Scarpia, grabs the safe conduct document, and flees to the prison. There, she tells Mario he must fake his death in front of the firing squad, but the plan is foiled. After the shooting, Mario is, in fact, dead. Scarpia's men arrest her, but she pushes away from them announcing she and Scarpia will meet before God, and leaps to her death.

Otello
(based on the Shakespeare drama)
GIUSEPPE VERDI

Verrett performed the falsely accused wife of Otello, Desdemona. Set in fifteenth-century Cyprus, the Moorish general and Cypriot governor, Otello, returns victorious after defeating the Turks at sea. His ensign, Iago, bitterly jealous of the general's fame and good fortune, plots the downfall of the Moor because he elevated Cassio to captain above Iago. Iago intends to use Cassio's interest in the general's wife Desdemona as the vehicle. Iago plies the captain with drink and tricks him into a brawl with another soldier. When Otello arrives at the commotion, he angrily demotes Cassio in rank. Desdemona arrives and calms her husband and they reaffirm their love and devotion to each other. But Iago suggests to Cassio that he ask Desdemona to intervene in his behalf to Otello. Shortly afterwards, Desdemona pleads with her husband on Cassio's behalf. His angry response causes her to wipe his brow with a handkerchief, which the Moor throws to the ground. Emilia, Desdemona's attendant, retrieves it, and she is forced to give it to Iago. When Otello vents his rage on Iago, the latter tells the general he heard Cassio uttering Desdemona's name in his sleep and has seen Desdemona's handkerchief in Cassio's hand. Otello swears revenge. Fueled by Iago's tricks, Otello confronts the innocent Desdemona and swoons in jealous rage with Iago standing over him in glee.

Desdemona has no hope but her prayers. Overcome by fury, Otello strangles her. Seeing the lifeless Desdemona, Emilia calls for help and reveals Iago's treachery. Otello stabs himself in remorse.

Fidelio
LUDWIG VAN BEETHOVEN

Verrett portrayed the heroic Leonora (known as Fidelio). Set outside eighteenth-century Seville, Spain, the corrupt governor, Don Pizzaro, hides his imprisoned political opponent, Florestan. Florestan's wife, Leonora, has disguised herself as a man (calling herself Fidelio) and taken a job with the jailer, Rocco. Her disguise is good enough that Rocco's daughter, Marcellina, falls in love with Fidelio. But Leonora presses Rocco about a secret prisoner she suspects is Florestan.

The local minister suspects Don Pizzaro of wrongdoing and announces he will inspect the prison. Don Pizzaro decides he must do away with Florestan quickly and enlists a hesitant Rocco in the plot to dig the grave. Suspecting foul play, Leonora and Rocco dig the grave. Leonora recognizes Florestan. Pizzaro plans to kill Florestan, Rocco, and Leonora to cover up his treachery, but when he draws his dagger, Leonora draws a pistol on him. The minister arrives not a moment too soon. Florestan and Leonora rejoice at their reunion. Florestan is released and pardoned, Pizzaro is arrested, and a crowd celebrates the reunion of husband and wife.

Iphigenie en Tauride
CHRISTOPH WILLIBALD GLUCK

Verrett portrayed the role of Iphigenie, the long-estranged daughter of Agamemnon and Clytemnestra, who has become a priestess of the goddess Diana. At the temple of Diana, on the island of Tauris in antiquity, Iphigenie questions Oreste. Either he or his friend Pylade, recent Greek arrivals, will be sacrificed to appease the gods, by the order of King Thoas of Scythia. From Oreste Iphigenie learns for the first time the horrific story of Clytemnestra's murder of Agamemnon, and how Oreste, their son, killed her. Only a daughter, Electra, survives, he says, concealing his tormented identity.

Iphigenie decides to save the young Greek because of his resemblance to her brother. She orders Oreste to deliver a letter to her sister Electra, but he refuses to leave his friend Pylade behind. Pylade agrees to take the letter. Oreste will stay behind and be sacrificed. Iphigenie is poised to strike with dagger in hand when she realizes he is, in fact, her brother. He is saved. Pylade comes to the rescue and kills Thoas. The goddess Diana pardons Oreste. And brother and sister are returned to Greece.

Alceste
CHRISTOPH WILLIBALD GLUCK

Verrett portrayed the self-sacrificing wife, Alceste. In Greek antiquity, King Admetus is near death. His wife, Alceste, is grief-stricken and offers to be the human sacrifice to spare the king. Admetus recovers and his people celebrate. He says he would have died for any of his subjects, but he does not know who has offered their life for his. When he learns it is Alceste, he is horrified at the idea of losing her and prefers his own death. Hercules, friend of Admetus, determines he will rescue them both and immediately leaves for Hades. Alceste resolves to cross over to the underworld and dies, but Hercules arrives, goes into Hades, and brings her back alive. Apollo announces that Hercules will be made a god because of his heroism, and this heroism appeases the gods for Alceste's sacrifice.

Médée
LUIGI CHERUBINI

Verrett performed the murderous Médée (Medea). In ancient Corinth, Dirce, the daughter of King Creon, is to be married to Jason, the famous warrior. He has abandoned the powerful Médée and taken their two children. Dirce fears that Médée will disrupt the wedding, but Jason hopes all will be well. An unknown veiled woman enters the court and reveals herself as Médée. Creon orders her exile. But Jason weakens under her pleas and brings their children to her for the day. Médée gives a diamond crown to Dirce as a wedding present. When informed how graciously Dirce received it, Médée quietly reveals it was poisoned with magic and Dirce will die. Médée also kills her children, to the horror of Jason, and sets fire to the temple.

Rigoletto
GIUSEPPE VERDI

Verrett recorded Maddalena, the seductive sister of the assassin Sparafucile. She lures victims into her brother's inn, and he murders them. Her latest victim is the wicked Duke of Mantua, whom the jester intends to have murdered. Maddalena succumbs to the Duke's charms and is spared. She instead lures the corrupt jester's disguised daughter into the inn to be murdered.

Cavalleria Rusticana
(Rustic Chivalry)

PIETRO MASCAGNI

Verrett performed the self-pitying peasant woman Santuzza. Recently jilted by Turiddu, Santuzza goes to his mother, Mama Lucia, to inquire about his whereabouts. She tells Mama Lucia that Turiddu is again pursuing Lola, wife of Alfio, a prosperous trader. As the town prepares for the Easter celebration, Santuzza, excommunicated for living openly with Turiddu, is forbidden to enter the church. Santuzza stops Turiddu on his way to church and begs him to return, but he is so rude, Santuzza tells Alfio about his wife's affair. Alfio challenges Turiddu to a duel. Alone with his mother, Turiddu expresses sympathy for Santuzza and goes off to fight. A child calls out that Turiddu has been killed. Santuzza faints.

Discography

Commercial Recordings on LP and CD

BEETHOVEN

Symphony No. 9
Everest SDBR 3162 (LP)

BELLINI

Norma
ABC 20017 (LP) // Angel AVC 34030 (LP)

BRAHMS

Alto Rhapsody
RCA ARL1-3001 (LP)//RCA 6716-2-RG (CD)

DONIZETTI

Anna Bolena
ABC ATS 20015 (LP)//Angel AVC 34031 (LP)

Lucrezia Borgia
RCA LSC 6176 (LP)//RCA 6642-2-RG (CD)

FALLA

El Amor Brujo
Columbia MS 6147 // CBS MPK 46449 (CD)

Prepared by Richard LeSueur and Christopher Brooks with assistance from Patricia Turner

GLUCK

Orfeo ed Euridice
RCA LSC 6169 (LP)//RCA 7896-2-RG (CD)

MAHLER

Symphony No. 3
RCA LSC 7046 (LP)

MASSENET

Arias; Chausson—"Poeme de l'amour et de la mer"
Fonit Cetra LIC 9006 (LP)// Fonit Cetra CDC 90 (CD)

MENDELSSOHN

Elijah
RCA LSC 6190 (LP)

ROSSINI

Siege of Corinth
Angel SCLX 3819 (LP)//EMI CMS 7 64335-2 (CD)

STOKOWSKI

Stokowski Conducts Wagner
RCA LSC-2555 (LP)

STRAVINSKY

Oedipus Rex
Columbia MS 6472 (LP)//Columbia M31129 (LP)

A Sermon, a Narrative, and a Prayer
Columbia MS 6647 (LP)

VERDI

Don Carlo
Angel SDL 3774 (LP)//EMI CDS7 47701-8 (CD)//Angel AVC 3406 (CD)

La Forza del Destino
RCA LSC 6413 (LP)// RCA 7971-2-RG (CD)

Luisa Miller
RCA LSC 6168 (LP)

Macbeth (Abbado)
DG 2709 062 (LP)//DG (new release)

Macbeth (Chailly)
London 417 525-2 (CD)

VERDI (continued)

Requiem
DG 2707 120 (LP)//DG 415 976-2 (CD)

Rigoletto
London 425 864-2 (CD)

Il Trovatore
London 430 694-2 (CD)

VIVALDI

Sacred Music
RCA LSC 2935 (LP)

OTHER RECORDINGS

Carnegie Hall Recital
RCA LSC 2835 (LP)

Great Opera Duets with Montserrat Caballé
RCA LSC 3153 (LP)//RCA 60818-2 (CD)

How Great Art Thou
Kapp SK 3394 (LP)

Recital of Spanish Songs
RCA LSC 2776 (LP)

Shirley Verrett in Opera
RCA LSC 3045 (LP)// RCA 09026 61457-2 (CD includes extras)

Singin' in the Storm
RCA LSC 2892 (LP) (only part reissued from other material)

Grand Gala in der Oper
RCA (German) RK 42876 (LP)

Met Stars in the New World
Metropolitan Opera 216 (CD) ("Oh! Glory")

Opera's Greatest Drinking Songs
RCA 09026 68095-2 (CD) (Lucrezia Borgia, "Brindisi")

Noncommercial Recordings on LP and CD

BERLIOZ

Les Troyens (RAI)
Arkadia CDMP 461.4

BIZET

Carmen (London, 1973)
GLH 804

DONIZETTI

La Favorita (New York, 1975)
BJR 148 (LP)

Maria Stuarda (Florence, 1967)
Hunt CD 543

Maria Stuarda (New York City, Carnegie Hall, 1967)

Maria Stuarda (Teatro alla Scala, 1971)
Myto 2 MCD 911.37 (CD)

Maria Stuarda (New York)
MRF 13 (LP)

MEYERBEER

L'Africaine (San Francisco)
Opera Disc 1003/05 (LP)//BJR 131 (LP)//Legato Classics LCD 116-3 (CD)

PURCELL

Dido and Aeneas
Arkadia HP 619.1

ROSSINI

Mose (RAI 1968)
Freuenz 011-040//Arkadia MP 491.2// LO 7724-25

Stabat Mater (Rome, 1967)
Voce 6 (LP)// Verona 27060 (CD)//Melodram MEL 28012 (CD)
//Cetra ARCD 2041 (CD)

SAINT-SAENS

Samson et Dalila (Teatro alla Scala, 1970)
Hope 217 (LP)//Frequenz (CD)//Foyer 2 CF-2031 (CD)// Arkadia MP 495.2

VERDI

Macbeth (Teatro alla Scala, 1975)
Myto 2MCD 962.145

Un Ballo in Maschera (Teatro alla Scala, 1977)
Legendary LR 176 (LP)

Don Carlo (Vienna, 1970)
Hope 235 (LP)//Legendary LR 163 (LP)

VERDI (continued)
Recital
(no date or place given; includes complete Mozart *Exsultate* and Chausson "Chanson
perpetuelle" with ensemble; John Wustman, piano) Opera Society OSCD 223 (CD)

Collections (reissued from other material)

Pavarotti, Verrett, Kraus
(*Favorita,* Eugene Ormandy, 1975, Philadelphia; Eve Queler, 1975, New York)
BLV 107.009

Arias
MGS 109 (LP) (w/Sills, Farrell, Baker, Gedda, etc.)

Great Soprano Cabalettas
Legato LCD 161 (*Macbeth,* "Or tutti sorgete")

Rossini Arias
UORC 104 (LP) (*Stabat Mater,* aria)

10 Sopranos in 10 Arias
HRE 216 (LP) (*Norma,* "Casta diva")

12 Outstanding American Singers
Legendary LR 139 (LP) (*Forza del Destino,* "Pace, pace mio dio," 11/3/77)

Commercial Videocassettes

BEETHOVEN

Symphony No. 9
Kulture

MASCAGNI

Cavalleria Rusticana
VAI

MEYERBEER

L'Africaine (San Francisco)
Home Vision

SAINT-SAENS

Samson et Dalila (San Francisco)
Various

VERDI

Macbeth (Chailly)
London

Shirley Verrett
Kulture

Great Arias with Domingo and Friends
VIEW

Pavarotti 30th Anniversary Concert
Uni/London Classics

Acknowledgments

I t is daunting yet gratifying to reflect on how many people gave their time, expertise, and energy to the completion of this project. It is a pleasure to thank them here. As grateful as Christopher Brooks and I are, it is difficult to convey here our full appreciation for their encouragement, input, and support.

Several institutions provided research or logistical support, most notably the University of Michigan School of Music, Virginia Commonwealth University's African American Studies Program, and Oakwood College.

Specific assistance at the University of Michigan was offered by Willis Patterson, Paul Boylan, Karen Wolff, Fay Burton, and Brenda Wimberly, among many others. Similar assistance was offered to Christopher at Virginia Commonwealth University by Njeri Jackson, Daniel Reeves, Melanie Kohn Day, Edgar Toppins, Audrey Smedley, Babatunde Lawal, Norma Jean Scott, Sue Bass, and Michael Walker.

We would also like to acknowledge the help of several people at Oakwood College who came to the assistance of one of its alums: Roy Malcolm, Minneola Davis, Joyce Williams, and Sherman Cox.

In the area of editorial assistance, many deserve mention. Along with the late John Ardoin, there was Dika Newlin, whose comments were invaluable in the early stages of this work. Others who deserve credit for crucial editorial input and guidance are Jewelle Gomez, John H. Whaley, Jr., Rashard Wright, and my friend Maurice Berger. My comments on bigotry on pages 19 through 20 first appeared in Maurice's book, *White Lies*. Carole Hall's dogged persistence throughout the editorial process at John Wiley & Sons deserves our highest praise and respect. At Wiley, we also thank associate managing editor Hope Breeman and copyeditor Patricia Waldygo.

I want to thank my dear colleagues and friends Claudio Abbado, Plácido Domingo, Sarah Caldwell, Luciano Pavarotti, and Zubin Mehta for their time and comments. Other friends and colleagues in the business whose input was invaluable include Herbert Breslin and Edgar Vincent.

It was necessary for Christopher to interview several people who were involved at some stage in my career and who brought to light some occurrences that I had long forgotten. Since the inception of this book, several dear loved ones have passed on, including Gideon Waldrop, whose support dated from my student days in New York. There are two in my immediate family who also did not survive to see this book in print, but their spirits and lives are infused throughout its pages. They are my brother Milton Verrett and my beloved mother, Elvira, who has now joined her husband, Leon Sr., in God's lasting embrace. Thanks must be extended to my sister, Elvira Verrett Smith, and brother David Verrett, my cousins John and Joseph McCoy, my long-time friend and accompanist Warren Wilson, and Richard Dyer. Simonetta Lippi and Robert Baxter were also of great assistance. We also wish to thank Bernetia Brooks for her expert handling of the many travel arrangements associated with interviews, research, and accommodations.

We gratefully acknowledge Edythea Ginis Selman, our agent, whose support and tireless efforts went above and beyond the ordinary. We have been truly fortunate to have such a dedicated coach and friend.

Denise Bethel of Sotheby's was extremely helpful in the photograph detective work that has enhanced this book. Thanks should also be extended to John Penino, Francesca Franchi, Jack Mitchell, and Milton Feinberg. Richard LeSueur's and Patricia Turner's assistance with the discography was a major component in this undertaking.

There is a seemingly nebulous area that we have called general support, but without it, this work might not have seen the light of day. There are so many to thank in this area, including Murry DePillars, who gave Christopher a copy of *Shirley Verrett Diva* years before this work was undertaken. Brenda and Eric Kahari provided Christopher with accommodations while he was doing research in South Africa.

Others are Carolyn Parker, Donna Shepherd, Arthur Majola, David Hiley, Patricia Cummins, Charles Hackett, Jr., Gwendolyn Howard, Rachelle Schlosser, Alfonzo Mathis, Yvette Perry-Kahari, Ken Hopson, Gerald Waldman, and Louis Mabre-Cargill. Without you, we might not have arrived at this place.

I want to thank my daughter, Francesca, and my two grandchildren, Tamarquis and Anastasia. When they are old enough to read this work, they will have some idea of why their grandmother was always concerned about discipline and organization.

My most profound thanks go to my husband Louis LoMonaco, my soulmate for more than forty years.

Shirley Verrett

Index

Note: Page numbers in *italics* indicate photographs.